Emerging and Frontier Markets

Emerging and Frontier Markets

The New Frontline for Global Trade

Marcus Goncalves and José Alves

BEP BUSINESS EXPERT PRESS

First published in 2015 by
Business Expert Press, LLC
222 East 46th Street, New York, NY 10017
www.businessexpertpress.com

ISBN-13: 978-1-63157-019-3 (paperback)
ISBN-13: 978-1-63157-020-9 (e-book)

Business Expert Press Economics Collection

Collection ISSN: 2163-761X (print)
Collection ISSN: 2163-7628 (electronic)

Cover and interior design by Exeter Premedia Services Private Ltd.,
Chennai, India

First edition: 2015

10 9 8 7 6 5 4 3 2 1

Printed in the United States of America.

To my forever-beautiful wife, Carla, and my son Samir, both living here on earth, and to my children Andrea and Joshua, who are now living in Heaven. I also would like to express my gratitude to my father, Mario M. Goncalves, for planting the seeds of research in me while a child, and to my father-in-law, Don Fernando Davalos, for the many insightful discussions on foreign affairs.

To God be the glory!

Marcus Goncalves
Summer 2014

Abstract

In today's fast-paced global economy, markets are sifting very swiftly, and the balance of trade and even political influence are following suit. It is important, therefore, that international business professionals, academics and students of global trade and international markets, and anyone interested on the latest developments taking place in global trade to be able to understand, compare and contrast the primary categories of emerging market business development, including its sub-categories, or maybe more appropriately, its sibling, the frontier markets.

There is no doubt that today's global markets present both great opportunity and significant risk for business development and investment. Established and mature markets have been supposedly providing safety and security for labor and capital, but the last seven years or so have changed such perspective when we witness advanced economies struggling with debt and lack of growth, while competition is at an all time high. Hence, understanding emerging and frontier markets present some of the most significant opportunities for international business professionals and investors. This book, an expanded and enhanced version of the Part II of our "big" book published a few months ago (*Advanced Economies and Emerging Markets: Perspectives for Globalization*), dives deeper at the opportunities and challenges faced by emerging and frontier markets, comparing the risks and opportunities in its main markets so that students and researchers, as well as investors and casual readers interested in this topic, can gain a better understanding of which markets provide the best opportunities. Our hope is that readers will find this information useful in their forward-looking international business careers and business strategies.

Marcus Goncalves, Fall 2014.

Keywords

ASEAN, BRICS, CIVETS, EAGLE, emerging markets, frontier markets, global trade, globalization, international business, international trade, MENA, trading blocs

Contents

Acknowledgments

There were many people who helped us during the process of writing this book. It would be impossible to keep track of them all. Therefore, to all that we have forgotten to list, please don't hold it against us!

We would like to thank Dr. Patrick Barron, professor at the Graduate School of Banking at the University of Wisconsin, Madison, and of Austrian economics at the University of Iowa, in Iowa City for his contributions on the issue of currency wars in chapter 5.

Many thanks also to ambassador M.K. Bhadrakumar, former diplomat in the Indian Foreign Service with assignments in the Soviet Union, South Korea, Sri Lanka, Germany, Afghanistan, Pakistan, Uzbekistan, Kuwait, and Turkey for his valuable insights and contributions to foreign policy issues in the MENA region.

CHAPTER 1

The IMF is Being Hit by BRICS

Overview

According to a recent study from the Peterson Institute,* a think-tank, from 1960 to the late 1990s just 30 percent of countries in the developing world, for which figures are available, managed to increase their output per person faster than the United States, thus achieving what is called "catch-up growth." That catching-up was somewhat apathetic; the gap closed at just 1.5 percent a year. From the late 1990s, however, the tables were turned. The researchers found 73 percent of emerging economies outpacing the United States, and doing so on average by 3.3 percent a year. Some of this was due to slower growth in America, but not all.

This outstanding growth of emerging markets in general and in partic-ular the BRICS (Brazil, Russia, India, China, and South Africa) has trans-formed the global economy in many ways, as commodity prices soared and the cost of manufactures and labor sank. Such growth also caused a significant decline on global poverty rates, which has tumbled, even though income inequality has grown around the world. Social mobility has decreased at similar rate. In addition, gaping economic imbalances has fueled an era of global financial vulnerability and contributed to the foundation for a global crisis. A growing and vastly more accessible pool of labor in emerging economies has played a significant part in both wage stagnation and rising income inequality.

China's pivot toward liberalization and global markets came at a pro-pitious time in terms of politics, business, and technology. Rich econ-omies were feeling relatively relaxed about globalization and current

---

* Conducted by Arvind Subramanian and Martin Kessler.

account deficits. At the time China and India were experiencing astronomic growth rates, the United States was not paying much attention. The Bill Clinton administration was characterized by an economic boom and market confidence. No one was concerned about the growth of Chinese industry or offshoring jobs to India.

The BRICS period arrived at the end of a century in which global living standards had diverged remarkably. Toward the end of the 19th century, America's economy overtook China's to become the largest on the planet. By 1992, China and India—home to 38 percent of the world's population—were producing just seven percent of the world's output, while six rich countries which accounted for just 12 percent of the world's population produced half of it. In 1890, an average American was about six times better off than the average Chinese or Indian. By the early 1990s he was doing 25 times better.

The bloc was originally known as "BRIC" before the inclusion of South Africa in 2010. Jim O'Neill coined the acronym in a 2001 paper entitled, "Building Better Global Economic BRICs."[1] The acronym has come into widespread use as a symbol of the apparent shift in global economic power away from the developed G-7 economies toward the developing world. The BRICS members are all emerging economies, either at a developing or newly industrialized stage, but distinguished by their large, fast-growing economies[2] and significant influence on regional and global affairs. All five countries are members of the G-20.

As of 2013, these five BRICS countries represent almost three billion people, with a combined nominal GDP of $16.039 trillion,[3] and an estimated $4 trillion in combined foreign reserves.[4] Impressively, their growing rates and the size of their economies sets them aside in a special way, as depicted in Figure 1.1. If we weigh their GDP in purchasing-power parity* (PPP) terms, these countries are the only $1 trillion dollar economies outside the rich, world club, OECD.

Advanced economies such as the EU, view the BRICS as less interested in shared ideas of a multilateral world, and more inclined toward

---

* An economic theory that estimates the amount of adjustment needed on the exchange rate between countries in order for the exchange to be equivalent to each currency's purchasing power.

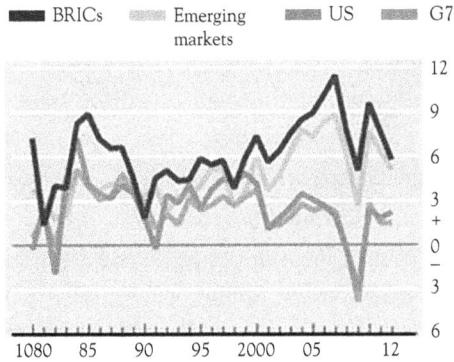

Figure 1.1 **The significant growth of the BRIC compared with emerging markets (overall) and the U.S. economy**

Source: IMF, The Economist

a nationalistic, multipolar world that emphasizes their own newly found strengths and interests. The result is fading authority and consensus on the world stage. The cold war *spheres of influence* between two powers are long gone. The new world order of U.S. dominance is diminishing. But no clear leadership or rules have yet replaced this. New struggles of trends such as human rights and democracy—and sovereignty—still have to be decided.

The shift toward the emerging economies will continue. But its most tumultuous phase seems to have more or less reached its end. Growth rates in all the BRICS have dropped. The nature of their growth is in the process of changing, too, and its new mode will have fewer direct effects on the rest of the world. The likelihood of growth in other emerging economies having an effect in the near future comparable to that of the BRICS in the recent past is low; they do not have the potential for catch-up the BRICS had in the 1990s and 2000s. The BRICS' growth has changed the rest of the world economy in ways that will dampen the disruptive effects of any similar surge in the future. The emerging giants will grow larger, and their ranks will swell, but their tread will no longer shake the Earth as once it did.

Recent developments, such as the danger of a property bubble in China, a decline in world trade, and volatile capital flows in emerging markets, could derail the global economic recovery and have a lasting impact. Arguably, in our view, 2013's economic deceleration to a large extent reflects the inability of global leaders to address the many challenges that were already present from 2001 to 2012.

Policymakers around the world remain concerned about high unemployment and the social conditions in their countries. The political brinkmanship in the United States continues to affect the outlook for the world's largest economy, while the sovereign debt crises and the danger of a banking system meltdown in peripheral eurozone countries remain unresolved. The high levels of public debt coupled with low growth, insufficient competitiveness, and political gridlock in some European countries are still stirring financial markets' concerns about sovereign default and the viability of the euro.

Given the complexity and the urgency of the situation, advanced economies around the world, in particular the United States and European countries are facing difficult economic management decisions with challenging political and social ramifications. Although European leaders do not agree on how to address the immediate challenges, there is recognition that, in the longer term, stabilizing the euro and putting Europe on a higher and more sustainable growth path will necessitate improvements to the competitiveness of the weaker member states.

Meanwhile, emerging markets are coping with the consequence of advanced economies' debt. In our view, given the expected slowdown in economic growth in China, India, and other emerging markets, reinforced by a potential decline in global trade and volatile capital flows in the next five to eight years, it is not clear which regions of the world can drive growth and employment creation in the short to medium term, but we believe the BRICS will play a major role in this process. Africa, as well as the whole MENA bloc, should see high growth levels in the next decade.

When we look at advanced economies as compared to emerging markets, the IMF[5] accurately estimated that, in 2012, the eurozone would have contracted by 0.3 percent, while the United States would have continued to experience a weak recovery with an uncertain future. Large emerging economies such as the BRICS are growing somewhat less than they did in 2011, but still growing at around 4–5 percent annually. Meanwhile, other emerging markets such as ASEAN also continue to show robust growth rates, around 5–7 percent, while the MENA as well as sub-Saharan African countries continue to gain momentum.

According to John Hawksworth and Dan Chan at PWC,[6] the world economy is projected to grow at an average rate of just over three percent per annum from 2011 to 2050, doubling in size by 2032 and nearly doubling again by 2050. Meanwhile, China is projected to overtake the United States as the largest economy by 2017 in PPP terms and by 2027 in market exchange rate terms. India should become the third 'global economic giant' by 2050, well ahead of Brazil, who is expected to become the fourth largest economy, ahead of Japan. Hawksworth and Chan also argue that Russia may overtake Germany to become the largest European economy before 2020 in PPP terms and by around 2035 at market exchange rates. Emerging economies such as Mexico and Indonesia could be larger than the UK and France by 2050, and Turkey larger than Italy.

The American or EU citizen who has travelled to India knows that his money stretches further than it does at home. To be precise, one can buy 2.8 times as much in India with a dollar's worth of rupees than one can with a dollar in the United States, according to the IMF.[7] This is because India's prices are only about 35 percent of America's, when converted into a common currency at market exchange rates. This magic is not unique to India of course. It applies across most developing countries. This is not true, however, when Americans visit countries like Switzerland, where prices are 175 percent of America's level, Denmark at 153 percent, or Australia with 149 percent.

In the biggest emerging economies, however, this magic is fading. Ten years ago, Brazil's price level was only 40 percent of America's, but as of July of 2013, it was 90 percent. China's also has risen from 39 percent to 67 percent over the same period, while Russia's has also soared from 31 percent to almost 83 percent. Taken together, the BRICs have become notably more expensive over the past decade. Their combined price level rose rapidly toward advanced economies levels from 2003 to 2011, before plateauing in the past two years.

This dramatic convergence of price levels is an underrated economic force. It is one telling reason why the BRICS' dollar GDP is now worth exceedingly more than anyone expected back in 2003, when O'Neill released the first of his long-range projections of the BRICS' economic fate over the next half-century. At the time, the projections raised eyebrows. Now that the BRIC economies have faltered, O'Neill's whole thesis has been sneered at. But, looking back at his attempt to look forward, O'Neill was, if anything, too conservative about his forecast. The BRICS combined dollar GDP will be 70 percent bigger in 2013 than O'Neill/Goldman Sachs had projected ten years ago.

Some of that over performance is due to the fact the BRICS have grown faster over the past decade than Goldman Sachs expected. China, for instance, is still growing faster than envisioned, despite its slowdown from double-digits growth rates. The same is not true for the other three countries, although a big part of the overrun is due to the fact the BRICS became pricier faster than Goldman Sachs foresaw. The following is a short profile of the BRICS, their strengths and weaknesses as of 2013.

Brazil

Following more than three centuries under Portuguese rule, Brazil gained its independence in 1822, maintaining a monarchical system of government until the abolition of slavery in 1888 and the subsequent proclamation of a republic by the military in 1889. Brazilian coffee exporters politically dominated the country until populist leader Getulio Vargas rose to power in 1930. Brazil is by far the largest and most populous country in South America. The country underwent more than a half-century of populist and military government until 1985, when the military regime peacefully ceded power to civilian rulers.

Brazil continues to pursue industrial and agricultural growth and development of its interior. Exploiting vast natural resources and a large labor pool, it is today South America's leading economic power and a regional leader, one of the first in the area to begin an economic recovery since 2008. Highly unequal income distribution and crime remain pressing problems. Characterized by large and well-developed agricultural, mining, manufacturing, and service sectors, Brazil's economy outweighs that of all other South American countries, and Brazil is expanding its presence in world markets.

Since 2003, Brazil has steadily improved its macroeconomic stability, building up foreign reserves, and reducing its debt profile by shifting its debt burden toward real denominated and domestically held instruments.

In 2008, Brazil became a net external creditor and two ratings agencies awarded investment grade status to its debt. After strong growth in 2007 and 2008, the onset of the global financial crisis hit the country in 2008. Brazil experienced two quarters of recession, as global demand for Brazil's commodity-based exports declined and external credit dried up. However, Brazil was one of the first emerging markets to begin a recovery. In 2010, consumer and investor confidence revived and GDP growth reached 7.5 percent, the highest growth rate in the past 25 years. But rising inflation led the government to take measures to cool the economy; these actions and the deteriorating international economic situation slowed growth to 2.7 percent in 2011 and 1.3 percent in 2012. Unemployment is at historic lows and Brazil's traditionally high level of income inequality has declined for each of the last 14 years.

Brazil's historically high interest rates have also made it an attractive destination for foreign investors. Large capital inflows over the past several years have contributed to the appreciation of the currency, hurting the competitiveness of Brazilian manufacturing and leading the government to intervene in foreign exchange markets and raise taxes on some foreign capital inflows. President Dilma Rousseff has retained the previous administration's commitment to inflation targeting by the central bank, a floating exchange rate, and fiscal restraint. In an effort to boost growth, in 2012 the administration implemented a somewhat more expansionary monetary policy that has failed to stimulate much growth.

According to Professor Klaus Schwab's Global Competitiveness Report[8] at the World Economic Forum, Brazil has made significant improvement in its macroeconomic condition, despite its still-high inflation rate of nearly seven percent. Schwab argues that, overall, Brazil's fairly sophisticated business community enjoys the benefits of one of the world's largest internal markets (seventh in the world), which allows for important economies of scale and continues to have fairly easy access to financing for its investment projects.

Notwithstanding these strengths, the country also faces important challenges, beginning with the lack of trust in its politicians, which remains low, as well as government efficiency, which is also low, due to excessive government regulation and wasteful spending. The quality of transport infrastructure, which was the cause of recent riots in Brazil during the fall of 2013, remains an unaddressed long-standing challenge. The quality of education is another challenge for the government, affecting Brazil's ability to compete abroad, unable to match the increasing need for a skilled labor force. Moreover, despite the red tape, government bureaucracies, and increasing efforts to facilitate entrepreneurship, especially for small companies, the time needed to start a business remains among the highest in Schwab's countries sample (130th and 139th, respectively). Taxation still is perceived to be too high and to have distortionary effects to the economy.*

With regards to social sustainability, Brazil's overall good performance masks a number of environmental concerns, such as the deforestation of the Amazon; the country possesses one of the highest rates of deforestation in the world. In general, outside of Brazil, the other four BRICS (Russia, India, China, and South Africa) all reveal significant weaknesses in both dimensions of sustainable competitiveness.

In April 2014, Finance Minister Guido Mantega held that the Brazilian economy is expected to expand 2.3 percent in 2014, which was slightly below his February's estimate of 2.5 percent. For the first half of 2014, economic data seemed to support his assertions showing a deceleration of the economy, as suggested by the government. Economic activity rose a timid 0.2 percent month-on-month in February, which was down from the 2.3 percent expansion tallied in January. Industrial output fell a monthly 0.5 percent in March, which was also down from the flat reading tallied in April. In addition, forward-looking indicators registered strong deteriorations in April, as both consumer and business confidence fell to the lowest levels in nearly five years. Will the World Cup, which starts in June, change such trend? Historically, such events do change positivity these economic outlooks, but unfortunately, it tends to be a temporary phenomenon.

Notwithstanding, Brazil's economic data remains positive. As depicted in Figure 1.2, unemployment and public debt have consistently decreased since 2009, and per capita GDP has grown about 33 percent in the past five years (mean of 6.6 percent increase annually).

---

* Ibidem.

	2009	2010	2011	2012	2013
Population (million)	193.2	194.9	196.7	198.4	199.9
GDP per capita (USD)	8,412	10,997	12,586	11,329	11,206
GDP (USD bn)	1,626	2,144	2,475	2,247	2,240
Economic growth (GDP, annual variation in %)	−0.3	7.3	2.7	1.0	2.3
Domestic demand (annual variation in %)	0.0	10.9	3.7	0.6	3.6
Consumption (annual variation in %)	4.4	6.9	4.1	3.2	2.3
Investment (annual variation in %)	−6.7	21.3	4.7	−4.0	6.3
Industrial production (annual variation in %)	−7.1	10.2	0.4	−2.3	2.3
Retail sales (annual variation in %)	5.9	10.9	6.6	8.4	4.3
Unemployment rate	8.1	6.7	6.0	5.5	5.4
Fiscal balance (% of GDP)	−3.3	−2.5	−2.6	−2.5	−3.3
Public debt (% of GDP)	42.5	39.7	37.1	36.0	34.3
Money (annual variation in %)	8.8	16.7	18.7	9.1	10.9
Inflation rate (CPI, annual variation in %, eop)	4.3	5.9	6.5	5.8	5.9
Inflation rate (CPI, annual variation in %)	4.9	5.0	6.6	5.4	6.2
Inflation (PPI, annual variation in %)	−4.1	13.9	4.1	9.1	5.1

Figure 1.2 Brazil economic data 2009–2013

Source: FocusEconomics.com

Russia

Founded in the 12th century, the Principality of Muscovy was able to emerge from over 200 years of Mongol domination (13th–15th centuries) and to gradually conquer and absorb surrounding principalities. In the early 17th century, a new Romanov Dynasty continued this policy of expansion across Siberia to the Pacific. Under Peter I (ruled 1682–1725), hegemony was extended to the Baltic Sea and the country was renamed the Russian Empire. During the 19th century, more territorial acquisitions were made in Europe and Asia.

Defeat in the Russo-Japanese War of 1904–1905 contributed to the Revolution of 1905, which resulted in the formation of a parliament and other reforms. Repeated devastating defeats of the Russian army in World War I led to widespread rioting in the major cities of the Russian Empire and to the overthrow in 1917 of the imperial household. The communists under Vladimir Lenin seized power soon after and formed the Union of Soviet Socialist Republics (USSR). The brutal rule of Iosif Stalin (1928–53) strengthened communist rule and Russian dominance of the Soviet Union at a cost of tens of millions of lives.

The Soviet economy and society stagnated in the following decades until General Secretary Mikhail Gorbachev (1985–91) introduced *glasnost* (openness) and *perestroika* (restructuring) in an attempt to modernize communism, but his initiatives inadvertently released forces that by December 1991 splintered the USSR into Russia and 14 other independent republics. Subsequently, Russia has shifted its post-Soviet democratic ambitions in favor of a centralized semi-authoritarian state in which the leadership seeks to legitimize its rule through managed national elections, populist appeals by President Putin, and continued economic growth. Russia has severely disabled a Chechen rebel movement, although violence still occurs throughout the North Caucasus.

Russia has undergone significant changes since the collapse of the Soviet Union, moving from a globally isolated, centrally planned economy to a more market-based and globally integrated economy. Economic reforms in the 1990s privatized most industries, with notable exceptions in energy and defense-related sectors. The protection of property rights is still weak and the private sector remains subject to heavy state interference.

In 2011, Russia became the world's leading oil producer,[9] surpassing Saudi Arabia. Russia is also the second-largest producer of natural gas, holding the world's largest natural gas reserves, the second-largest coal reserves, and the eighth-largest crude oil reserves. Russia is also a top exporter of metals such as steel and primary aluminum. Notwithstanding, Russia's reliance on commodity exports, as in Brazil's, makes it vulnerable to boom and bust cycles that follow the volatile swings in global prices. Hence, the government, since 2007, embarked on an ambitious program to reduce this dependency and build up the country's high technology sectors, but with few visible results so far.

The economy had averaged seven percent growth in the decade following the 1998 Russian financial crisis, resulting in a doubling of real disposable incomes and the emergence of a middle class. The Russian economy, however, was one of the hardest hit by the 2008–2009 global economic crisis as oil prices plummeted and the foreign credits that Russian banks and firms relied on dried up.*

According to the World Bank[10] the government's anti-crisis package in 2008–2009 amounted to roughly 6.7 percent of GDP. The economic decline bottomed out in mid-2009 and the economy began to grow again in the third quarter of 2009. High oil prices maintained Russian growth in 2011–2012 and helped Russia reduce the budget deficit inherited from 2008–2009, which helped Russia reducing unemployment to record lows and lower inflation.

Russia joined the WTO in 2012, which will reduce trade barriers in Russia for foreign goods and services and help open foreign markets to Russian goods and services. At the same time, Russia has sought to cement economic ties with countries in the former Soviet space through a Customs Union with Belarus and Kazakhstan, and, in the next several years, through the creation of a new Russia-led economic bloc called the Eurasian Economic Union (EEU).

Nonetheless, Russia is experiencing several challenges. The country has had difficulty attracting foreign direct investment and has experienced large capital outflows in the past several years, leading to official programs to improve Russia's international rankings for its investment climate. Russia's adoption of a new oil-price-based fiscal rule in 2012 and a more flexible exchange rate policy have improved its ability to deal with external shocks, including volatile oil prices. Russia's long-term challenges also include a shrinking workforce, rampant corruption, and underinvestment in infrastructure.

Nevertheless, according to Klaus Schwab[11] at the World Economic Forum, Russia has sharply improved its macroeconomic environment due to low government debt and a government budget that has moved into surplus, although the country still hasn't managed to address its weak public institutions or the capacity for innovation. Hence, the country

---

* Ibidem.

still suffers from inefficiencies in the goods, labor, and financial markets, where the situation is deteriorating for the second year in a row.

Russia's weak level of global competition, caused by inefficient anti-monopolistic policies and high restrictions on trade and foreign ownership, contributes to this inefficient allocation of Russia's vast resources, hampering higher levels of productivity in the economy.* Moreover, as the country moves toward a more advanced stage of economic development, its lack of business sophistication and low rates of technological adoption will become increasingly important challenges for its sustained progress. On the other hand, its high level of education enrollment, especially at the tertiary level, its fairly, good infrastructure, and its large domestic market represent areas that can be leveraged to improve Russia's competitiveness.

According to a revised estimate released in May 2014 by Focus-Economics.com,[†] the Russian economy expanded 0.9 percent over the same period in Q1 of 2013, confirming concerns that the country has been facing an economic deceleration. Notwithstanding, also in May 2014, Russia and China signed a $400 billion deal in which the former will sell gas to the latter for 30 years starting in 2018. The deal is the largest gas contract Russia has ever entered into, which can potentially improve Russia's overall economic data.

Figure 1.3 provides Russia's economic data from 2009 through 2014. Unemployment and inflation rates have consistently decreased since 2009; per capita GDP has grown over 100 percent in the past five years (about 20 percent annual increase). While political tensions eased after Russia withdrew its troops from the Ukrainian border, capital outflows totaled $63.7 billion, which was the largest outflow since 2011 and exceeded all outflows tallied in 2013. Such outflow of capital was due to the two rounds of sanctions imposed on Russia in March and April remain in force and the threat of stronger measures has already served to erode investor confidence and trigger a massive capital flight.

---

* Ibidem.

[†] http://focus-economics.com/countries/russia.

	2009	2010	2011	2012	2013
Population (million)	142.7	142.9	142.4	141.9	141.4
GDP per capita (USD)	7,841	10,673	13,246	14,438	15,718
GDP (USD bn)	1,119	1,525	1,886	2,049	2.223
Economic growth (GDP, annual variation in %)	−7.8	4.5	4.3	3.4	1.3
Consumption (annual variation in %)	−5.1	5.5	6.8	7.9	4.7
Investment (annual variation in %)	−14.4	5.9	10.2	5.3	−0.1
Industrial production (annual variation in %)	−9.2	7.3	5.1	3.4	0.4
Retail sales (annual variation in %)	−4.8	6.2	6.9	6.5	3.9
Unemployment rate	8.4	7.5	6.6	5.5	5.5
Fiscal balance (% of GDP)	−5.4	−3.9	0.8	−0.0	−0.7
Public debt (% of GDP)	8.3	9.0	9.5	10.5	11.3
Money (annual variation in %)	17.7	31.1	22.3	11.9	14.6
Inflation rate (CPI, annual variation in %, eop)	8.8	8.8	6.1	6.6	6.5
Inflation rate (CPI, annual variation in %)	11.7	6.9	8.4	5.1	6.8
Inflation (PPI, annual variation in %)	13.8	16.7	12.0	5.1	3.7

Figure 1.3 Russia economic data from 2009 through 2013

Source: FocusEconomics.com

India

The Indus Valley civilization, one of the world's oldest, flourished during the third and second millennia B.C. and extended into northwestern India. Aryan tribes from the northwest infiltrated the Indian subcontinent about 1500 B.C., and then merged with the earlier Dravidian inhabitants creating the classical Indian culture. The Maurya Empire of the 4th and 3rd centuries B.C., which reached its apex under Ashoka,* united much of South Asia. The Golden Age ushered in by the Gupta dynasty (fourth to sixth centuries A.D.) saw a flowering of Indian science, art, and culture. Islam spread across the subcontinent over a period of 700 years. In the 10th and 11th centuries, Turks and Afghans invaded India and established the Delhi Sultanate. In the early 16th century, the Emperor Babur established the Mughal Dynasty, which ruled India for more than three centuries.

---

* Ashoka Maurya (304–232 BCE) was an Indian emperor of the Maurya Dynasty who ruled almost the entire Indian subcontinent from 269 BCE to 232 BCE.

European explorers began establishing footholds in India during the 16th century. By the 19th century, Great Britain had become the dominant political power on the subcontinent. The British Indian Army played a vital role in both World Wars. Years of nonviolent resistance to British rule, led by Mohandas Gandhi and Jawaharlal Nehru, eventually resulted in Indian independence, which was granted in 1947. Large-scale communal violence took place before and after the subcontinent partition into two separate states, India and Pakistan.

The neighboring nations have fought three wars since independence, the last of which was in 1971 and resulted in East Pakistan becoming the separate nation of Bangladesh. India's nuclear weapons tests in 1998 emboldened Pakistan to conduct its own tests that same year. In November 2008, terrorists originating from Pakistan conducted a series of coordinated attacks in Mumbai, India's financial capital. Despite pressing problems such as significant overpopulation, environmental degradation, extensive poverty, and widespread corruption, economic growth following the launch of economic reforms in 1991 and a massive youthful population are driving India's emergence as a regional and global power.

India is developing into an open-market economy, but there remain traces of its past autarkic policies. Economic liberalization measures, including industrial deregulation, privatization of state-owned enterprises, and reduced controls on foreign trade and investment, began in the early 1990s and have served to accelerate the country's growth; growth that has averaged fewer than seven percent per year since 1997.

India's diverse economy encompasses traditional village farming, modern agriculture, handicrafts, a wide range of modern industries, and a multitude of services. Slightly more than half of the work force is in agriculture, but services, particularly information technology and information systems (IT&IS) are the major source of economic growth, accounting for nearly two-thirds of India's output, with less than one-third of its labor force. India has capitalized on its large educated English-speaking population to become a major exporter of information technology services, business outsourcing services, and software workers.

In 2010, the Indian economy rebounded robustly from the global financial crisis, in large part due to strong domestic demand, and growth exceeded eight percent year-on-year in real terms. However, India's economic growth began slowing in 2011 due to a slowdown in government spending and a decline in investment, caused by investor pessimism about the government's commitment to further economic reforms. High international crude prices have also exacerbated the government's fuel subsidy expenditures, contributing to a higher fiscal deficit and a worsening current account deficit.

In late 2012, the Indian Government announced additional reforms and deficit reduction measures to reverse India's slowdown, including allowing higher levels of foreign participation in direct investment in the economy. The outlook for India's medium-term growth is positive due to a young population and corresponding low dependency ratio, healthy savings and investment rates, and increasing integration into the global economy.

India has many long-term challenges that it has yet to fully address, including poverty, corruption, violence and discrimination against women and girls, an inefficient power generation and distribution system, ineffective enforcement of intellectual property rights, decades-long civil litigation dockets, inadequate transport and agricultural infrastructure, accommodating rural-to-urban migration, limited non-agricultural employment opportunities, and inadequate availability of basic quality of life and higher education.

On the topic of education, in his New York Times bestseller *Imagining India: the Idea of a Renewed Nation*, the co-chairman of Infosys Technologies, Nandan Nilekani argues that "reforms that expand access are thus the most crucial for the disempowered. They are critical in bringing income mobility to the weakest and poorest groups. And this mobility is at the heart of the success of free markets: we tend to forget that a prerequisite to productivity and efficiency is a large pool of educated people, which requires in turn easy and widespread access to good schools and colleges."[12]

Nilekani argues that the government of India ignores such challenges of fairness and equality at their peril. He contends that if discontent is left to fester, it will trigger enormous backlashes against open market policies, which actually is happening with Wal-Mart's expansion in the country. In August 2013, an article in the Business Standard[13] discussed Wal-Mart's ongoing Enforcement Directorate (ED) investigation into its investment in the Bharti Group, a business conglomerate headquartered in New Delhi, India, where in 2010 the retailer giant made an investment in the form of compulsory convertible debentures (CCD). In addition, Wal-Mart was concerned with the political uncertainty in India, with the general election slated for 2014, along with the possibility of a statewide block to foreign direct investment (FDI) in retailing as a potential barrier for the company in that country.

Hence, as of 2013, India is the worst performer among the BRICS, with concerns in both areas of sustainability. Regarding social sustainability, India is not able to provide access to some basic services to many of its citizens; only 34 percent of the population has access to sanitation. The employment of much of the population is also vulnerable, which combined with weak official social safety nets, makes the country vulnerable to economic shocks. In addition, although no official data are reported for youth unemployment, numerous studies indicate that the percentage is very high.[14]

According to Amin,[15] India's economy was once ahead of Brazil and South Africa, but it now trails them by some 10 places, and lags behind China by a margin of 30 positions. The country continues to be penalized for its disappointing performance in areas considered basic factors of competitiveness. The country's supply of transport and energy infrastructure remains largely insufficient and ill adapted to the needs of the economy. Indeed, the Indian business community repeatedly cites infrastructure as the single biggest hindrance to doing business, well ahead of corruption and bureaucracy. It must be noted, however, that the situation has been slowly improving since 2006.*

The picture is even bleaker in the health and basic education sectors. According to the World Economic Forum's Global Competitiveness Report,[16] despite improvements across the board over the past few years, poor public health and education standards remain a primary cause of India's low productivity. Turning to the country's institutions, discontent within the business community remains high regarding lack of reforms and the perceived inability of the government to push them through. Indeed, public trust in politicians has been weakening for the past three

---

* Ibidem.

years. Meanwhile, the macroeconomic environment continues to be characterized by large and repeated public deficits and the highest debt-to-GDP ratio among the BRICS. On a positive note, inflation returned to single-digit territory in 2011.

Despite these considerable challenges, India does possess a number of strengths in the more advanced and complex drivers of competitiveness. This reverse pattern of development is characteristic of India. It can rely on a fairly well developed and sophisticated financial market that can channel financial resources to good use, and it boasts reasonably sophisticated and innovative businesses environment. As argued by Vinay Rai and William Simon in their book titled *Think India*,[17] there is a "new India rising up, and it is going to change the world, from Bollywood to world financial markets, from IT to manufacturing, for service to design." "In the India of today," Rai and Simon continue, "activity in construction, in manufacturing, in innovation, abounds everywhere from large cities to small towns and rural villages. Every sector of the economy, without exception, is growing. And not just growing, but at starling rates that reach fifty to a hundred percent annually."*

Rai and Simon argue that India is not Japan, Brazil, the EU, or even China, as India's people, with their diversity, openness, practicality, innovation, and service orientation, are the country's real strength. Indians creative energy, unleashed after hundreds of years of slavery and foreign rule, are driving modern India to new heights. Just imagine, by 2020, one-half of the world population of people under age of twenty-five will be in India! Mumbai has today some of the most expensive real estate in the world, with over 18 million clustered around the crescent-shaped bay, with a density more than triple of Tokyo. Electronic City, an industrial park that's home to over hundred electronics and software firms in Bangalore, India's Silicon Valley, is the dynamic epicenter of 21st-century India. Figure 1.4 provides an overall outlook for India's economic data between 2009 and 2013. Per capita GDP has grown consistently since 2009 through 2012, although not significantly as Brazil and Russia, at an average rate of about 7.52 percent a year, for a total of 30 percent from

---

* Ibidem.

	2009	2010	2011	2012	2013
Population (million)	1,178	1,195	1,211	1,227	1,243
GDP per capita (USD)	1,160	1,427	1,563	1,509	–
GDP (USD bn)	1,366	1,705	1,893	1,852	–
Economic growth (GDP, annual variation in %)	8.6	8.9	6.7	4.5	–
Consumption (annual variation in %)	7.4	8.7	9.2	5.0	–
Investment (annual variation in %)	7.8	11.1	12.6	0.8	–
Industrial production (annual variation in %)	5.3	8.2	3.0	1.1	–0.1
Public debt (% of GDP)	72.5	67.5	66.8	66.6	–
Money (annual variation in %)	17.0	16.1	4.3	10.4	9.1
Inflation rate (CPI, annual variation in %, eop)	14.3	9.0	9.0	11.2	6.7
Inflation rate (CPI, annual variation in %)	12.2	10.6	8.4	10.2	9.5
Inflation (PPI, annual variation in %)	3.8	9.6	9.0	7.4	6.0

Figure 1.4 India's economic data from 2009 through 2013

Source: FocusEconomics.com

2009 through 2012 (no data was available for 2013). Public debt has also decreased significantly, a trend across all BRICS countries.

The rising of consumerism class is impressive. Their new spending power will make India the biggest cash-drawer worldwide for consumer goods and services.* The Indian consumer, due to colonial prejudices toward moneylenders, had hitherto considered taboo the buying of a house or a car on credit. Now that attitude is being debunked as the enthusiasm of Indians to consume grows, as their disposable incomes continues to rise. Hence, their new enthusiasm to take out a loan to pay for everything from television sets to a trip overseas is making bankers from around the world levitate, although in our view, it may not necessarily be a good thing for Indian families to enter into debt.

More and more banks are investing in India, either by establishing presence there or buying stake in Indian banks. The list of foreign banks in India today is impressive, including global stalwarts such as Deutsche Bank, Citigroup, Goldman Sachs, and investment banks such as JM Morgan Stanley, Barclays, and Merrill Lynch.

---

* Ibidem.

Larry Summers, the former president of Harvard University, said in 2006 that Harvard had made a "fundamental error of judgment" in not recognizing India's potential and promise early enough. A mistake, according to Summers, that Harvard would correct by setting up a dedicated "India Center" with an initial funding of $1 billion.

Back in 2006, the World Economic Forum's (WEF) Global Competitiveness Report* ranked India highest among all BRIC nations, the 43rd most competitive country in world—out of 148 countries surveyed—versus China's 54th at the time. In 2013, India dropped its ranking significantly, to 60th, versus China's even more significant rise to 29th. The rest of the BRICS countries, Brazil, Russia, and South Africa, by comparison, rank 56th, 64th, and 53rd respectively.[18] Stalled reforms, slowing growth, and a sliding rupee have singled India out as an underperformer on the world stage. India's ranking declined by three places to 59th position in the Global Competitiveness Index 2012–2013 of the WEF due to disappointing performance in the basic factors underpinning competitiveness.

The fact remains, however, that India has several advantages over China, according to the WEF Competitiveness report:[†]

- China has less chance for innovation in its relatively closed state-controlled market. India, the largest democracy in the world, has a free market and a free press, which empowers its people to be innovative and creative, even at the grassroots levels.
- India's growing workforce of people below the age of 25 is a major competitive weapon in its arsenal, the benefits of which will soon start trickling in. China's one-child policy, although under revision, while reducing pressure of a population growing too fast and is under revision is making the nation age faster as well.
- Many Indians speak fluent English while most Chinese don't.

---

* http://www.weforum.org/pdf/Global_Competitiveness_Reports/Reports/ gcr_2007/gcr2007_rankings.pdf, (last accessed on 2/02/2012).

† http://www.weforum.org/pdf/Global_Competitiveness_Reports/Reports/ gcr_2007/gcr2007_rankings.pdf, (last accessed on 2/02/2012).

- Both India and China (even more so than India) are known for manufacturing, but India has lured several fortune 500 companies to set up high-end/high-tech research and development centers on their soil.
- Efficient capital markets, quality of public institutions, and a sound judicial system accounts for India besting its competitors.[19]

The Goldman Sachs analysis[20] that puts the United States in third place economically by 2050, behind India and China, while it seems so unlikely to many, seems more logical when you recognize that the brightest 25 percent of India population outnumber the entire population of the United States. Will the same still be true in 2050? If we do the math, the answer is a resounding yes.

In 2014, opposition candidate Narendra Modi from the Bharatiya Janata Party (BJP) won the general elections by a landslide and will become the first prime minister to lead a party with an absolute parliamentary majority since 1989. The BJP-led National Democratic Alliance (NDA) won in 336 out of the 543 constituencies, according to the results the Election Commission of India presented in May 2014. The BJP won an astonishing 282 constituencies, whereas the main opposition party, the Indian National Congress (INC) only won in 44. The results allow Modi and the NDA to form a strong government. Markets reacted to the results with an optimistic surge as Modi's campaign was centered on deregulation of business and fostering foreign direct investment, a policy setting that he put in place during his time as Chief Minister of the State of Gujarat.

China

For centuries China stood as a leading civilization, outpacing the rest of the world in the arts and sciences, but in the 19th and early 20th centuries, the country was beset by civil unrest, major famines, military defeats, and foreign occupation. After World War II, the communists under Mao Zedong established an autocratic socialist system that, while ensuring

China's sovereignty, imposed strict controls over everyday life and cost the lives of tens of millions of people.

After 1978, Mao's successor Deng Xiaoping and other leaders focused on market-oriented economic development and by 2000 output had quadrupled. For much of the population, living standards have improved dramatically and the room for personal choice has expanded, yet political controls remain tight. Since the early 1990s, China has increased its global outreach and participation in international organizations.

Since the late 1970s, China has moved from a closed, centrally planned system to a more market-oriented one that plays a major global role, becoming in 2010, the world's largest exporter. Reforms began with the phasing out of collectivized agriculture, and expanded to include the gradual liberalization of prices, fiscal decentralization, increased autonomy for state enterprises, creation of a diversified banking system, development of stock markets, rapid growth of the private sector, and opening to foreign trade and investment.

China has implemented reforms in a gradualist fashion. In recent years, China has renewed its support for state-owned enterprises in sectors it considers important to economic security, explicitly looking to foster globally competitive national champions. After keeping its currency tightly linked to the U.S. dollar for years, in July 2005 China revalued its currency by 2.1 percent against the U.S. dollar and moved to an exchange rate system that references a basket of currencies. From mid-2005 to late 2008 cumulative appreciation of the renminbi against the U.S. dollar was more than 20 percent, but the exchange rate remained virtually pegged to the dollar from the onset of the global financial crisis until June 2010, when Beijing allowed resumption of a gradual appreciation.

The restructuring of the economy and resulting efficiency gains have contributed to a more than tenfold increase in GDP since 1978. Measured on a purchasing power parity (PPP) basis that adjusts for price differences, in 2012, China stood as the second-largest economy in the world after the United States, having surpassed Japan in 2001. The dollar values of China's agricultural and industrial output each exceed those of the United States. China is also second to the United States in the value of services it produces. Still, per capita income is below the world average.

According to U.S. CIA's World FactBook,[21] the Chinese government faces numerous economic challenges, including:

- Reduction of its high domestic savings rate and correspondingly low domestic demand.
- Sustaining adequate job growth for tens of millions of migrants and new entrants to the work force.
- Reducing corruption and other economic crimes.
- Containing environmental damage and social strife related to the economy's rapid transformation. Economic development has progressed further in coastal provinces than in the interior, and by 2011 more than 250 million migrant workers and their dependents had relocated to urban areas to find work.

One consequence of population control policy is that China is now one of the most rapidly aging countries in the world. Deterioration in the environment, notably air pollution, soil erosion, and the steady fall of the water table, especially in the North, is another long-term problem. China continues to lose arable land because of erosion and economic development. The Chinese government is seeking to add energy production capacity from sources other than coal and oil, focusing on nuclear and alternative energy development.

In 2010–2011, China faced high inflation resulting largely from its credit-fueled stimulus program. Some tightening measures appear to have controlled inflation, but GDP growth consequently slowed to fewer than 8 percent for 2012. An economic slowdown in Europe contributed to China's, and is expected to further drag Chinese growth in 2013. In addition, debt overhangs from the stimulus program; particularly among local governments, and a property price bubble currently challenges policy makers. The government's 12th Five-Year Plan, adopted in March 2011, emphasizes continued economic reforms and the need to increase domestic consumption in order to make the economy less dependent on exports in the future. However, China has made only marginal progress toward these rebalancing goals.

Therefore, China's competitiveness performance notably has weakened in the past few years. Social sustainability is partially measured for

	2009	2010	2011	2012	2013
Population (million)	1,335	1,341	1,347	1,354	1,361
GDP per capita (USD)	3,740	4,429	5,452	6,092	6,810
GDP (USD bn)	4,992	5,938	7,346	8,249	9,267
Economic growth (GDP, annual variation in %)	9.2	10.5	9.3	7.7	7.7
Consumption (annual variation in %)	11.4	10.6	14.6	10.1	–
Investment (annual variation in %)	30.5	24.5	24.0	20.6	19.6
Industrial production (annual variation in %)	11.0	15.7	13.9	10.0	9.7
Retail sales (annual variation in %)	15.5	18.4	17.1	14.3	13.1
Unemployment rate	4.3	4.1	4.1	4.1	4.1
Fiscal balance (% of GDP)	−2.3	−1.7	−1.1	−1.7	−1.9
Public debt (% of GDP)	17.7	16.8	15.2	14.9	–
Money (annual variation in %)	27.7	19.7	13.6	13.8	13.6
Inflation rate (CPI, annual variation in %, eop)	1.9	4.6	4.1	2.5	2.5
Inflation rate (CPI, annual variation in %)	−0.7	3.3	5.4	2.6	2.6
Inflation (PPI, annual variation in %)	−5.4	5.5	6.0	−1.7	−1.9

Figure 1.5 China economic data from 2009 through 2013

Source: FocusEconomics.com

China, as the country does not report data related to youth unemployment or vulnerable employment. However, the available indicators[22] show a somewhat negative picture, with rising social inequality and general access to basic services such as improved sanitation remaining low.

As depicted in Figure 1.5, China's economic data remains positive. GDP per capita has grown from $3,740 in 2009 to $6,810 in 2013, an increase of over 82 percent (or about 16 percent annually) in just five years. Unemployment has held sturdy at an average of 4.1 percent annually, while public debt has also decreased substantially.

According to the Global Competitiveness Report,* after five years of incremental but steady progress, China has lost some competitive advantages. Without a doubt, the country continues to lead the BRICS economies by a wide margin, ahead of second-placed Brazil, China boasts $8.2 billion in nominal GDP versus Brazil's $2.4 billion. Although China's decline is small, its global competitiveness deterioration is more

---

* Ibidem.

pronounced in those areas that have become critical for China's competitiveness, namely financial market development, technological readiness, and market efficiency.

For market efficiency, insufficient domestic and foreign competition is of particular concern, as the various barriers to entry appear to be more prevalent and more important than in previous years. On a more positive note, China's macroeconomic situation remains very favorable, despite a prolonged episode of high inflation. China runs a moderate budget deficit, boasting a low, albeit increasing, and government debt-to-GDP ratio of 26 percent, while its gross savings rate remains above 50 percent of GDP.

The rating of its sovereign debt is significantly better than that of the other BRICS and indeed of many advanced economies. Moreover, China receives relatively high marks when it comes to health and basic education, as enrollment figures for higher education continues to be on the rise, even though the quality of education, in particular the quality of management schools, and the disconnect between educational content and business needs in the country remain important issues.

South Africa

Dutch traders landed at the southern tip of modern day South Africa in 1652 and established a stopover point on the spice route between the Netherlands and the Far East, founding the city of Cape Town. After the British seized the Cape of Good Hope area in 1806, many of the Dutch settlers traveled north to establish their own republics. The discovery of diamonds in 1867 and gold in 1886 stimulated wealth and immigration, while intensifying the subjugation of the native inhabitants. The Dutch traders resisted British invasions but were defeated in the Boer War in 1899–1902. The British and the Afrikaners, as the Dutch traders became known, ruled together beginning in 1910 under the Union of South Africa, which became a republic in 1961 after a whites-only referendum.[23] In 1948, the National Party was voted into power and instituted a policy of apartheid, or the separate development of the races, which favored the white minority at the expense of the black majority. The African National Congress (ANC) led the opposition to apartheid and many top ANC leaders, such as Nelson Mandela, spent decades in South Africa's prisons. Internal protests and insurgency, as well as boycotts by some Western nations and institutions, led to the regime's eventual willingness to negotiate a peaceful transition to majority rule. The first multi-racial elections in 1994 brought an end to apartheid and ushered in majority rule under an ANC-led government.

Since then, South Africa has struggled to address apartheid-era imbalances in decent housing, education, and health care. ANC squabbling, which has grown in recent years, pinnacled in September 2008 when President Thabo Mbeki resigned, and Kgalema Motlanthe, the party's General-Secretary, succeeded him as interim president. Jacob Zuma became president after the ANC won general elections in April 2009.

South Africa is a middle-income, emerging market with an abundant supply of natural resources. It has a well-developed financial, legal, communications, energy, and transport sectors and a stock exchange that is the 15th largest in the world. Even though the country has modern infrastructure that support a relatively efficient distribution of goods to major urban centers throughout the region, some factors are delaying growth.

From 1993 until 2013, South Africa GDP growth rate averaged 3.2 percent reaching an all time high of 7.6 percent in March of 1996. The economy began to slowdown in the second half of 2007 due to an electricity crisis. State power supplier Eskom encountered problems with aging plants and meeting electricity demand necessitating load-shedding* cuts in 2007 and 2008 to residents and businesses in the major cities. Since then Eskom has built two new power stations and installed new power demand management programs to improve power grid reliability. Subsequently, the global financial crisis reduced commodity prices and world demand. Consequently, in 2009, South Africa's GDP fell nearly two percent, to a record low of −6.3 percent in March of 2009, but it

---

* A load shedding, also referred to as rolling blackout, is an intentionally engineered electrical power shutdown where electricity delivery is stopped for non-overlapping periods of time over different parts of the distribution region. Load shedding is a last-resort measure used by an electric utility company to avoid a total blackout of the power system.

has recovered since, at an annualized 0.70 percent in the third quarter of 2013 over the previous quarter.*

South Africa export-based economy is the largest and most developed in Africa. The country is rich in natural resources and is a leading producer of platinum, gold, chromium, and iron. From 2002 to 2008, South Africa grew at an average of 4.5 percent year-on-year, its fastest expansion since the establishment of democracy in 1994. However, in recent years, successive governments have failed to address structural problems such as the widening income inequality gap between rich and poor, low-skilled labor force, high unemployment rate at nearly 25 percent of the work force, deteriorating infrastructure, high corruption, and crime rates.

As a result, since the recession in 2008, South Africa growth has been sluggish and below African average. South Africa's economic policy has focused on controlling inflation, however, the country has had significant budget deficits that restrict its ability to deal with pressing economic problems. The current government faces growing pressure from special interest groups to use state-owned enterprises to deliver basic services to low-income areas and to increase job growth.

Sub-Saharan Africa has grown impressively over the last 15 years, registering growth rates of over five percent in the past two years, while the region continues to exceed the global average and to exhibit a favorable economic outlook. Indeed, the region has bounced back rapidly from the global economic crisis, when GDP growth dropped to two percent in 2009. These developments highlight its simultaneous resilience and vulnerability to global economic developments, with regional variations. Although growth in sub-Saharan middle-income countries seems to have followed the global slowdown more closely, such as in South Africa, lower-income and oil-exporting countries in the region have been largely unaffected.

As mentioned earlier in this section, South Africa is ranked 52nd in 2013, the best economy in sub-Saharan Africa, and the third among the BRICS economies. The country benefits from the large size of its economy. Particularly impressive is the country's financial market development,

---

* http://www.tradingeconomics.com/south-africa/gdp-growth, (last accessed on 10/20/2013).

	2012	2013(e)	2014(p)	2015(p)
Real GDP growth	2.5	1.9	2.7	3
Real GDP per capita growth	1.7	1.2	2	2.3
CPI inflation	5.7	5.7	5.7	5.3
Budget balance % GDP	−4.2	−4.1	−4.1	−3.9
Current account balance % GDP	−5.2	−6.5	−6.4	−6.4

Figure 1.6 Microeconomics indicators for South Africa

Source: AfricanEconomicOutlook.org

indicating high confidence in South Africa's financial markets at a time when trust is returning only slowly in many other parts of the world. South Africa also does reasonably well in more complex areas, such as business sophistication, and innovation, benefiting from good scientific research institutions and strong collaboration between universities and the business sector in innovation.

Nonetheless, the 2014 strikes in South Africa have again crippled the economy. The economy contracted 0.6 percent q/q annualized in the March quarter, the first contraction since the 2009 global downturn, and fears have increased of a first-half recession. Year-on-year growth was 1.6 percent. Mining fell an annualized 25 percent, its biggest drop in 47 years. Figure 1.6 provides microeconomic indicators for the country.*

According to WEF's 2013's Global Competitiveness report,[24] these combined attributes make South Africa the most competitive economy in the African region, but in order to further enhance its competitiveness, the country will need to address some weaknesses. Out of 148 countries surveyed by WEF, South Africa still rank 113th in labor market efficiency, a drop of 18 places from 2012 position, due to its rigid hiring and firing practices, a lack of flexibility in wage determination by companies, and significant tensions in labor-employer relations.

The educational sector is another challenge, as efforts also must be made to increase the university enrollment rate in order to better develop

---

* The authors attempted to use macroeconomic data from Focus Economics for consistency in data analysis across all other BRICS countries, however data was not available.

its innovation potential. Combined efforts in these areas will be critical in view of the country's high unemployment rate of 24.7 percent, although it has improved since 2012, at which time the rate was at 25.7 percent. In addition, South Africa's infrastructure, although good by sub-Sahara's standards, requires upgrading. The poor security situation remains another important obstacle to doing business in South Africa. The high business costs of crime and violence and the sense that the police are unable to provide sufficient protection from crime do not contribute to an environment that fosters competitiveness. Another major concern remains the health of the workforce, which WEF* ranked 132nd out of 148 economies, as a result of high rates of communicable diseases and poor health indicators.

BRICS' Global Influential Ascend

Over the last decade, the BRIC, now BRICS, term has come to symbolize the growing power of the world's largest emerging economies and their potential impact on the global economic and, increasingly, political order. All five members of BRICS are current members of the United Nations Security Council. Russia and China are permanent members with veto power, while the rest are non-permanent members currently serving on the Council.

Whether the BRICS represents a cohesive group or just a clever acronym, however, is still debatable. Arguably, there are many differences between these countries, from values and economics to political structure and geopolitical interests, which far outweighs commonalities. One main commonality among these countries is a mild anti-Americanism and generally internal or domestic challenge, including but not limited to institutional stability, social inequality, and demographic pressures.

There is a common agreement, however, of how important the BRICS bloc is for each of the members in terms of the symbolism of creating for themselves an important role on the global stage, as well as an alternate perspective on the global economic order, and the desire to wield greater influence over the rules governing international commerce and economic

---

* Ibidem.

policy. As of 2014, the five nations combined hold less than 15 percent voting rights in both the World Bank (WB) and the International Monetary Fund (IMF), despite the fact their economies are predicted to surpass the G7 economies in size by 2032.

The BRICS, as the biggest emerging markets, are uniting to tackle under-development and currency volatility, as well as pooling foreign-currency reserves to ward off balance of payments or currency crises. The plan calls for an implementation of an institution that encroaches on the roles of the World Bank and IMF. At the time of this writing, the leaders of the BRICS bloc were getting ready to approve the establishment of a new development bank during an annual summit in the eastern South African city of Durban.*

Meanwhile, the IMF seems to be fermenting over the BRICS. After years promoting and showcasing them, in November of 2013 it admitted the bloc had either "exhausted their catch-up growth models, or run into the time-honored problems of supply bottlenecks and bad government."[25] We believe, however, the IMF was caught off guard by the aggressiveness of the emerging market rout when the U.S. Federal Reserve began to reconsider its quantitative easing policies in May 2013, threatening to decrease the dollar liquidity that has fuelled the booms, and masked the woes, in Asia, Latin America, and Africa. This dependence on the dollar has disrupted growth in many regions of the world, especially those more dependent on the U.S. consumer marker and the dollar as a currency.

This issue is not new. In the last decade, a few Latin American countries—the most dollarized region in the world—began introducing measures to create incentives to internalize the risks of dollarization, the development of capital markets in local currencies, and de-dollarization of deposits. These all contributed to a decline in credit dollarization globally, but predominantly in Latin America and the BRICS countries. Bolivia, Paraguay, Peru, and Uruguay have been gradually declining in financial dollarization.

---

* There have been speculations that the location of this new BRICS' IMF-like bank will be based in Durban, South Africa.

Coping with De-dollarization

For several decades, dollarization has greatly complicated the policy response in several crises and near-crisis episodes, especially for emerging economies. In some cases, it has been the primary source of financial vulnerability that triggered a crisis not only for BRICS countries, but also for other emerging countries such as the CIVETS and the MENA blocs. The urge to *de-dollarize*, or to withdraw from U.S. Treasury bills and the dollar, is a direct result of foreign countries' mistrust in the U.S. government's ability to control its massive budget deficits. As depicted in Figure 1.7, according to the IMF,[26] the degree of dollarization has declined sharply in Latin America over the past decade.

The same trend holds true for other emerging markets around the world. A case in point is Iran. On March 20, 2012, as Iran was celebrating its greatest holiday of the year, New Year's Eve, it not only celebrated the beginning of a new year but also the end of the dollar as an acceptable currency for payment of its oil.

Although the holiday, known as Nowruz, is typically commemorated by a symbolic purging of the home and spiritual representation of

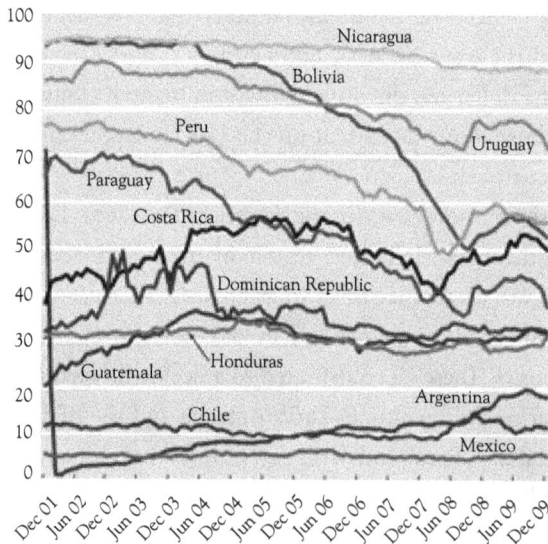

Figure 1.7 Latin America de-dollarization has been high in the past decade

Source: IMF

creation and fertility. In 2012, Iran celebrated it by changing its policy for payment of oil. Essentially, Iran made the decision to no longer accept the U.S. dollar as payment for oil, and instead, decided to accept other currencies and commodities.

Ever since President Obama signed one of the most severe sanction bills against Iran into law, (H.R. 2194), which prohibits any person or business from investing more than 20 million dollars in Iranian petroleum resources, Iran appears determined to phase out the dollar as a form of payment for its oil and derived products. However, if Iran continues to follow through with its decision to refuse dollars-for-oil, it may trigger an intense reaction from the U.S. government, especially for the dollar-reserve currency, mainly supported by the Saud family's determination to accept only dollars for oil, the so-called petrodollars.

The charter of the Iranian oil bourse, a commodity exchange which opened more than five years ago, calls for the commercialization of petroleum and other byproducts in various currencies other than the U.S. dollar, primarily the euro, the Iranian rial, and a basket of other major (non-U.S.) currencies. While there are three other major U.S. dollar-denominated oil markers in the world (North America's West Texas Intermediate crude, North Sea Brent Crude, and the UAE Dubai Crude), there are just two major oil bourses: the New York Mercantile Exchange (NYMEX) in New York City, and the Intercontinental Exchange (ICE) in London and Atlanta.

Iran sits on the largest oil and gas reserves in the world, as depicted in Figure 1.8. Consequently, the country has been developing a fourth oil market where U.S. dollars are not accepted for oil trade. In fact, Iran has proposed the creation of a Petrochemical Exporting Countries Forum (PECF), aimed at financial and technological cooperation among members, as well as product pricing and policy making in production issues—not unlike the Organization of the Petroleum Exporting Countries (OPEC). The British newspaper, The Guardian, cites Iran, Saudi Arabia, United Arab Emirates (UAE), Russia, Qatar, and Turkey as potential members of PECF.

In the wake of such tensions, India is pondering whether to use gold or yen as payment for oil. India has expanded on this conundrum by proposing the setup of a multilateral non-dollarized bank that would be

Proved oil reserves by country, 2013
Top 20 countries

Country	Billions of barrels of crude oil
Venezuela	298
Saudi Arabia	268
Canada	173
Iran	155
Iraq	141
Kuwait	104
United Arab Emirates	98
Russia	80
Libya	48
Nigeria	37
Kazakhstan	30
China	26
Qatar	25
United States	23
Brazil	13
Algeria	12
Angola	10
Mexico	10
Ecuador	8
Azerbaijan	7

0   40   80   120   160   200   240   280   320

Billions of barrels of crude oil

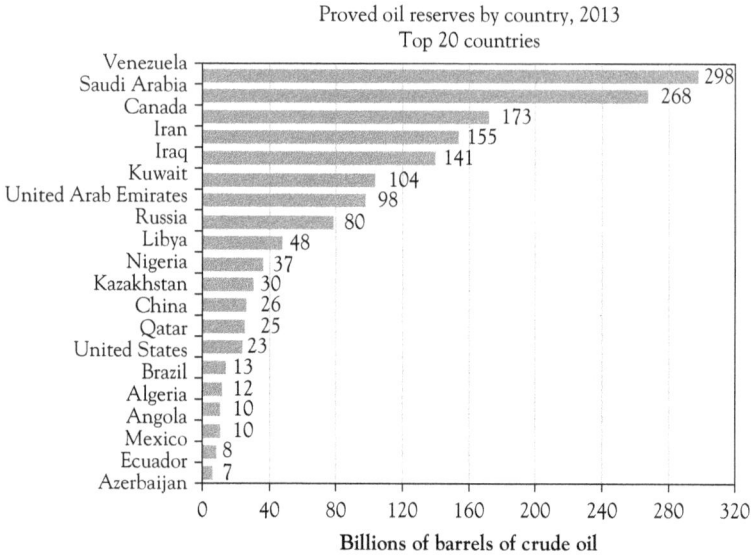

Figure 1.8 Iran's oil reserves is the 4th in the world

funded exclusively by emerging nations to include the BRICS countries for the purpose of financing projects in those countries.

The policy debate about de-dollarization, notwithstanding the United States and Iran conflicts, has heated up around the world. Is de-dollarization a realistic goal for the world? If so, how might it be implemented? Can Iran, the BRICS, the CIVETS, ASEAN, and the MENA countries trigger a chain of events that may threaten to crumble the U.S. dollar as the world's premiere reserve currency? What would be the consequences to the United States, and the world economy, if the dollar was no longer the OPEC measure for oil prices? Certainly, the United States would no longer enjoy the lowest price of gasoline as a non-oil producer nation. The price of fuel would likely skyrocket, increasing the price of all other commodities which ultimately would impact the microeconomics in advanced economies.

While dollarization is a sensible response of economic agents to political or economic uncertainties, its adverse effects often motivate countries, especially emerging economies, to reduce its level. Dollarization is also a rational reaction to interest rate arbitrage opportunities. It may have some benefits, and in extreme cases may be the only viable option available to a country. In such cases, dollarization can be the choice of policymakers or a result of private agents' decision to stop using the local currency. However, most countries seek to limit the extent of dollarization, owing to its potential adverse effects on macroeconomic policies and financial stability. These include a reduction or loss of control of monetary and exchange rate policy, a loss of seigniorage,* and increased foreign exchange risk in the financial and other sectors.

Often key policies that encourage de-dollarization, especially among the emerging markets, focuses on policymakers' intentions to gain greater control of monetary policy, often drawing on the experiences of past countries' successful de-dollarization experiences. We believe durable de-dollarization depends on a credible disinflation plan and targeted microeconomic measures. An effective de-dollarization policy makes the local currency more attractive to local consumers, more than foreign currency. De-dollarization, therefore, entails a mix of macroeconomic and microeconomic policies to enhance the attractiveness of the local currency in economic transactions and to raise awareness of the exchange-risk related costs of dollarization, thus providing incentives to economic agents to de-dollarize voluntarily. It may also include measures to force the use of the domestic currency in tandem with macroeconomic stabilization policies.

On May 16, 2008, Yekaterinburg, Russia hosted the official diplomatic meeting and in June 2009, the BRICS held their first summit in Yekaterinburg. The Yekaterinburg Summit discussions were dominated with negative criticism against the U.S. dollar, with Russion President Putin going so far as to publicly endorse the yuan as a global reserve currency. The group later agreed to replace the U.S. dollar by the IMF's special drawing rights (SDR).

CitiGroup economists have proposed the idea of the 3-G (Global Growth Generators) countries, comprised of 11 countries' economies identified as sources of growth potential and of profitable investment opportunities, in an attempt to effectively put an end to the BRICS bloc.[27] There is also a geostrategic move to pit India as a linchpin in the Pivot of Asia strategy announced in 2010, intended as a new direction for

---

* Seigniorage is the difference between the value of money and the cost to produce and distribute it.

U.S. foreign and strategic policy in the Asia-Pacific region. It was a policy designed under the assumption that U.S. interventions in other regions were winding down. As Secretary of State, Hilary Clinton noted,

> In the last decade, our foreign policy has transitioned from dealing with the post-Cold War peace dividend to demanding commitments in Iraq and Afghanistan. As these wars wind down, we will need to accelerate efforts to pivot to new global realities. . . . In the next 10 years, we need to be smart and systematic about where we invest time and energy, so that we put ourselves in the best position to sustain our interests, and advance our values. One of the most important tasks of American statecraft over the next decade will therefore be to lock in a substantially increased investment—diplomatic, economic, strategic, and otherwise—in the Asia-Pacific region. . . . U.S. commitment there is essential. It will help build that architecture and pay dividends for continued American leadership well into this century, just as our post-World War II commitment to building a comprehensive and lasting transatlantic network of institutions and relationships paid off many times over—and continues to do so. The time has come for the U.S. to make a similar investment as a Pacific power, a strategic course set by President Barack Obama from the outset of his administration and one the is already yielding benefits.[28]

The United States wants to ally with India, Japan, Thailand, South Korea and the Philippines. Could it be that the United States wants to form a sort of *Pacific Rim-region* alliance, to effectively divide the two prominent BRICS nation, India and China, and effectively generate a global discourse to hedge China from becoming an attractor against American hegemony?

At the moment there is no clear answer. Even academicians have expressed concern about the potential demise of the dollar and the role it plays in global markets, as it guarantees the strength to American society and the military. Joshua Zoffer, staff writer of The Harvard International Review, sums up concerns of a strong BRICS IMF-like development bank and the weakening influence of the dollar in an essay titled *Future of Dollar Hegemony*:

"As the issuer of the international reserve currency, the U.S. has garnered two unique economic benefits from dollar hegemony. First, in order for other countries to be able to continually accumulate dollar reserves by purchasing dollar-denominated assets, capital has to flow out of the U.S. and goods must flow in. As a result, the value of the dollar must be kept higher than the value of other currencies in order to decrease the price of imported goods. While this arrangement has come at the cost of an ever-growing current account deficit, it has also subsidized US consumption and fueled the growth of the US economy.

The second benefit of this system is its effect on the market for U.S. government debt. The largest market in the world for a single financial asset is the multi-trillion dollar market for American bonds. This market, considered by many to be the most liquid in the world, allows any nation or large investor to park massive amounts of cash into a stable asset with a relatively desirable rate of return. While the depth and stability of U.S. financial markets as a whole were part of the original reason nations gravitated toward the dollar as a reserve currency, the explosive growth of U.S. government debt has made US Treasury bonds the center of the foreign exchange market and the most widely held form of dollar reserves. The use of the U.S. Treasury securities in currency reserves has created an almost unlimited demand for U.S. debt; if the federal government wishes to issue debt, someone will buy it if only as a way to acquire dollar holdings. This artificially high demand means that the U.S. can issue debt at extremely low interest rates, especially relative to its national debt and overall economic profile. And while the U.S. has had to pay off its existing debt by issuing new securities, no nation wants to call in its debt for fear that it would devalue the rest of its dollar holdings. While precarious and arguably dangerous in the long term, *the reality is that as long as the dollar is the international reserve currency, the U.S. will have a blank check that no one wants to cash.**

---

* Emphasis added.

Whether we agree with U.S. fiscal policy, it is indisputable that the ability to finance its debt has allowed the U.S. to provide its citizens with a high standard of living and fund its enormous military programs. *Essentially, dollar hegemony has served as the backbone of U.S. primacy.** Domestically, the ability to run effectively unlimited budget deficits has allowed the U.S. to fund its massive entitlement programs and, more recently, afford sweeping bailouts at the height of the recession. The U.S. has used its unlimited allowance, afforded by dollar hegemony, to finance its high standard of living and maintain the prosperity required of a hegemon. More importantly, the U.S. has used the demand for American debt to fund its military apparatus."[29]

The BRICS effort to create their own IMF-like bank seems, to address not only a viable alternative for loans aside from the IMF, but also a counter-strategy to fend off advanced economies' strategies such as 3G and Pivot of Asia, thus reducing their exposure to the dollar-pegged polices.

BRICS Capitalization of an IMF-Like Development Bank

In early 2012, the BRICS countries, together representing 43 percent of the world's population and 18 percent of the world's GDP, met in New Delhi, India, for their fourth annual convention. In this meeting of five countries, now attracting more than half of total global financial capital, a plan was announced to establish a BRICS-focused development bank, to be funded solely by BRICS countries. If successful, such bank would enable the bloc to no longer rely on the WB and the IMF for funds, which, for nearly 70 years, have served as omniscient monetary levers for Western interests.

During the G-20 Summit in St. Petersburg, Russia, in September of 2013, the BRICS nations decided to fund their development bank with $100 billion. Russia, Brazil, and India agreed to contribute $18 billion to the BRICS currency reserve pool, while China agreed to contribute

---

* Emphasis added.

$41 billion and South Africa $5 billion.[30] The reserves are aimed at financing joint development ventures, and are set to rival the dominance of the World Bank and the IMF. It is unclear if the amount of initial capitalization will exceed the planned seed-capital, as very different sums of money are being mentioned. Nonetheless, assuming the BRICS countries maintain current growth trends, we believe within the next eight years the bloc may have the ability to fund this bank, thus challenging the IMF and Western advanced economies.

The BRICS countries officially announced the formation of the BRICS Bank in their fifth Summit at Durban, South Africa in 2013. The bank was first proposed in 2012 but the proposal was only approved a year later at a BRICS summit in South Africa. According to a Reuters' article,[31] South African Finance Minister Pravin Gordhan indicated that the bloc will have all preparatory work done for setting up its development bank by the group's next summit in July of 2014.

The group's other project, a $100 billion fund designated to steady currency markets, has also been off to a slow start, although some progress has been made, which marks an important step to the potential institutionalization of a post-western global order. This is causing a lot of debate around the glove, especially among advanced economies; mainly focusing on whether such bank is viable. In our views, such an event can only be compared to the one in San Francisco, during the Summit of the Allies in 1945, when new institutions were being founded for the post-Second World War world order.

The bloc has struggled to take coordinated action on most issues in the past year after the scaling back of U.S. stimulus prompted an exodus of capital from their markets, but they hope their leaders will officially launch the bank at their July 2014 meeting in Brazil. This IMF-like BRICS development bank, which will focus on funding infrastructure projects without the neo-liberal prescriptions imposed by the World Bank, is funded with an initial capital of $100 billion. Since there is reticence from some of the members to contribute more than $10 billion, China will be the major contributor. China is no stranger to money lending. In 2010 it helped create and fund the Chiang Mai Initiative (CMI), a multilateral currency swap arrangement among the ten members of the ASEAN, Japan, and South Korea, which draws from a foreign exchange reserves pool worth $120 billion. That pool expanded to $240 billion in 2012.[32] It wouldn't be surprising if a sudden push for an *Asian Monetary Fund* was to be developed.

In addition to crafting its own economic and monetary policies, another implication for a BRICS' "IMF-like" international bank is the possibility of an alternative global currency to the dollar. What would the world prefer: debased fiat money of the Anglo-American led debtor countries or a currency backed by nations whose citizens are enriched with savings and where economies are producing needed goods and services?

Looking back to Bretton Woods, one cannot ignore the massive debt incurred by the U.S. Treasury alone: $16.7 trillion at the time of this writings, and rising. Estimated U.S. population as of summer of 2013 was 316,669,430, so each citizen's share of this debt is about $52,881.59. The National Debt has continued to increase an average of $1.93 billion per day since September 30, 2012. Conversely, the BRICS have accumulated impressive cumulative reserves topping US$4 trillion. In the short term, this plan is contingent on the extent to which it reconciles the competing agendas of the BRICS nations.

A bank such as this could become attractive for emerging markets, considering the track record of the IMF and World Bank austerity policies in the region, which are very mixed. There is little doubt that many nations would welcome an alternative to these institutions, which would make the BRICS development bank very influential, if we consider the fact that many policymakers believe that the current economic crisis has led to unwielded power of both the World Bank and the IMF, and that this power is uncontested.

There remains the issue of limited IMF and World Bank power. The aftermath of the Asian financial crisis saw a number of countries in Asia and Russia hoarding foreign exchange reserves precisely so they did not have to repay the IMF or World Bank again, or comply with their austerity plans not often prescribed to advanced economies and which resorts to monetization of the debt. The proposed BRICS development bank represents an important new development, that, potentially further circumscribes the influence of those institutions. At least in theory, the BRICS bank could erode the role and status of the IMF and the World Bank. Although it may take a few years before the bank is operational, in the long term this BRICS bank could have a significant impact on the IMF, the World Bank, and global development, as the bank would have access to a vast and growing emerging market. We caution though that the power struggle between nations could lead to difficulties.

At present, China holds vast foreign exchange reserves and is likely to play a major role in the BRICS bank. South Africa, with the weakest economy among the BRICS, due to increased reliance on minerals prone for eventual depletion, may have the most to gain from the establishment of the bank. Nevertheless, we believe the entire BRICS bloc could benefit from the international clout the new bank would wield.

Meanwhile, American politicians plan on increasing the U.S. debt even further by at least $1 trillion a year into the foreseeable future—the stock market rebounds every time the Federal Reserve Bank suggests the potential for more stimulus—the European sovereign debt crisis is an ongoing financial crisis that has made it nearly impossible for some countries in the eurozone to refinance their government debt. During the early summer of 2012, Spain's borrowing costs skyrocketed to seven percent yield on the 10-year bond after Moody's downgraded its bond rating. As of summer 2013, yield fell to five percent, as a result of ECB backstop, but we don't believe it to be sustainable. Spain's borrowings costs will likely continue to rise as a result of the U.S.'s own challenges in jumpstarting its economy.

Also in summer of 2013, Italy, too, is struggling to sell its bonds, being forced to pay the most in nearly a year to sell three-year paper at auction. Italian debt has underperformed that of Spain due to political turmoil involving its former premier Silvio Berlusconi whose outcomes could bring down the Italian government.

A bias we could not avoid during the research of this book is that we are avid believer in a free-market system. Hence, we also believe government programs and monetary stimulus tend, all too often, to be a waste of money. Every policy, rule, and regulation sponsored by government and imposed onto its citizens—i.e. printing of fiat money throughout most of the advanced economies—appears to be a type of price fixing; in this case, to promote currency debasement. In the long run such strategies simply aren't sustainable. It only degrades society's wealth and over time pools more and more of society's assets into the hands of unscrupulous leaders and financiers. Inevitably, the printing press creates an overabundance of money, which in turn makes people feel rich and overspend, creating yet another (false!) boom that will lead to another real bubble. Eventually the bubble bursts, turns to a bust and the cycle repeats itself.

With that in mind, and with the two major world currencies and economies struggling to stabilize, global markets may begin to falter if the continued monetary dominance of an Anglo-American currency is still warranted, as it was in Bretton Woods' times. Even more worrisome is the lack of real compromise over the prospect of money and power among these major global markets: the United States and the EU. Meanwhile, the BRICS, led by China, seem to favor an alternative to the U.S. dollar, especially considering these countries are asked to rely on a monetary system with increasingly shaky economic fundamentals, and currently barred from trading with Iran, if they want to continue trade relations with the United States.

It is no surprise then that the BRICS are pushing for the rapid realignment of control for international funding. In all likelihood, struggling countries, mainly from Africa, East Europe, and Latin America, also may express their desire to align themselves with this new *BRICS Monetary Fund*. It is even possible that other resource rich nations, such as Chile, Bolivia, and Indonesia, may wish to engage as well.

We would not be surprised if the United States continues to overheat its monetary printing press, to the delight of Wall Street, to the point where some savings rich Western nations, such as Germany, Switzerland, and the Nordic Countries may also be tempted to join the BRICS in their quest for an international reserve standard based on sounder currency. We would argue for monetary competition in lieu of currency value fixing, as money has proven over the course of history to be whatever we decided it would be.

CHAPTER 2

CIVETS

A New Strong and Fast Emerging Market

Overview

Until recently, the best notorious work of Goldman Sach's economist Jim O'Neill was probably the development of the BRIC* acronym. Now, however, the new grouping of Colombia, Indonesia, Vietnam, Egypt, Turkey, and South Africa countries, dubbed CIVETS is becoming well know as well. Although it is not certain who created the acronym, some assert HSBC's chief executive Michael Geoghegan while others claim the Economist Intelligence Unit, all parties believe this new bloc is becoming the next big strategy for growth, foreign investments, and global policy influence.

The authors believe that the future of robust global growth and development are being concentrated in the emerging markets. These emerging economies don't have the debt problems with which advanced economies are dealing. We also believe most of the world's consumption will continue to grow with emphasis on emerging market as the merging middle class demands also continue to grow.

While advanced economies, including the UK, those in Europe and North America are deemed to be in a long period of stagnation, much like the BRICS and MENA, the CIVETS countries are home to large youth populations and a fast-growing middle class. These new emerging

---

* Later turned into BRICS, by the BRIC nations themselves with the inclusion of South Africa, although in this chapter we keep this country as part of CIVETS, as originally intended by those whom coined the term.

economies are becoming the perfect storm for Western capital investment seeking new opportunities.

According to HSBC, in its Business Without Borders* newsletter, while the past decade was all about the BRICS countries the next will be focused on the CIVETS. The article goes as far as suggesting that CIVETS "rising middle class, young populations and rapid growth rates make the BRICs look dull in comparison."† In concept, we tend to agree with HSBC's assessment of the CIVETS and BRICS, as it will be discussed throughout this section.

Although we believe in the strength and positive factors surrounding the BRICS in relation to advanced economies, we also acknowledge that there is little in the way of shared interests to unite the BRICS countries. Russia and China are authoritarian states, while Brazil and India are noisy democracies. Brazil and South Africa, both big agricultural and mineral resources exporters seeking freer trade, have little in common with India, which protects its farmers with high tariff barriers. Russia, whose economy is based largely on energy exports, has little in common with China, a net oil importer. China, with over 1.3 billion people, is more than 25 times bigger than South Africa's 50 million. But the BRICS are a model of solidarity when compared to the CIVETS.

The organization of the CIVETS into a cohesive coherent group could be analogous to herding cats; interesting enough, the word civet also is used to refer imprecisely to a number of cat-like creatures of different genii and species. We also worry that some countries that should have been part of the bloc are not, such as Mexico, Myanmar, Nigeria, and Kenya.

For instance, Thailand, with a population of 69 million, an average age of 34, and a GDP growth forecast of more than six percent in 2012 (adjusted to 4.5 in 2015)‡ is not part of the group. Egypt's poor economic performance of late can be considered temporary fallout from the Arab Spring upheavals, but what about South Africa, which in the nearly

---

* https://globalconnections.hsbc.com/us/en
† Ibidem
‡ http://www.worldbank.org/en/publication/global-economic-prospects/regional-outlooks/eap#2

18 years since the advent of majority rule has chalked up an average annual GDP growth of 3.3 percent? If compared to South Africa, Bangladesh could have been included, as it boasts a population of 150 million with median age of 23, and GDP growth averaging six to eight percent. Let's not forget Nigeria, with a population of 140 million people with average age of 19, and an average GDP growth of 6.9 percent since 2005 (adjusted to 4.2 for 2014). Nonetheless, according to the HSBC, "the six countries in the group are posting growth rates higher than five percent, with the exception of Egypt and South Africa, and are trending upwards. Lacking the size and heft of the BRICs, these upstarts nevertheless offer a more dynamic population base, with the average age being 27, soaring domestic consumption and more diverse opportunities for businesses seeking international expansion."*

Despite the various opinions, including ours, on which countries should have been part of the CIVETS acronym, the bloc's economies are being considered the new strong and fast growth markets in the world, and the reasons for that is easily illustrated by its economic figures. As depicted in Figure 2.1, CIVETS markets have been outperforming the

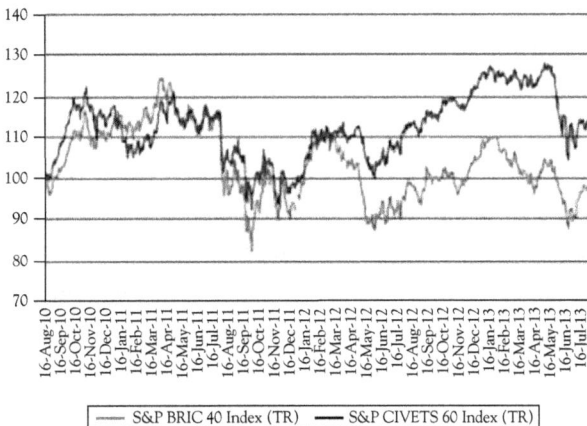

Figure 2.1 **CIVETS market performance through 2007 exceeded the BRIC**

Source: Seeking Alpha,e PREVINVEST calculation on market data and LesEchos. http://blogs.lesechos.fr/echosmarkets/vous-aimez-les-bric-vous-allez-a5662.html

---

* Ibidem.

BRICS since 2009. Half of Turkey's 72 million inhabitants are under the age of 28 and its economy is expected to be the second-fastest growing in the world by 2018. To date, there are more than 900 British companies already operating in Egypt, a country poised to expect a doubling of its population over the next 25 years. South Africa's infrastructure investment programs are providing a huge opportunity to companies that can contract expertise, goods, and services into them over a generation or more. Advanced economies are benefiting from this boom by way of bolstering their own growth.

Governments in advanced economies are taking notice of such positive trends and making commitments to expand their presence in those emerging markets and assist their own multinational companies to access these markets in order to hit ambitious export-led growth targets. In England, for example, the Department for Business, Innovation and Skills is offering assistance to 50,000 small and medium size enterprises (SMEs) to expand their exports into these high-growth markets by 2015.[1] The government is offering financial and diplomatic levers to assist those businesses. The United States is pushing for a Pivot of Asia strategy, and in the EU, Martin Hutchinson, a noted commentator, author and long-time international merchant banker, tells the European Business Review magazine that the next hot emerging-market economies is in fact the CIVETS, or the new BRICs.[2]

Notwithstanding historic political upheaval in Egypt over the last year, large amounts of FDI are finding its way to that country. The UK remains the country's largest investor, with investments of about £13 billion pounds ($20.8 billion). Egyptian's transition government has signaled a wish to speed up economic reform along with the formation of a new democracy in order to attract more outside investment, but already high inflation alongside political uncertainty tops the agenda for the immediate future. That said, thereafter it is expected that the Egyptian economy will grow at a rate of three percent annually.

Its highly mobile, well-educated youth is an important part of Egypt's business opportunity. But a second reason economies like those of Egypt or Turkey are appealing is that they provide a relatively hospitable back door into the emerging potential in neighboring, harder-to-access countries in the BRICS, ASEAN and the MENA regions. We argue that these blocs are in many ways interdependent. As measured by its economic results, 2012 was a good year for the CIVETS bloc. Only Indonesia didn't perform well. South Africa's economy also performed well, despite some labor strife at its palladium mines. Egypt fought off domestic and regional geopolitical headwinds for much of 2012, but its economy remained resilient.

Those are two examples of the fact that each CIVETS nation faces its own issues in the years ahead. Figure 2.2 provides a comparison between the BRICS and the CIVETS countries. Looking closely one can identify a multitude of ways in which these economies intertwine, land resources and opportunities to each other, and open up non-traditional ways to many other emerging and advanced economies.

	BRIC Countries	CIVETS Countries
Countries	Brazil, Russia, India, and China	Colombia, Indonesia, Vietnam, Egypt, Turkey, and South Africa
Name by	Goldman Sachs	Economist Intelligence Unit (EIU)
Growth rate during next 20 yrs	4.9% (prediction by EIU)	4.5% (prediction by EIU)
Population comparison	Brazil-201 mn; Russia-139 mn; India-1.2 bn, and China-1.3 bn.	Colombia-44 mn; Indonesia-242.9 mn; Vietnam-89.5 mn; Egypt-80 mn; Turkey-77 mn; South Africa-49.9 mn
International reach	Have own companies that are destined to be very important outside their own countries	Lack established multinational corporations (MNCs)
Economic power	Already changing the rules of the game	Do not have the economic power to "reshape the global economic order." Combined GDP will only amount to one-fifth the size of the G7 nations' combined GDP by 2030

Figure 2.2 A comparison between the BRIC and the CIVETS economies

Source: WealthOpinion, Knowledge@Wharton.pinion, Knowledge@Wharton. http://wealthy-opinions.blogspot.com/2011/03/bric-countries-vs-civets-countries.html

For instance, a British company, Faun Trackway, landed a contract to supply temporary helipads to the Colombian government's anti-narcotraffic forces, which provided them a gateway into the U.S. market because those forces are bankrolled by American state budgets. In South Africa, the British Prime Minister David Cameron has backed an African Union's idea to launch an African free trade area by 2017, which would in turn simplify and standardize trade tariffs and infrastructure among member states, allowing investors to benefit not only from the South African economy, but also many other leading economies in Africa, such as the MENA bloc.

The following is a breakdown of the CIVETS countries, their economies' threats, opportunities, and challenges.

Colombia

Colombia is emerging as an attractive driving force in the South American region. The country boasts 44 million people and a GDP of $231 billion, which certainly positions itself for future growth. In a world in which resources prices are likely to tick upwards due to Chinese and Indian demand, Colombia's agricultural and natural-resources orientation is in high demand globally. In addition, should the U.S. Congress ever actually ratify the United States-Colombia Free Trade Agreement, which was signed back in November 2006, there should be a further boost to the Colombian market.

Colombia is the oldest democracy in Latin America,[3] but it has suffered several conflicts with guerrilla groups for more than 40 years, threatened its stability. This has changed dramatically, however, since the implementation of the policy *seguridad democrática*[4] (democratic security) implemented in 2003, which has improved significantly the reputation of the country around the world. Improved security measures have led to a 90 percent decline in kidnappings and a 46 percent drop in the murder rate over the past decade, which has helped per-capita GDP double since 2002. As of 2011, and depicted in Figure 2.3, Colombia's GDP growth has been larger than Latin America, the eurozone, and the United States, with only China surpassing it. Colombia's sovereign debt was promoted to investment grade by all three ratings agencies (Fitch, S&P, and

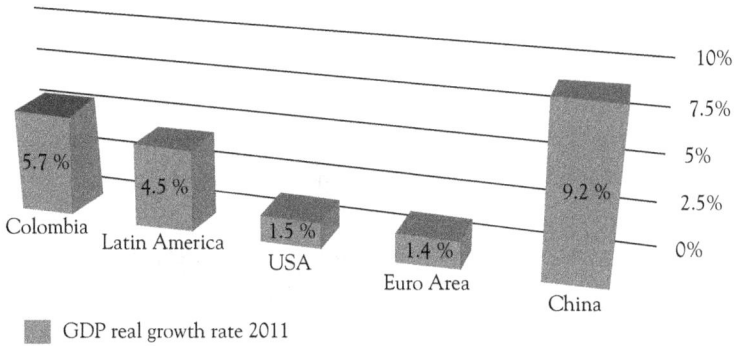

GDP real growth rate 2011

Figure 2.3 Colombia GDP growth rate

Source: IMF

Moody's) recently. In addition, Colombia has substantial oil, coal and natural gas deposits, and as of 2010, a total FDI of $6.8 billion in 2010, with the United States as its principal partner.

Colombia's economy is slowly returning to growth, over 3.5 percent on average for the past few years. Its unemployment rate, however, is among the highest in the region. Its currency, the peso, is rising on the country's commodities boom, and fiscal deficit remains a challenge. As of August 2010, Colombia had a budget deficit of 3.6 percent of its GDP, which according to The Daily Market,[5] is still reasonable. Inflation rate in 2013 was 2.6 percent and external debt a modest 47 percent of GDP.

There has been a surge of new policies favoring entrepreneurism and creation of businesses, which allow foreigners to integrate into this market.[6] Foreign investment in Colombia has increased fivefold between 2002 and 2010[7], increasing significantly its infrastructure. The oil boom since 2010[8] has provided a major boost to its economic recovery, and the country is being proactive in devising strategies to avoid the Dutch disease as billions of dollars in FDI are injected in the country's economy.

Indonesia

Indonesia is a country with 243 million people and a GDP of $521 billion. The country boasts a substantive and well-diversified economy, with agriculture, natural resources, and substantial manufacturing. The level of corruption in the government and society, however, is very high, but still lower than in Russia. The country is situated strategically between China and India, meaning it should benefit as both those behemoths grow.

After emerging as the third-fastest-growing member of the G20 in 2009, Indonesia has continued to display strong growth performance. For the past half-decade, Indonesia's annual GDP growth rate has averaged about six percent, the fastest in Southeast Asia, due in large part to a consumer-spending boom. According to Moody's, the compound credit loan growth rate in the country has been over 22 percent for the past six years, while non-mortgage consumer credit nearly tripled in the last five years. During this time, credit card use has greatly proliferated, with the number of credit cards jumping by 60 percent, while the actual value of transactions almost tripled. This prompted the Bank of Indonesia, the country's central bank, fearing a consumer debt crisis, to limit the number of credit cards a single person is allowed to hold, while barring Indonesians who earn less than $330 dollars a month from being issued credit cards.

In addition, ultra-low interest rates in ailing advanced economies, combined with the U.S. Federal Reserve's multi-trillion dollar QE programs, has led to a $4 trillion tsunami of *hot money*** flowing into emerging market assets since 2008. As depicted in Figure 2.4 this has enabled Indonesia to grow at a very fast pace, following the footsteps of China and India's fast economic growth.

Multinational corporations from advanced economies have taken notice of Indonesia's consumer spending boom. Automakers including Nissan, Toyota, and General Motors have committed to spend up to $2 billion dollars to expand their manufacturing operations in the country in the next few years. Cheap financing also has been fueling a surge in motorcycle sales, which grew 13.9 percent in August 2013 from a year earlier.

---

* According to Investopedia, "Money that flows regularly between financial markets as investors attempt to ensure they get the highest short-term interest rates possible. Hot money will flow from low interest rate yielding countries into higher interest rates countries by investors looking to make the highest return. These financial transfers could affect the exchange rate if the sum is high enough and can therefore impact the balance of payments. http://www.investopedia.com/terms/h/hotmoney.asp.

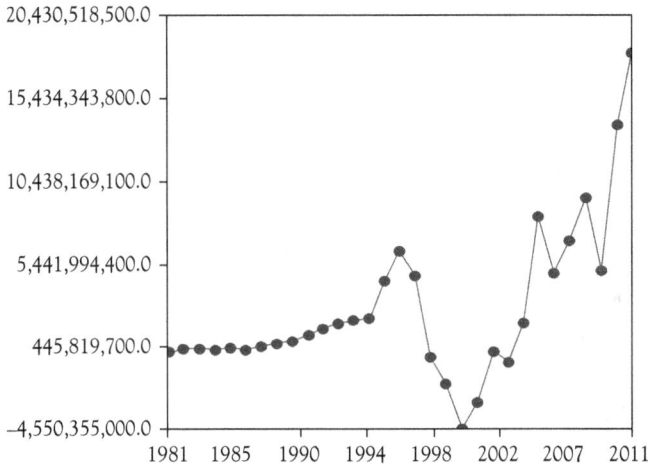

Figure 2.4 Foreign direct investment in Indonesia more than tripled since 2008

Source: IndexMundi.com

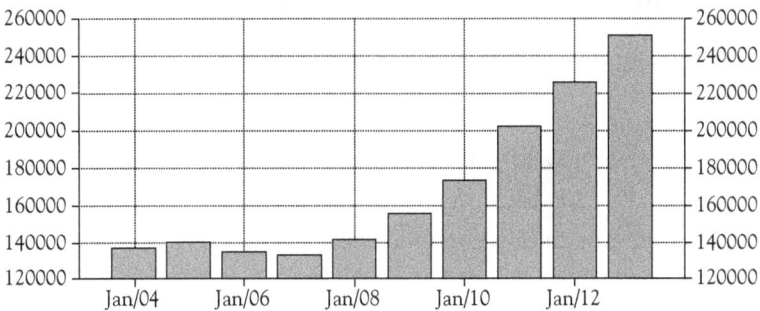

Figure 2.5 Indonesia external debt has nearly doubled since 2008

Source: Trading Economics

Retail sales that have been growing at an annual rate of 10–15 percent in recent years have attracted numerous Western consumer brands like L'Oreal, Unilever, and Nestle that are seeking to cash in on Indonesia's consumer spending boom.[9]

The huge inflows of hot money into the country have benefited many foreign holders of Indonesian local currency government bonds, which rose from 14 percent to 34 percent, while the country's external debt nearly doubled, as depicted in Figure 2.5. These massive capital inflows into Indonesia, however, have contributed to a nearly 50 percent strengthening of the rupiah currency's exchange rate against the U.S. dollar. It also pushed the country's 10-year government bond yields down to record lows of five percent from its 10–15 percent before the 2008 global economic crisis range. This was bad for the local economy, which experienced a major rise in inflation rates, causing the Bank of Indonesia to cut their benchmark interest rate from 12.75 percent to just 5.75 percent to stem export-harming currency appreciation.

Infrastructure spending and high commodity prices boosted most of the investment growth in 2009, but such record low interest rates have also fueled an increasing credit and consumption boom in Indonesia, with domestic consumer spending accounting for nearly 60 percent of the country's overall economy. In addition, the country has the lowest unit labor costs in the Asia-Pacific region, and a very ambitious government committed to attract even higher FDI into its economy, in an attempt to turn the nation into a manufacturing hub. But despite all the positive trends, corruption is still a major problem in the country.

Vietnam

Vietnam, while new to global trade, only becoming a member of the WTO in 2007, has been one of the fastest-growing economies in the world for the past 20 years, with the World Bank projecting an average of 5.54 percent, annually in 2014 and the next few years. Its membership in the ASEAN, and its proximity to China may very well lead the country to become a new potential manufacturing hub as its labor costs are lower than those of China. Foreign investors rank Vietnam as an attractive destination for future investments. The country is one of the most popular destinations for expansion within the ASEAN region.[10] It has been hailed as the next China, and with good reason: Vietnam has a culture that's similar to the Red Dragon in that it's an ex-Communist, one-party state, and attracts FDI due to its cheap labor costs.

After the death of its leader Le Duan in 1986, Vietnam began making the transition from a planned economy to a socialist-oriented market economy after suffering an inflation rate of 700 percent and a stagnant economy.[11] The Communist Party launched a broad economic reform package called Doi Moi ("Renewal"), very similar to the Chinese model (economic openness mixed with communist politics), achieving similar results. Between 1990 and 1997 Vietnam's economy grew at eight percent per annum, with similar results in the following years.

This rapid growth from the extreme poverty of 1986 has given rise to advanced economies—especially Westerns—consumerist habits, particularly among the new rich of Vietnam, causing a widening gap of social inequality and rise in inflation up to 12 percent. In light of stable increases in GDP per capital and average disposable incomes during recent years, the still high percentage of food in the CPI basket emphasizes the substantial, negative impact of high inflation on Vietnam's economy. The rise of food and fuel prices in the world market also imposes a burden on Vietnamese consumers. About 43 percent of disposable income is spent on food and eating activities, which means that the majority of people's consumption budget currently goes to the food sector, giving it substantial revenues as compared to other industries. As the wet markets serve as the main retail channel of most types of food, it is fair to say that nearly 40 percent of people spending will go to these wet markets for food purchases. Revenue of food "industry" will mostly be concentrated in the traditional markets, not on fast-food chains, restaurants, or retail chains as in the United States.

In Vietnam, the stronger integration with the world economy gives rise to sprawling of modern commercial centers, luxurious shopping complexes, and gigantic malls in big cities. The traditional consumption habits, however, still prevail and steer most people to traditional markets, sometimes called flea markets or wet market. These traditional markets are the major channel of retail dating back more than a thousand years ago since the very first urban areas arose and society formed an organized structure under the rule of dynasties. According to Vietnam Association of Retail,* there are now approximately 9000 traditional markets nationwide and up to 80 percent of all retail sales are conducted through these traditional channels. In all, as depicted in Figure 2.6, retail businesses in Vietnam continues to soar.

---

* Voice of Vietnam, http://english.vov.vn/Economy/Vietnam-Retailers-Association-to-be-set-up/22869.vov, (last accessed on 11/03/2013).

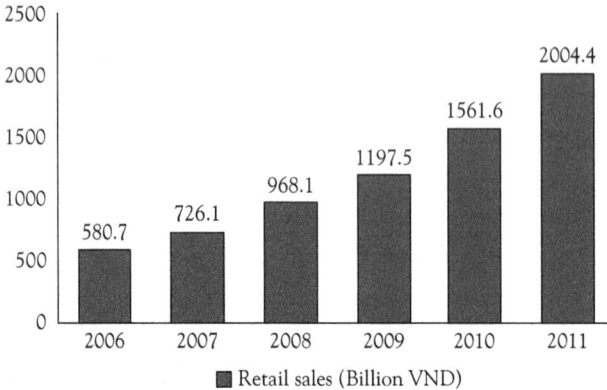

Figure 2.6 Revenue from retail sales and services in Vietnam 2006–2011

According to statistics from the Ministry of Industry and Finance,[12] as of May 2012, there are approximately 638 supermarkets and 117 malls across the nation. The number of newly established supermarkets and malls after five years of joining the WTO (2007–2011), is 27 percent higher than in the five year period prior to the WTO integration. Hence, the Communist Party leaders are very keen on maintaining the growth rate, so that within the next ten years the nation can attain the status of an industrialized country.* Whether the country will be able to achieve this status within such timeframe is yet to be seen, but Vietnam has unquestionably attained relatively stable macroeconomic conditions.

According to the World Bank,[13] as of 2013, the country has been able to maintain a moderate level of inflation at 6.7 percent, while also maintaining a stable exchange rate. The dong depreciated by 1.6 percent in the past 12 months, based on average exchange rates by commercial banks. Simultaneously, the government has been able to increase foreign reserves. It has grown from 2.2 months of import cover at the end of first quarter of 2012 to 2.8 months at the end of first quarter of 2013. This while reducing sovereign risks, with the country's credit default swap (CDS) about 250 basis points in June 2013 compared to about 350 in June 2012.

As a result of strong foreign investment, which accounted for 66 percent of Vietnam total exports, Vietnam's solid export growth has been significant. The total export value rose by 16 percent in the first half

---

* Ibidem.

of 2013 compared to the same period last year, with a wider diversification of export composition although more concentrated on high-tech products, such as cell phones and parts, surpassing the country's traditional exports of crude oil, garment, and footwear. In fact, cell phones, electronics, and computers, now account for nearly a fifth of Vietnam total exports. Most significantly, in 2012, Vietnam achieved its first ever surplus in trade balance since 1992.

But there are some concerns looming over Vietnam's economic outlook. The total FDI ratio has recently declined from a record 11.8 percent in 2008 to about 7.7 percent in the first half of 2013, and other ASEAN countries, such as Indonesia and Thailand, are performing better, while new competitors, such as Myanmar, closing in. Vietnam's growth has actually slowed down since the onset of economic reforms in the late-1980s. Real GDP grew by 5.25 percent in 2012, which although impressive if compared to advanced economies, is the lowest level since 1998.

The World Bank has predicted that the country's economy during 2010–2013 would grow at a slower pace than Indonesia and the Philippines; the first time in nearly two decades. The main cause for the slowdown is the decline in FDI and consequently, low Purchasing Managers Index (PMI), which has remained below 50 marks for most of 2012 and 2013. (PMI below 50 signals contraction in production.) There also has been a slowdown in retail sales and services, from 24 percent in 2011 to 16 percent in 2012, and to 11.9 percent in the first half 2013. Figure 2.7 provides a snapshot of Vietnam's economic achievements and challenges.

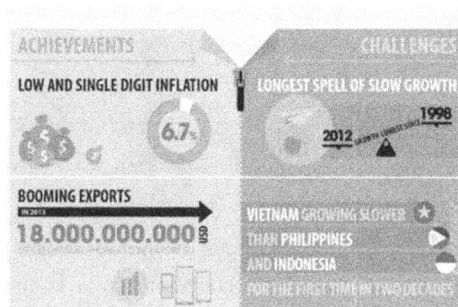

Figure 2.7 Vietnam's economic achievement and challenges as of July 2013

Source: The World Bank

Egypt

Occupying the northeast corner of the African continent, Egypt is bisected by the highly fertile Nile valley, where most economic activity takes place. Egypt's economy was highly centralized during the rule of former President Gamal Abdel Nasser but opened up considerably under former Presidents Anwar El-Sadat and Mohamed Hosni Mubarak. Cairo, from 2004 to 2008, aggressively pursued economic reforms to attract FDI and facilitate GDP growth. Notwithstanding the relatively high levels of economic growth in recent years, living conditions for the average Egyptian remains poor, which has contributed to major public discontentment.

The first year after the fall of the Egyptian president, Hosni Mubarak, in February 2011 was very disruptive for Egypt's economy. After 30 years of dictatorship, elections brought to power the Muslim Brotherhood, who promised to be inclusive and tolerant. But since the Brotherhood Muhammad Morsi became president at the end of June of 2012, the political climate in the country has become even more chaotic. Egyptian society is ever more polarized, and protests frequently turned into violence. The security forces vacillate between support for the Islamists and deep-seated suspicion of them. All the while Egypt's economy has continued to slide toward major disarray, as most economic indicators point to challenging times.

Following the political unrest, the Egyptian government drastically increased social spending to address public dissatisfaction, but political uncertainty at the same time caused economic growth to slow significantly, reducing the government's revenues. Tourism, manufacturing, and construction were among the hardest hit sectors of the Egyptian economy. Subsequently, the government had to resort to the utilization of foreign exchange reserves to support the Egyptian pound. At the time of this writing, it is clear that Egypt will likely seek a loan from the IMF, or perhaps from the newly former BRICS development bank.

Since the revolution, according to YaLibnan, a leading specialized source of Lebanese news,[14] the Egyptian pound has slid about 10 percent, while unemployment hit 20 percent. As of fall 2013, FDI is withering, and total reserves have fallen from $35 billion to $10 billion in the past four years. Many of Egypt's most dynamic businessmen have fled the country, fearing they will be arraigned for complicity with Mr. Mubarak, while the government threatens to reverse a number of privatizations. Meanwhile, the price of food is soaring at a time when the average family spends nearly half of its income to feed itself, forcing a quarter of Egypt's 83 million people to live below the poverty line.

According to the Pew Center's Global Attitudes Project more than 70 percent of Egyptians are unhappy with the way the economy was moving, and 49 percent believe that a strong economy is more important than a good democracy. We believe the number of people disillusioned with the revolution is likely to increase as the economy weakens further. Hafez Ghanem, Senior Fellow, Global Economy and Development with the Brookings Institution,[15] argues that the Egyptian economy is unlikely to collapse suddenly, but in the absence of a serious macroeconomic stabilization program it will continue to deteriorate gradually. Against the backdrop of mounting political unrest and insecurity, socio-economic conditions continue to deteriorate: the unemployment rate is rising, especially among youth (39 percent of the 20–24 age group are unemployed), and rural-urban income disparities remain wide.

The approach of a new Constitution in January 2014 was a key milestone of the transition roadmap issued in July 2013 after the ouster of President Morsi. However, an uncertain political outlook in 2014 continues to undermine economic recovery prospects. The Egyptian economy is plagued with low growth, increasing unemployment, and inflation, as shown in Figure 2.8, excluding corruption, as the country witnessed more than 6,000 corruption investigations and several high profile incriminations since February 2011. The future of Egypt's economy will depend

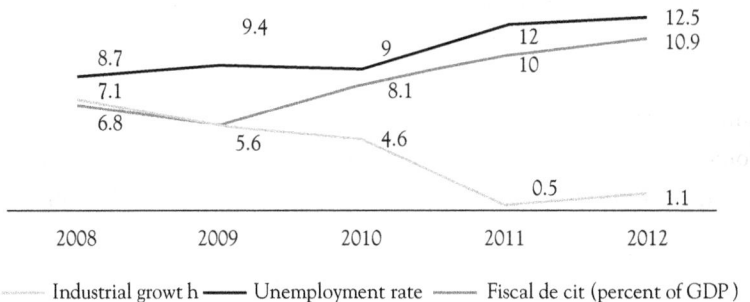

Figure 2.8 Egypt's selected economic indicators

Source: Brookings Institution

on how well it transitions to democracy. We must consider the fact that Egyptian politics are polarized and it is difficult to see how serious economic reforms would be implemented without first reaching compromise on some problematic political issues. The economic outlook for the rest of 2014 remains weak. Growth will remain fragile, the fiscal deficit unsustainably high, and public debt in excess of 100 percent of GDP, as Egypt continues to implement expansionary macroeconomic policies with the help of aid from the Gulf countries.

Ashraf El-Arabi, Planning and International Cooperation Minister, argues that Egypt's economic growth rate in the second quarter of 2012–2013 fiscal years would likely be 0.2 percent lower than the previous quarter, while in the first quarter the economy grew by 2.6 percent, with a forecasted growth for October-December 2012 period in the neighborhood of 2.4 percent. Although Egypt has opened its markets to global trade and investment, non-tariff barriers continue to constrain trade freedom. The investment regime has been stable, but flows have slowed significantly due to the challenging economic and political situation, and the central bank has imposed controls on capital transfers. The state-dominated financial system has been stressed, with negative impacts from the global crisis exacerbated by domestic turbulence.

It's clear that Egypt is facing a major economic crisis, and needs to implement credible reforms to stabilize the economy, control corruption, and lay the foundation for inclusive growth. Such reforms would normally include a reduction in the fiscal deficit to bring the domestic debt under control and a further depreciation of the Egyptian pound to encourage exports and tourism.

The Egyptian government is negotiating with the IMF to obtain support for such a stabilization program. IMF support is desirable because it would open the doors for increased assistance from other bilateral and multilateral donors, and thus help ease the pain of stabilization. The revolution severely retrained economic growth in Egypt. Growth predictions by the World Bank* are to reach only one percent in 2013, compared with 5.2 percent prior to the revolution.

---

* "The World Bank: World Development Indicators Database. Gross Domestic Product 2013," PPP, (last accessed on 09/18/2013).

Analysts expected Egypt to regain its growth trajectory once political stability returned, which has not been the case so far, as the political instability persists. Egypt does possess many assets, including fast-growing ports on the Mediterranean and Red Sea linked by the Suez Canal, a growing tourism network, and vast untapped natural gas reserves. Nonetheless, as long as the political unrest endures, chances for an economic rebound are nominal. Hence, Egypt's economy is expected to grow 2.6 percent in 2014, well below the 3.5 percent projected by the government.[16] A Reuters poll also suggested growth would pick up to four percent only starting in 2015. Figure 2.9 provides a snapshot of the severe downturn of Egypt's GDP growth since 2008.

Given its challenges vis-à-vis politics and economics transition, Egypt has been experiencing an extended period of instability. Much-needed improvements in economic policy have been delayed, and the effectiveness of reforms that might have helped to open markets and improve productivity have been undercut by the tenuous rule of law and the legacy of Egypt's socialist past. Deeper institutional reforms are needed to spur lasting economic growth and development. Those reforms include

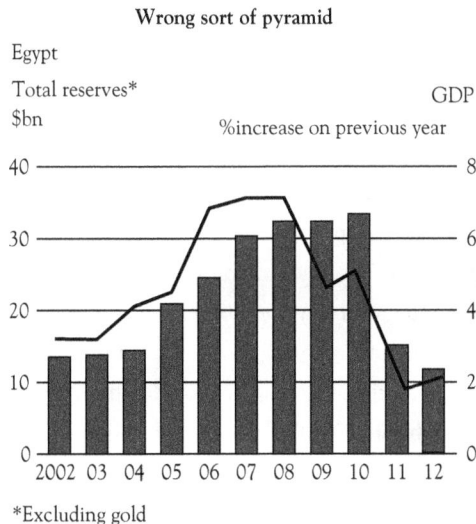

Wrong sort of pyramid

Egypt

Total reserves*
$bn

GDP

%increase on previous year

*Excluding gold

Figure 2.9 A snapshot of the severe downturn of Egypt's GDP growth since 2008

Source: IMF

strengthening the judicial system, better protection of property rights, and more effective action against growing corruption.

Turkey

Located between Europe and major energy producers in the Middle East, Caspian Sea and Russia, Turkey was founded in 1923 from the Anatolian remnants of the defeated Ottoman Empire. After a period of one-party rule, an experiment with multi-party politics led to the 1950 election victory of the opposition Democratic Party and the peaceful transfer of power. Since then, Turkey's political parties have multiplied and democracy has been disrupted by periods of instability and intermittent military coups in1960, 1971, and 1980, which in each case ultimately resulted in a return of political power to civilians.

Turkey has a dynamic economy that has trading links with the European Union but without the constraints of the eurozone or EU membership. The country joined the UN in 1945 and NATO in 1952. In 1964, Turkey became an associate member of the European Community. Over the past decade, it has undertaken many reforms to strengthen its democracy and economy, and began accession membership talks with the EU in 2005. The country is a founding member of the OECD (1961) and the G-20. Since December 31, 1995, the country is part of the EU Customs Union.

An aggressive privatization program has reduced state involvement in basic industry, banking, transport, and communication, and an emerging cadre of middle-class entrepreneurs is adding dynamism to the economy and expanding production beyond the traditional textiles and clothing sectors. According to a survey by Forbes magazine[17] in March 2013, Istanbul, Turkey's financial capital, boasted a total of 37 billionaires (up from 30 in 2012), ranking fifth in the world behind London and Hong Kong in fourth (43 billionaires), New York (62 billionaires), and Moscow (84 billionaires). Turkey's major cities and its Aegean coastline attract millions of visitors every year.

Its ostensibly free-market economy increasingly is driven by its industry and service sectors, although its traditional agriculture sector still accounts for about 25 percent of employment. Turkey has major natural-gas pipeline projects that make it an important energy corridor between Europe and Central Asia. The automotive, construction, and electronics industries are rising in importance and have surpassed textiles within Turkey's export mix. In 2006, oil began to flow through the Baku-Tbilisi-Ceyhan pipeline, marking a major milestone that will fetch up to one million barrels per day from the Caspian to market. Several gas pipeline projects also are moving forward to help transport Central Asian gas to Europe via Turkey, which over the long term will help address Turkey's dependence on imported oil and gas to meet 97 percent of its energy needs.

In 2011, the World Bank[18] placed Turkey as the world's 15th largest GDP-PPP and 18th largest Nominal GDP. After Turkey experienced a severe financial crisis in 2001, Ankara adopted financial and fiscal reforms as part of an IMF program. Then, according to data from the OECD,[19] following weak growth in 2012, the economy began to regain momentum as consumption and investment contracted and offset a surge in exports. Growth is projected to surpass to above three percent in 2013 and, as the global recovery gathers strength, to pick up to 4.5 percent in 2014. Inflation and current account deficit, however, remain above comfort levels.

According to the OECD,* a tight fiscal stance decided upon has been set for 2013 and 2014, but policymakers should allow the economy to stabilize and have flexibility to consider some temporary stimulus should conditions turn out much worse than projected. Internationally comparable general government accounts would help implement and assess the stance of fiscal policy. Monetary policy needs to reduce inflation without undermining the recovery and without pushing up the real exchange rate thus hurting competitiveness. Disinflation would limit the costs on this front. Structural reforms to accelerate formalization and productivity gains remain crucial for strong and sustainable growth.

As depicted in Figure 2.10, the reforms strengthened the country's economic fundamentals and ushered in an era of strong growth, averaging more than six percent annually until 2008, growing faster than any other OECD country. Global economic conditions and tighter fiscal policy,

---

* Ibidem.

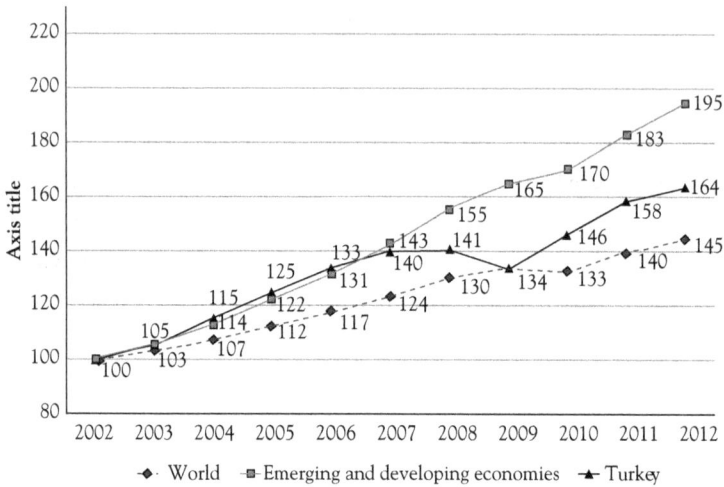

Figure 2.10 Turkey's real GDP growth 2002–2012

Source: Conference Board Database

however, caused GDP to contract in 2009, but Turkey's well-regulated financial markets and banking system helped the country weather the global financial crisis. GDP rebounded strongly to 9.2 percent in 2010 and continue to grow, as exports returned to normal levels following the recession.

Despite impressive growth over the past decade, as a group, Turkish performance lagged significantly behind emerging and advanced economies, but starting in 2009 real GDP rose by 95 percent compared to Turkey's 64 percent. Real GDP in large emerging markets such as China, India, Bangladesh, and Indonesia all grew more rapidly than in Turkey, as it did in many smaller African and Latin American countries. Turkey's rank in global GDP improved marginally over the decade, as in purchasing-power adjusted terms, it went from 17th to 16th in global GDP rankings, surpassing Australia. Measured by current exchange rates, however, the country rose from 21st to 17th, surpassing Taiwan, Switzerland, Belgium, Netherlands, and Sweden, but falling behind Indonesia.* Notwithstanding, Turkey's performance, when leveraged against the

---

* Note that such comparisons of rankings over time using current dollars can be misleading due to movements in real exchange rates.

emerging markets, is less distinguished, but it is significant when compared to advanced economies. The IMF is predicting Turkey's real GDP to be at 3.8 percent in 2013, falling back to 3.5 percent in 2014.[20]

Growth dropped to approximately three percent in 2012. Turkey's public sector debt to GDP ratio fell to about 40 percent, and at least one rating agency has upgraded Turkey's debt to investment grade in 2012. Turkey remains dependent on often volatile, short-term investment to finance its large trade deficit. The stock value of FDI stood at $117 billion at year-end in 2012. Inflows have receded because of continued economic turmoil in Europe and the United States, the source of much of Turkey's FDI. Turkey's relatively high current account deficit, uncertainty related to monetary policy-making, and political turmoil within Turkey's region leave the economy vulnerable to destabilizing shifts in investor confidence.

South Africa

South Africa is another resource-rich economy, with 49 million people and a GDP of $280 billion, which positions the country with a decent-sized economy. The IMF,[21] however, argues South Africa faces low growth, widespread unemployment, and a high reliance on foreign capital inflows.

Rising commodity prices, renewed demand in its automotive and chemical industries and spending on the World Cup have helped South Africa; a diversified economy rich in resources such as gold and platinum, resume growth after it slipped into recession during the global economic downturn.

Despite considerable success on many economic and social policy fronts over the past 19 years, South Africa faces a number of long-standing economic problems that still reflect the long-lasting and harmful legacy of apartheid. Unemployment remains excessively high, and educational outcomes are poor on average and extremely uneven, which aggravates the excess supply of unskilled labor as well as worsening income inequality. In addition, the prospects for sustained improvements on the quality of life of its people are compromised by environmental challenges, notably climate change and water issues.

%, year-on-year

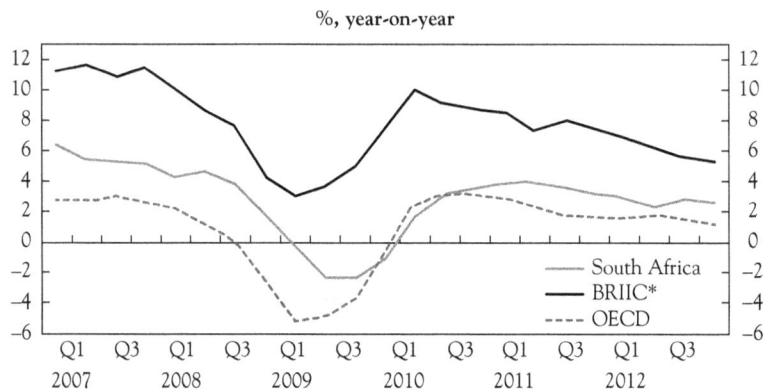

* Brazil, Russian federation, India, Indonesia and China

Figure 2.11 South Africa GDP growth

Source: OECD Quarterly National Accounts database and OECD Economic Outlook 92 database

The OECD[22] argues that South Africa needs to achieve rapid, inclusive economic growth while at the same time making the transition to a low-carbon economy and effectively managing the country's scarce water resources. Tackling the key problems effectively will require continued and skillful management of macroeconomic policies, but above all improved implementation of structural policies, with education being a particularly critical area. As shown in Figure 2.11, the global economic crisis that started in 2008, and the weak global economic outlook is not helping the country.

South Africa has posted, however, major achievements since the transition to majority rule in 1994. Per capita GDP has increased by 40 percent in inflation-adjusted terms. The poverty rate has dropped by 10 percent, and schools and hospitals have been built in previously underserved areas, while government-financed houses have been made available to many in need and social transfers now reach more than half of all households. In addition, the country has strong macroeconomic policy institutions. The government's medium-term fiscal policy framework has been a pillar for the country's prudent fiscal policy, while monetary policy has anchored inflation expectations.

Many see the nation as a gateway to investment into the rest of Africa, including HSBC, which sees long-term growth potential in mining, energy, and the chemical firm, Sasol Ltd. Notwithstanding, South Africa, and the whole continent of Africa, is rich in minerals and oil. China has an economy that requires them in abundance. Since the mid-1990s the economy of sub-Saharan Africa has grown by an average of five percent a year. At the start of this period Africa's trade with China was negligible. It is now worth roughly $200 billion a year. Most of Africa's exports are raw materials. China sends manufactured goods back in return.

Natural resources make up a quarter or more of export revenues for nearly half of the 45 countries in sub-Saharan Africa. Nine of them, including Nigeria and Angola, which have two of Africa's largest economies, benefit from exports of oil and gas. Yet mining and oil are far from the whole story in South Africa. The IMF[23] recently (2013) warned that South Africa is trailing other emerging markets and must quickly implement reforms if it wants to avoid a crisis, pointing to painfully high unemployment and a plethora of other economic troubles staking the country. The country's growth has underperformed and vulnerabilities have increased considerably, including continued sluggish growth of two percent in 2013 and 2.9 percent in 2014.

But while much of the world staggered in the wake of the global financial meltdown, South Africa has managed to stay on its feet—largely due to its prudent fiscal and monetary policies. The country is politically stable and has a well-capitalized banking system, abundant natural resources, well-developed regulatory systems as well as research and development capabilities, and an established manufacturing base. The World Bank ranked South Africa as an "upper middle-income country." It is the largest economy in Africa. It was admitted to the BRIC group of countries of Brazil, Russia, India, and China in 2011.

With a world-class and progressive legal framework, South African legislation governing commerce, labor and maritime issues is particularly strong, and laws on competition policy, copyright, patents, trademarks and disputes conform to international norms and standards. The country's modern infrastructure supports the efficient distribution of goods throughout the southern African region.

The economy has a marked duality, with a sophisticated financial and industrial economy having grown alongside an underdeveloped informal economy. It is this "second economy" which presents both potential and a developmental challenge.

In its 2012–2013 Global Competitiveness report,[24] the World Economic Forum ranked South Africa second in the world for the accountability of its private institutions, and third for its financial market development, "indicating high confidence in South Africa's financial markets at a time when trust is returning only slowly in many other parts of the world." The country's securities exchange, the JSE, is ranked among the top 20 in the world in terms of size.

South Africa's success in reforming its economic policies is best reflected by its GDP figures, which reflected an unprecedented 62 quarters of uninterrupted economic growth between 1993 and 2007, when GDP rose by 5.1 percent. With South Africa's increased integration into the global market, there was no escaping the impact of the 2008–2009 global economic crises, and GDP contracted to 3.1 percent.

While the economy continues to grow—driven largely by domestic consumption—growth is at a slower rate than previously forecasted. It is projected to grow at 2.7 percent in 2013, 3.5 percent in 2014 and 3.8 percent in 2015. According to figures from the National Treasury, total government spending will reach R1.1 trillion rand in 2013. This represents a doubling in expenditure since 2002–03 in real terms.

To ensure that there is a similar improvement in service-delivery outcomes, the government is deploying measures to strengthen the efficiency of public spending and to root out corruption. Under its inflation-targeting policy, implemented by the South African Reserve Bank (SARB), prices have been fairly steady. In January 2013, the annual consumer inflation rate was 5.4 percent, dipping from December 2012's 5.7 percent. Stable and low inflation protect living standards, especially of working families and low-income households.

The country's outlook is affected both by national concerns, such as unrest in and pressure on the mining industry, as well as international sluggishness, with Europe as one of South Africa's chief export destinations. However, trade and industrial policies encourage local firms to explore new areas of growth based on improved competitiveness. China, India, and Brazil offer significant opportunities. Infrastructure, mining, finance, and retail developments across Africa are helping to fuel a growth trajectory in which South Africa can participate.

The Problem of Corruption

According to Transparency International* (TI), many of the CIVETS, as well as the BRICS and the MENA, countries experience major challenges with corruption. Figure 2.12 provides a global picture of 2011 corruption scores according to LexixNexis'[†] RiskRadar[‡]. When we look at the BRICS, for example, Chinese firms have the weakest overall performance among the bloc nations. In its report titled *Transparency in Corporate Reporting: Assessing Emerging Market Multinationals*[25] TI analyzed 100 of the fastest growing companies based in 16 emerging markets. Three quarters of the businesses scored less than five out of ten, where zero is the least transparent. Scores were based on publicly available information about anti-corruption measures, transparency in reporting, how the companies structure themselves and the amount of financial information they provide for each country in which they operate.

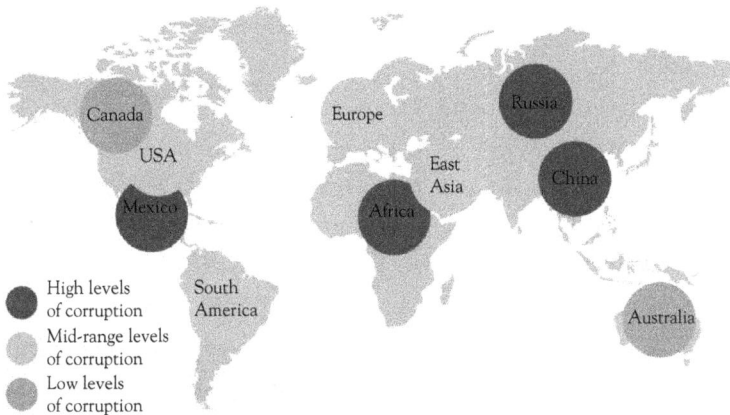

Figure 2.12 2011 Global corruption index

Source: LexisNexis

---

* http://www.transparency.org/country

† http://www.theriskradar.com/tag/corruption/

‡ The RiskRadar is a content platform for people who wish to keep abreast of the latest developments in AML and anti-bribery and corruption. The RiskRadar is powered by LexisNexis.

Chinese companies accounted for more than a third of the assessed businesses. According to TI China must take "immediate action"* to raise standards. Companies in India scored best out of the BRICS with a result of 5.4. The studies credit this to national laws obliging publication of key financial information on subsidiaries. Some 75 of the 100 companies in the report come from BRICS nations, which have contributed 50 percent of world growth since the financial crisis. The study said about 60 percent of the firms evaluated does not disclose information about political contributions. TI called on companies in emerging markets to disclose to the public what they are doing in terms of prevent corruption as well as their relationship with their governments. It added legislation forcing companies to publish what they pay to governments in every country where they operate.

To continue to foster consistent growth, emerging markets must be partners in playing their part in the global fight against corruption. As emerging market companies expand their global influence they should seize the opportunity to become active participants in the role of stopping corruption internationally.

Government infrastructure contracts in the CIVETS bloc, as well as BRIC and MENA in general, might be hard to access without breaking the U.S. 1977 Foreign Corrupt Practice Act (FCPA) or the 2011 UK Bribery Act, making such companies exposed to DOD and SEC prosecutions. This is because requests for bribes are increasing in state procurement processes at both the provincial and local government levels. This could be a major problem for emerging market growth, not only the CIVETS. As defined by the U.S. Department of Justice,†

> The FCPA of 1977 was enacted for the purpose of making it unlawful for certain classes of persons and entities to make payments to foreign government officials to assist in obtaining or retaining business. Specifically, the anti-bribery provisions of the FCPA prohibit the willful use of the mails or any means of instrumentality of interstate commerce corruptly in furtherance of any

---

* Ibidem.
† http://www.justice.gov/criminal/fraud/fcpa/

offer, payment, promise to pay, or authorization of the payment of money or anything of value to any person, while knowing that all or a portion of such money or thing of value will be offered, given or promised, directly or indirectly, to a foreign official to influence the foreign official in his or her official capacity, induce the foreign official to do or omit to do an act in violation of his or her lawful duty, or to secure any improper advantage in order to assist in obtaining or retaining business for or with, or directing business to, any person.

Fraud in the construction sector, according to Grant Thornton,* a global think-tank based in the UK, could be worth as much as $860 billion dollars globally, which is about 10 percent of industry revenues, and it could hit $1.5 trillion by 2025.

It is important to note, however, corruption is not only a challenge in emerging markets. Advanced economies are plagued by it also, either as the proverbial "cost for doing business in emerging markets" or for accepting bribes or being victims of extortion. Across Australia, Canada, India, the UK, and the United States it is evident that fraud in the development of infrastructure is commonplace and in some cases endemic.

In the UK, the three biggest areas of construction fraud are bid rigging, or alterations to contracts and false misrepresentation, which spans use of illegal workers, falsifying reports, results or certificates, and non-compliance with regulations. Grant Thornton's report refers to *breakfast clubs*,† where contractors meet to decide who will win the latest contract. In New York, the think-tank calculated that five percent of construction projects' were awarded to five Mafia families alone (2011). The problem is that many companies are not aware of their increased level of liability or new legal risks that threaten their business. The drive for growth is also increasing corporate corruption risk as businesses expand into emerging markets where corruption tends to be more prevalent. In countries such as the UK, Canada, and Australia, the propensity of bid rigging has been

---

* http://www.grant-thornton.co.uk/
† Ibidem.

normalized to the extent that it might even be perceived as legal, according to Grant Thornton's report.

To prevent fraud, policymakers in emerging market need to combat the practice by making the issue a priority in national agendas. They need to devise processes to scrutinize in-country multinational firms and their own corporations—in particular; they would be well serviced to not forget to extend this same scrutiny to its government agencies. Policymakers must be able, and capable, to place aside reputational issues and prosecute fraudulence. The use of information systems and technology, in an effort to tap into big data to identify and predict fraud is paramount. Governments also must encourage whistleblowing, and provide full support and cooperation to these practices listed in this book.

Watch the EAGLEs

In the aftershock of the financial crisis and subsequent Great Recession of 2007–2008, the emerging markets, not the world's debt-ridden advanced economies, have been the most resilient in the face of global distress. As Chief Economist and Leader of PwC's Emerging Markets practice Harry Broadman puts it, "Going through the financial crisis, the most resilient economies—measured by GDP or trade volumes—have been the emerging markets."[26] Broadman argues that, while the BRICS still serve as a proxy of sorts for any emerging markets debate, there is much going on beyond the BRICS that business leaders and international business professionals should know.

As discussed earlier in this book, something interesting happened to emerging markets as they continued to develop; they became the engines of global economic growth. The BRICS and many other countries are undergoing the kind of economic transformation that South Korea, Japan, and European countries experienced during the post-World War II boom. Much of the economic progress in emerging markets is happening at an accelerated pace due, at least in part, to technological advancement, sound economic policymaking, and reduction in poverty as a result of health, education, and other social reforms. Hence, from 1996 to 2010, emerging markets countries grew at more than twice the rate of advanced economies, at a rate of about five percent versus two percent annual

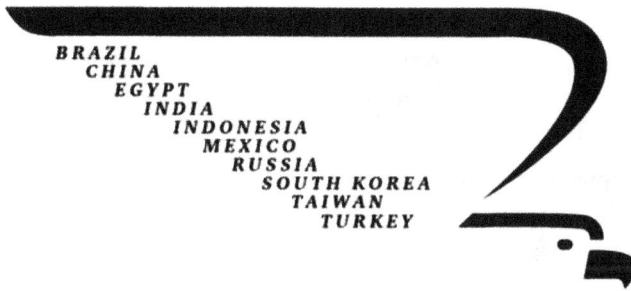

Figure 2.13 The 10 EAGLEs countries

Source: BBVA

GDP growth, respectively. Even more impressive is that, recently, income disparity between certain emerging markets and developed markets is declining rapidly as well.

The ubiquitous success of the term BRICS has spawned a whole new set of alphabet-soup-like terms for different groupings of emerging markets. One is the CIVETS, as discussed earlier in this chapter. But a new acronym, the EAGLEs, has emerged, defining the 10 Emerging And Growth-Leading Economies, as depicted in Figure 2.13.

The EAGLEs are a grouping of key emerging markets developed by Banco Bilbao Vizcaya Argentaria (BBVA) Research. The EAGLE economies are expected to lead global growth in the next 10 years; growth that is expected to be larger than the average of the G-7 economies. This is a dynamic concept where country members can change over time according to their forecasted performance relative to developed economies. The membership of the EAGLEs is subjected to a yearly revision and can change according to their forecasted economic performances relative to developed economies.

As global economic growth shifts from advanced to emerging countries there have been increasing interest in identifying the emerging markets that will become global leaders, as well as increasing the lobbying of some countries to be included in the BRICS definition. However, many economists have argued that the BRICS concept is outdated and have proposed alternative definitions. The EAGLEs concept is similar to other proposals in going beyond BRICs, such as the CIVETS, Next 11 or 7 percent club, but its methodology differs from others' in several ways:

- Its main focus is on the incremental GDP (IGDP) these economies will generate, instead of paying attention to the current or expected size of their GDP. This creates a situation where having big size or a high growth rate is not enough on its own to be a key world player, as it is a combination of both that really matters.
- It gives less relevance to economic size and population, which may be misleading.
- It is not a closed group and the concept is not linked to an acronym formed by a given set of countries.
- The cut-off is explicit. In order to become an EAGLE member, each country's expected IGDP in the next 10 years needs to be greater than the one anticipated for the average of the G-7.
- The results are based on a shorter horizon—10 years—than the ones considered in other cases, ranging from 20 to 50 years.

It is important to note, however, that no matter how sliced and diced, most emerging markets will continue to enjoy growth that dwarfs that of the advanced economies. The IMF and the WB project that, in 2025, the pace of growth in emerging markets still will be double that of advanced economies. Much of this growth will result from what is known as *South-South commerce*, or commerce among emerging markets, as opposed to the more familiar *North-South commerce*, which is advanced economies investing in emerging markets to make products cheaply and then exporting predominantly to advanced economies.

Emerging markets are trading increasingly more among themselves. In 1970, South-South trade was about seven percent of world trade. Today, it is 20 percent of world trade. That means that the usual suspects looking for market share in emerging markets, typically multinationals from advanced economies have an additional source of competition in successful emerging markets brands. Google could not compete with Baidu in China, and Wal-Mart is struggling to remain competitive over there. While there are some analysts in the United States that believe the Nike of China will be Nike (of the United States), chances are it will be Li Ning, China's third-largest athletic brand, after Nike and Adidas.

The same is true for Apple's iPhone, having a hard time competing with South Korean's Samsung's Galaxy line.

More recently, in May 2014, Russia and China closed a major energy deal, a 30-year, worth $400 billion dollars, to pipe natural gas from Russia's Far East to China. Not only this is another example of south-south commerce, but it has also prompted much concern on the impact such agreement may have on reshaping the global energy markets, tilting the balance of influence in Ukraine and, more broadly, in Europe, and also, on a longer run threat the petrodollar status around the world. The deal has impacted advanced economies such as of the EU, which may be forced to think of diversifying their gas imports away from Russia, fostering a more competitive market for liquefied natural gas (LNG) in Japan and South Korea, which together bought more than half of the world's supply in 2013.

This significant change in the structure of the global economy has ushered in a new era of South-South capital investment as well. In the past, the transparency and liquidity of the U.S. capital market proved an enormously strong lure for many global companies, no matter where they were based. While the United States still is one of the world's largest recipients of FDI, the growth of South-South FDI flows has taken off. If in the past emerging market investors used to invest on advanced economies, if you look today at where FDI from these markets are going, you will find that one-third of it is going directly to other emerging markets.

CHAPTER 3

The Strength of ASEAN Economies

Overview

The group of ten countries assembled in the Association of Southeast Asian Nations (ASEAN) has a common ambition that is not merely consolidating their economies. Their goal is to become the center of gravity of the entire Asian region, in order to multiply channels of dialogue and diplomacy among the main international players, with the objective of promoting peace, stability, and security in the new geopolitical environment of rising regional powers. The East Asia Summits (EAS) are a good example of the regional architecture ASEAN is trying to build with its partners. The project of economic integration summarized below is conceived as a tool to achieve wider strategic goals than merely promoting economic growth and development.

It's helpful to remind our readers of this wider perspective in the beginning of this chapter as we tapped into a trove of data and analysis from various international research institutions, including but not limited to the World Bank, the IMF, the OECD economic data forecasts, the Asian Development Bank, the ASEAN secretariat, the CIA Facebook 2014, Goldman Sachs, the Aseanist Times, the International Business Times, and the Economy Watch.

The ASEAN Economic Community

In January 2007, the ten Southeast Asian nations agreed to implement the ASEAN Economic Community (AEC) with four objectives: (a) a single market and production base; (b) a highly competitive economic region; (c) a region of equitable economic development; and (d) a region integrated into the global economy.

The AEC is a highly ambitious effort to enhance ASEAN's global competitiveness. Through the free flow of goods, services, and skilled labor, the project intends to establish an efficient *single market and production base* encompassing nearly 600 million people and $2 trillion in production. Business communities in the ASEAN hold that the regional economic integration would not disrupt their businesses, citing that it would even give even more opportunities rather than threats.

The ASEAN Business Advisory Council (ASEAN BAC) conducted a survey of 502 executives from companies of various sizes operating in the ASEAN region. The results of the survey, entitled *2013 ASEAN-BAC Survey on ASEAN Competitiveness,*[1] suggest that the ASEAN economic integration will pose a low or very low threat, 2.49 out of 5 (1 = very low to 5 = very high) to their organizations.

The survey was conducted in 2010, by ASEAN-BAC in collaboration with fellow scholars from Lee Kuan Yew School of Public Policy at the National University of Singapore. The integration of the regional politics and the economy within ASEAN, called ASEAN Economic Community (AEC), would take effect by the end of 2015, allowing free flow of economic activities and resources within the region. The survey showed that about 60 percent of the businesses in the region believed that AEC would provide high or very high opportunities for their organizations, as reflected by an average ratio of 3.59 out of 5 (1 = very low to 5 = very high).

The AEC areas of cooperation include human resources development and capacity building; recognition of professional qualifications; closer consultation on macroeconomic and financial policies; trade financing measures; enhanced infrastructure and communications connectivity; development of electronic transactions through e-ASEAN; integrating industries across the region to promote regional sourcing; and enhancing private sector involvement for the building of the AEC. In short, the AEC will transform ASEAN into a region with free movement of goods and services, investment, skilled labor, and freer flow of capital.

This agenda of economic convergence and interdependence has been viewed, since its outset, as one of the dimensions of the ASEAN Community, which member states decided to implement, to be effective by 2015. Economically speaking, with the implementation of the AEC, it is expected that ASEAN exports will expand by 42.6 percent, while imports will expand by 35.4 percent.

At the country level, the projections indicate a relatively low export increase of about 10.4–43.7 percent for the region's most export-oriented economies such as Brunei, Malaysia, Thailand, and Singapore, and relatively high increases of 55.4–101.1 percent for the CLMV (Cambodia, Laos, Myanmar, and Vietnam) Asian sub-group economies. Table 3.1 lists the forecasted effects on international trade for the region by 2015.

The result will be a small increase in the region's steady state trade surplus, attributed to the increased FDI inflows that the AEC is assumed

Table 3.1 Effects on international trade in the ASEAN region (2015)*

Change in exports, percent from baseline					
	AFTA	AFTA+	AEC	AEC+	AEC++
ASEAN	6.5	31.2	42.6	70.9	88.9
Cambodia	37.0	70.3	77.6	86.8	113.9
Indonesia	6.5	22.5	53.6	84.0	109.5
Laos	41.0	85.0	101.1	103.6	110.3
Myanmar	8.7	43.9	65.8	100.7	163.2
Malaysia	4.5	26.4	35.6	53.3	65.4
Philippines	2.9	25.4	45.4	67.3	82.4
Singapore	4.5	39.7	43.7	61.1	64.9
Thailand	8.8	27.8	33.6	63.5	85.5
Vietnam	15.4	49.0	55.4	160.1	239.5
Brunei	2.1	9.8	10.4	8.6	13.7
PARTNERS					
China	0.0	−0.7	−0.8	7.5	6.9
Japan	−0.1	−0.6	−0.5	8.4	7.6
Korea	−0.2	−1.1	−1.5	7.1	6.6
India	0.1	−0.1	−0.3	57.4	57.0
Australia	−0.1	−0.5	−1.0	5.3	4.4
New Zealand	−0.3	−0.5	−0.6	6.1	5.1
USA	0.0	−0.3	−0.8	−1.4	2.9
Europe	−0.1	−0.3	−0.9	−1.3	0.6
World	0.4	1.8	2.1	6.4	8.4

*See ASEAN Charter, ASEAN , Community 2015, and ASEAN Economic Community
Blueprint at ASEAN.org.

to generate. Those inflows will give rise to steady-state outflows of investment income (profits), which need to be covered by a larger trade surplus. Following is a brief highlight of each of the ASEAN country members as of spring 2014.

Brunei Darussalam

Brunei is a country with a small, wealthy economy that is a mixture of foreign and domestic entrepreneurship, government regulation, and welfare measures, and village tradition. The Sultanate of Brunei's influence peaked between the 15th and 17th centuries when its control extended over coastal areas of northwest Borneo and the southern Philippines. Brunei subsequently entered a period of decline brought on by internal strife over royal succession, colonial expansion of European powers, and piracy. In 1888, Brunei became a British protectorate, and independence only was achieved in 1984. It is noteworthy that the same family has ruled Brunei for over six centuries.

The country is supported almost wholly by exports of crude oil and natural gas, with revenues from the petroleum sector accounting for 60 percent of GDP and more than 90 percent of exports. Brunei is the third-largest oil producer in Southeast Asia, averaging about 180,000 barrels per day. It is also the fourth-largest producer of liquefied natural gas in the world. The government, however, understands the risks of having too much of the country's GDP relying on a single industry, and has demonstrated progress in its basic policy of diversifying the economy away from oil and gas.

Brunei's policymakers also are concerned that steadily increased integration into the world economy will undermine internal social cohesion, though it has taken steps to become a more prominent player by participating as an active player in the Asian Pacific Economic Cooperation (APEC) group.

According to Trading Economics,* Brunei's personal income tax rate is 0 percent (2013), while inflation rates are also extremely low at

---

* TE country indicators, http://www.tradingeconomics.com/brunei/inflation-cpi, (last accessed on 11/02/2013).

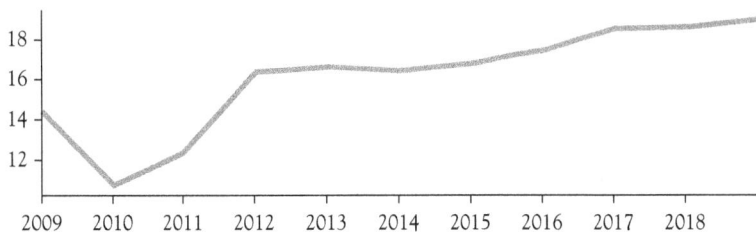

Figure 3.1 *Brunei's growing GDP*

Source: Quandl

0.30 percent (August 2013). The per capita GDP in Brunei is among the highest in Asia, and substantial income from overseas investment supplements income from domestic production.

As Figure 3.1 shows, the country's GDP in 2013 was $16.21 billion dollars, with an estimated GDP growth of $18.8 billion dollars by 2018.* The economy is projected to grow by an average of 2.4 percent from 2013 to 2017 as Southeast Asia recovers from a slowdown in 2011 and 2012, according to the OECD.[2] For Bruneian citizens the government provides for all medical services, subsidizes food and housing, and provides complimentary education through the university level. The government owns a 2,262 square mile cattle farm in Australia, larger than Brunei itself, which supplies most of the country's beef.[†] Eggs and chickens largely are produced locally, but most of Brunei's other foods are imported.

Agriculture and fisheries sectors are among the government's highest priorities in its efforts to diversify the economy, but while the country is best known for its substantial hydrocarbon reserves, the government also is starting to focus on green forms of energy, including solar. However, compared to some Southeast Asian neighbors, the Sultanate has set more modest goals and has been slower to develop alternatives to oil and gas.

The government actively encourages more FDI into the economy by offering new enterprises that meet certain criteria or a *pioneer status,* which exempts profits from income tax for up to five years, depending on

---

* According to Quandl country indicator, http://www.quandl.com/economics/brunei-all-economic-indicators.

† According to the U.S. Department of State report on Brunei, http://www.state.gov/r/pa/ei/bgn/2700.htm, (last accessed on 09/12/2013).

the amount of capital invested. The normal corporate income tax rate is 30 percent, but as stated earlier, there is no personal income tax or capital gains tax. Hence, increased investment in research and development (R&D),[3] combined with targeting niche markets, are two cornerstones of a strategy being rolled out by the government aimed at encouraging economic diversification. Japanese Mitsubishi has committed $2 million dollars investment in R&D, a figure that could expand multifold if results are satisfactory.

Brunei recorded a trade surplus of $719 million Brunei dollars ($578 million) in July of 2013. From 2005 until 2013, Brunei's Balance of Trade averaged $1,307 million Brunei dollars ($1,051 million) reaching an all-time high of $2,971 million Brunei dollars ($2,390 million) in September of 2008. As an oil producer, Brunei has been able to run consistent trade surpluses despite having to import most of what it consumes. Oil and natural gas account for over 95 percent of Brunei's exports, in addition to clothing.

Brunei mainly imports machinery and transport equipment, manufactured goods, food, fuels and lubricants, chemical products, and beverages and tobacco. Brunei's main trading partners are Singapore, Malaysia, China, Japan, the United States, and Germany. Singapore, however, is the largest trading partner for imports, accounting for 25 percent of the country's total imports in 2012. Japan and Malaysia are the second-largest suppliers. As in many other countries, Japanese products dominate local markets for motor vehicles, construction equipment, electronic goods, and household appliances. As of 2012, the United States was the third-largest supplier of imports to Brunei as of 2012.*

Cambodia

In 1995, the government transformed the country's economic system from a planned economy to its present market-driven system.[4] Hence, Cambodia currently follows an open market economy and has seen rapid economic progress in the last decade,[5] where growth was estimated at

---

* TE country indicators. http://www.tradingeconomics.com/brunei/imports, (last accessed on 11/02/2013).

seven percent while inflation dropped from 26 percent in 1994 to only six percent in 1995. Imports increased due to the influx of foreign aid, and exports, particularly from the country's garment industry.

In October 2004, King Norodom Sihanouk abdicated the throne and his son, Prince Norodom Sihamoni, was selected to succeed him. Local elections were held in Cambodia in April 2007, with little of the pre-election violence that preceded prior elections. National elections in July 2008 were relatively peaceful, as were commune council elections in June 2012.

Nonetheless, since 2004, amidst all Cambodia's political turmoil, garments, construction, agriculture, and tourism have driven Cambodia's economic growth, as depicted in Figure 3.2.[6] Agriculture has slowed but industry, while services expanded in 2013, maintaining economic growth at just above seven percent for the third consecutive year. Robust growth in services and expanding export industries drove economic growth of 7.2 percent in 2013. Services alone have remained the largest source of growth from the supply side, expanding by an estimated 8.4 percent in 2013. This stemmed largely from growth in wholesale and retail trading, real estate services, and tourism-related services. Bank credit to wholesale and retail trading increased by 24.5 percent to $2.5 billion and to real estate by 36.5 percent to $250.5 million. Tourist arrivals rose by 17.5 percent

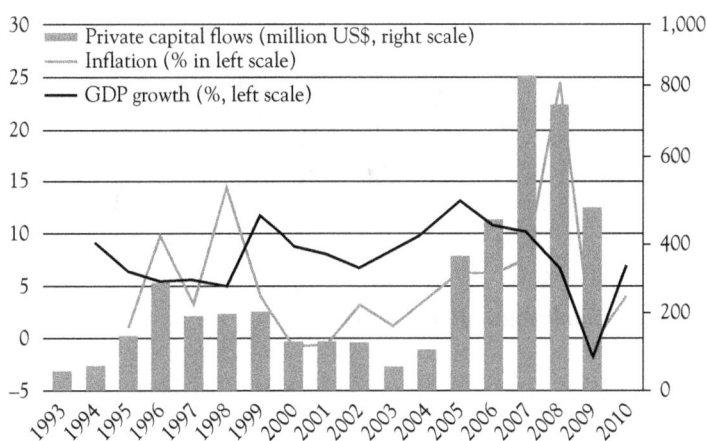

Figure 3.2 Cambodia's economic performance 1993–2010

Source: CamproPost

to 4.2 million. Political tensions and labor unrest suggest growth will ease in 2014 before picking up in 2015. Inflation, at modest rates last year, is seen edging higher in 2014. Spurring the development of small and medium-sized firms would help to sustain and diversify economic growth. GDP has climbed more than 6 percent per year between 2010 and 2012. In 2007, Cambodia's GDP grew by an estimated 18.6 percent.

In 2005, exploitable oil deposits were found beneath Cambodia's territorial waters, representing a potential revenue stream for the government, if commercial extraction becomes feasible.[7] Mining also is attracting some investor interest and the government has touted opportunities for mining bauxite, gold, iron and gems. The tourism industry has continued to grow rapidly with foreign arrivals exceeding two million per year since 2007 and reaching over 4.2 million visitors in 2013.* Cambodia, nevertheless, remains one of the poorest countries in Asia and long-term economic development remains a daunting challenge, due to endemic corruption, limited educational opportunities, high-income inequality, and poor job prospects.

As depicted in Figure 3.3, and according to the Council for the Development of Cambodia[8] (CDC), per capita GDP, although rapidly

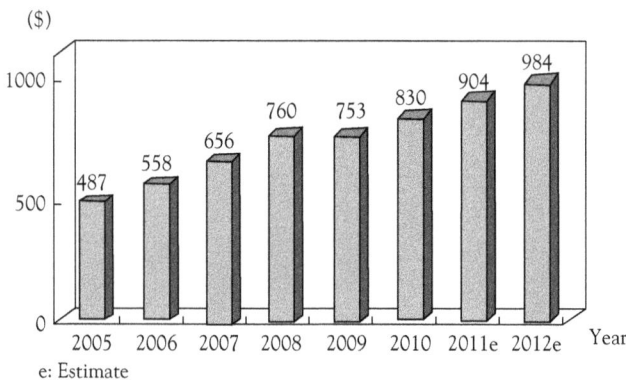

Figure 3.3 Cambodia's GDP per capita

Source: CDC

---

* Ministry of Tourism, of Cambodia (2014) Tourism Statistics Report 2013, http://www.tourismcambodia.org/images/mot/statistic_reports/tourism_statistics_annual_report_2013.pdf

increasing since 1998 when the Riel greatly depreciated against the dollar, is still low compared with most neighboring countries in ASEAN. In 2013, per capita GDP reached $830 dollars, an increase of approximately 70 percent from $487 dollars in 2005.

Cambodia's two largest industries are textiles and tourism, while agricultural activities remain the main source of income for many Cambodians living in rural areas.[9] The service sector is heavily concentrated on trading activities and catering-related services. About four million people live on less than $1.25 per day, and 37 percent of Cambodian children under the age of five suffer from chronic malnutrition. Over half of the population is under 25 years of age. This young population lacks education and productive skills. This is particularly true in the impoverished countryside, that also lacks basic infrastructure.

The major economic challenge for Cambodia over the next decade will be developing an economic environment in which the private sector can create enough jobs to handle Cambodia's demographic imbalance. The Cambodian government is working with bilateral and multilateral donors, including the Asian Development Bank, the World Bank, and IMF, to address the country's many pressing needs, as more than 50 percent of the government budget is received by donor assistance. Presently, Cambodia's main foreign policy focuses on establishing friendly borders with its neighbors, particularly Thailand and Vietnam, as well as integrating itself into the regional ASEAN and global WTO trading system.

Indonesia

Indonesia has the largest economy of the ASEAN. With the population exceeding 240 million, it is the fourth largest country in the world. Indonesia has a land area of around two million sq. km (736,000 sq miles) and a maritime area of 7.9 million sq. km. The Indonesian archipelago is the largest in the world and consists of over 16,000 islands, and stretches 5,000 km from east to west.

Despite the political turmoil of the late 1990s, Indonesia is politically stable today. Stability has not come easily but the democratic process prevailed with two consecutive mandates (to be concluded in 2014) of the first elected president, Dr Susilo Bambang Yudhoyono.

The reforms of 1999 ended the formal involvement of the armed forces in the government. Like other members of ASEAN, Indonesia has a market-based economy in which the government has traditionally played a major role. It has been a WTO member since 1995 and is now a proud member of the Group of Twenty Finance Ministers and Central Bank Governors, also known as G-20. Its economy is ranked as the 15th and 16th largest by the World Bank and the IMF, respectively.

Under President Suharto's "New Era," which extended from 1967 to 1997, the Indonesian economy grew in excess of seven percent until the Asian financial crisis, which was the lowest point of the economy and resulted in political instability. Since then, the rupiah has strengthened with the return of political and economic stability.

The banking sector and capital markets have been restructured. GDP growth, as depicted in Figure 3.4, rose steadily at four to six percent annually from 1998 to 2007. In 2008, there was a decline caused by a slump in exports and manufacturing and the global downturn that stunted its growth. During the second half of 2009, the growth rate did not gain new capital investment, which is attributed more to the lack of available credit and financing than any domestic economic issues. Indonesia recovered fairly quickly from the 2009 downturn and real GDP growth of six percent

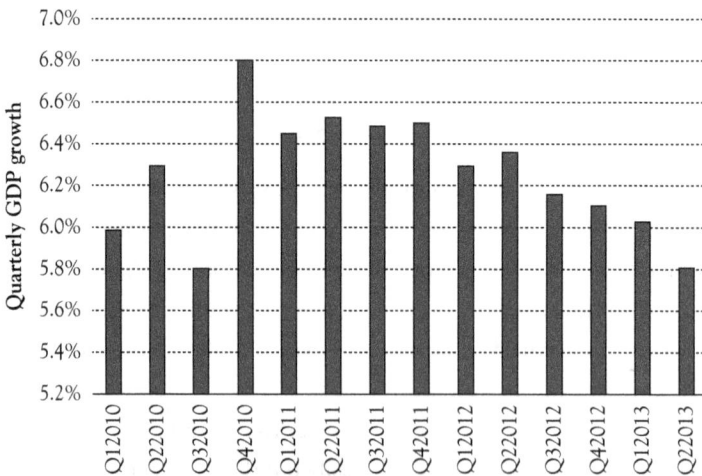

Figure 3.4 Indonesia GDP growth has declined since Q4 2010

Source: Badan Pusat Statistik

was reached in 2011. Subsequently, however, the country's economy has slowed and 5.8 percent was the real GDP growth at the end of 2013.

Indonesia has been a net petroleum exporter and a member of OPEC, but left the organization in 2008 and has been importing oil since. This was mainly due to maturation of existing fields. In 2007, Indonesia ranked second (after Qatar) in world gas production. The oil and gas sector contributed over 31 percent to total government revenue in 2008 and maintains a positive trade balance. Indonesia had proven oil reserves of 3.99 billion or 0.29 percent of the world's reserves. In 2008, its natural gas consumption was 33.8 billion cu m and proven natural reserves of 3 trillion cu m. Indonesia is also rich in minerals and has been exploring and extracting bauxite, silver, tin, copper, nickel, gold, and coal. A mining law passed in 2008 has reopened the coal industry to foreign investment. Indonesia exported 140 million tons of coal in 2008. The country ranks fifth among the world's gold producers.

The government made economic advances under the first administration of President Yudhoyono (2004–2009), introducing significant reforms in the financial sector, including tax and customs reforms, the use of Treasury bills, and capital market development and supervision. During the global financial crisis, Indonesia outperformed its regional neighbors and joined China and India as the only G-20 members posting growth in 2009.

The government has promoted fiscally conservative policies, resulting in a debt-to-GDP ratio of less than 25 percent, a fiscal deficit below three percent, and historically low rates of inflation. Fitch and Moody upgraded Indonesia's credit rating to investment grade in December 2011. Indonesia still struggles with poverty and unemployment, inadequate infrastructure, corruption, a complex regulatory environment, and unequal resource distribution among regions. In 2014, the government faces the ongoing challenge of improving Indonesia's insufficient infrastructure to remove impediments to economic growth, labor unrest over wages, and reducing its fuel subsidy program in the face of high oil prices.

LAOS

In its foreign relations, Laos has slowly shifted from hostility to the West and a pro-Soviet stance to a more amenable and open policy with its neighbors in the region. Laos remains a one-party communist state and the political environment is stable. The LPR has been in power since 1975 and rules by decree.

Laos became a full-fledged member of ASEAN and joined the WTO in 2010. The country is a member of many international organizations such as United Nations, ASEAN Free Trade Area (AFTA), Asian Development Bank (ADB), Food and Agriculture Organization (FAO), World Bank's International Bank of Reconstruction and Development (IBRD), and IMF.

The Laos government started encouraging private enterprise in 1986 and now is transiting to a market economy but with continued governmental participation. Prices are generally determined by the market and import barriers have been eased and replaced with tariffs. The private sector is now allowed direct imports and farmers own land and sell their crops in the markets. From 1988 to 2009, the economy grew significantly, as shown in Figure 3.5, at an average six to eight percent annually. According to the World Bank,* growth is projected at 7.2 percent in 2014, with

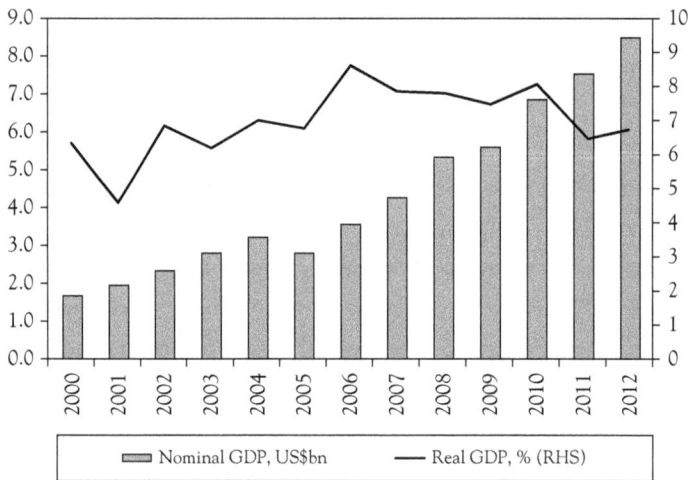

Figure 3.5 Laos's economic growth in GDP terms

Sources: Goldman Sachs; Forbes: Asian Development Bank

---

* http://www.worldbank.org/en/country/lao/publication/lao-pdr-economic-monitor-january-2014-managing-risks-for-macroeconomic-stability, (last accessed on 06/19/2014).

a moderate slowdown on the 8.1 percent recorded for 2013. Growth continues to be fueled by the resource sector, continued FDI-financed investment in hydropower, and accommodative macroeconomic policies.

The resource sector is expected to provide a smaller direct contribution to growth in 2014. This is due to most major projects are under construction and not expected to commence operation this year. It is also due to expected lower gold production, which is likely to offset some of the gains expected from higher copper production. Despite being rich in natural resources the country remains underdeveloped, however, and nearly 70 percent of the population lives off subsistence agriculture, which contributes to roughly 30 percent of the GDP.

Industry is a growing sector (11 percent) and contributes 33 percent of its GDP. The main activity is the extraction industry with mining of tin, gold, and gypsum. Other industries include timber, electric power, agricultural processing, construction, garments, cement, and tourism. The service sectors account for nearly 37 percent of GDP and four new banks have opened in the last two years. Laos operates a managed exchange rate and the Lao kip has been strengthening.

A new commercial banking law was introduced in 2006. Lending to the private sector more than doubled in 2008 to the equivalent of 15 percent of GDP. The country's first stock market launched in 2010 with 10 companies listed. A special economic zone is being set up in Savannakhet to promote foreign and domestic investment. Tourism has become a major revenue earner and has provided employment to many. In the 2012–2013, the fiscal deficit widened significantly, due to a combination of a large increase in public sector wages and benefits, and a decline in grants and mining revenues. The primary cause of the expanded deficit was due to an almost doubling of the total public expenditure on civil service wages and benefits. The 2013–2014 budget plan, however, indicates a slightly narrower fiscal deficit, but cuts in benefits will be offset by new recruitment as well as further increases in salaries paid to civil servants for two consecutive years. The government has discussed some revenue administration measures to help address the issue. In addition to revenue measures, there is a need for more prudent medium-term expenditure planning and execution by the government going forward.

Poverty has reduced substantially, from 46 percent in 1992 to 26 percent in 2009. Exports in 2009 including copper, gold, clothing, hydropower, wood and wood products, and coffee were sent mainly to Thailand (35 percent), Vietnam (16 percent) and China (9 percent). Imports were comprised mostly of machinery and equipment, vehicles, fuel, and consumer goods. The country is rich in hydropower generation, which provides almost 90 percent of electricity. There are no indigenous sources of oil and natural gas but PetroVietnam is exploring for oil and gas jointly with Laos. There are considerable untapped deposits of minerals and these are largely untapped. There are also ample sources of gemstones, especially high quality sapphires, agate, jade, opal, amber, amethyst, and pearls.

Numerous foreign mining companies are operating in Laos. In 2010, only China had mining projects here. The biggest source of income and investment continues to be hydropower and Laos hopes to become the "battery of Asia." It plans to increase exports of hydroelectricity to 20,000 MW per year by 2020. Thailand is its main customer and the two countries already have an electricity purchase contract for 5,000 MW scheduled for 2015. Investment in hydropower projects has been rising with accumulated investment in 2000–2009 standing at $2.65 billion with Thailand, $2.24 billion with China and $2.11 billion with Vietnam. Laos was previously a major source of opium but major steps were taken to quell production, which is now at its lowest level since 1975.

Infrastructure development, streamlining business regulations and improving finance have been identified as the main priorities for the government. Construction roads and buildings for the Southeast Asian Games in December 2012 and for the celebration of the 450th anniversary of Vientiane as the country's capital in 2010 have aided infrastructure development. A mini construction boom is being experienced around Vientiane. The manufacturing and tourism sectors are seen as the key sectors for private sector growth. The garment sector has created employment for over 20,000. There is still a vital a need to focus attention on ameliorating transportation and skill levels of workers.

Laos continues to remain dependent on external assistance to finance its public investment. In 2009, it launched an effort to increase tax collection and included value added tax (VAT), which has yet to be imposed. It also simplified investment procedures and expanded bank facilities for small farmers and entrepreneurs. Inflation is in check and has averaged five percent and the currency, the kip has been rising steadily against the U.S. dollar. In practice, the Lao economy is highly dollarized. Laos' bill on imported oil remains large. The country's international reserves have been strengthened through investments in hydropower and mining. The government maintains controls of the price of gasoline and diesel. The economy is expected to grow by around seven to eight percent annually.

Malaysia

Malaysia is one of ASEAN's more successful economies and has been declared a middle-income country. It boats a free market economy and is fully integrated into the global economy. It has benefited from the advantage of being located on the Straits of Malacca, one of the most important shipping lanes in the world that connect the trade route between the East and the West.

Stemming from agriculture and mining based economy in the 1970s, it has been able to transform (itself) into a high-tech industrialized nation. The country has a well-developed infrastructure and a vast array of natural resources. Over 59 percent of Malaysia is forested. It is a major producer of tin, palm oil, rubber, petroleum, copper, iron ore, natural gas and bauxite. Services account for 48 percent GDP, industry accounts for 42 percent and agriculture 10 percent.

The manufacturing sector is productive in electronics, hard drives, and automobiles. The service sector has become increasingly important and this includes growth in real estate, transport, energy, telecommunications, distributive trade, hotel and tourism, financial services, information and computer services, and health services. Malaysia has a well-diversified economy.

The economy has been growing at six to eight percent and GDP, as depicted in Figure 3.6, touched $381 billion in 2009. There was a decline, however, during the Asian financial crisis when the government fixed the exchange rate of its currency, the ringgit, to the U.S. dollar in order to leverage the decline.

Since 2006, the Malaysian ringgit has operated as a managed float. The country went through another steep decline during the global

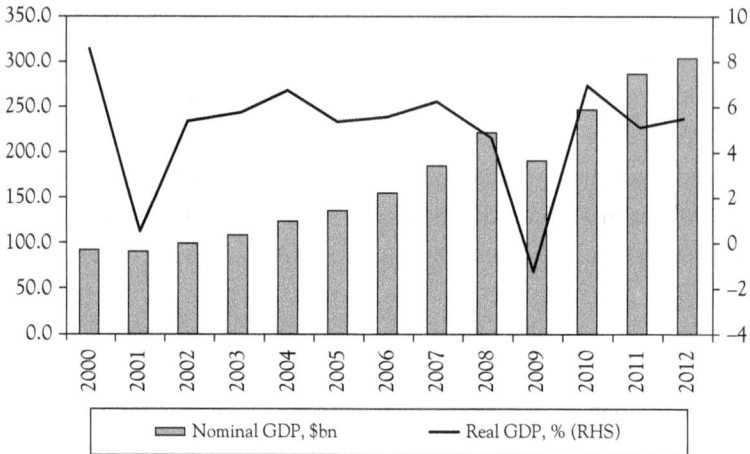

Figure 3.6 Malaysia economic growth is significant

economic stagnation of 2008–2009 but is slowly recovering. The government has injected the economy with a healthy stimulus package to jumpstart growth. Inflation, unemployment and poverty levels are low. The government has instituted banking and financial reforms. Local banks have been consolidated and fiscal liberalization is being introduced gradually. Greater incentives are being provided to invite foreign investment, especially in high-tech areas such as MSC Malaysia (MSC).[10]

The MSC Malaysia, formerly known as the Multimedia Super Corridor, is a Special Economic Zone (SEZ) in Malaysia, which was officially inaugurated by the fourth Malaysian Prime Minister Mahathir Mohamad on February 12, 1996. The establishment of the MSC program was crucial to accelerate the objectives of Vision 2020 and to transform Malaysia into a modern state by the year 2020, with the adoption of a knowledge-based society framework. Figure 3.7 provides an insight into Malaysia's growth outlook projections from 2013 through 2017 in various different sectors of the industry.

Exports remain the main driver of the economy, which totaled $226 billion in 2011. Oil and gas exports provide 40 percent of government revenue. Other top exports are electronic equipment, semiconductors, wood and wood products, palm oil, rubber, textiles, and chemicals. The present government is working to catapult the economy further up the value-added production chain and reduce dependency on exports. It is

	2013	2014	2015	2016	2017
Real GDP growth	5.0	5.1	5.2	5.2	5.2
Domestic demand	6.9	6.5	6.2	6.2	6.2
CPI inflation	2.2	2.4	2.6	2.4	2.2
Gross domestic investment	29.4	29.4	28.8	28.6	28.3
Gross national saving	35.3	35.1	34.0	33.6	33.1
Federal government overall balance	–3.9	–3.3	–2.8	–2.7	–3.0
Revenue	21.0	20.5	20.2	20.2	20.0
Expenditure and net lending	24.9	23.8	23.1	23.0	23.0
Federal government debit	53.1	52.3	50.8	49.5	48.8
Current account balance	20.1	21.0	21.0	21.6	22.7

Figure 3.7 Malaysia's growth outlook projections 2013–2017

Source: Tradingeconomics, IMF Global Outlook Report

actively promoting investments in biotechnology, pharmaceuticals, manufacturing of automotive components, tourism, research and development, manpower development, and environment management. There are 13 free industrial zones (FIZ) and 12 free commercial zones (FCZ) where raw materials, products, and equipment may be imported with minimum customs formalities.

A unique feature of the Malaysian economy is the New Economic Policy (NEP) launched in 1971 to reduce the socioeconomic disparity between the Malay majority and the Chinese minority. It was primarily an affirmative action system with the end goal of transferring 30 percent of the country's wealth to the *bumiputera* (natives) Malays. The policy was implemented through programs that give preferential treatment to Malays through special rights in ownership of land and property, businesses, civil service jobs, education, politics, religion and language. In 1991, this policy was renamed the National Development Policy (NDP); the modified NDP still espouses the original goals, income inequality had been reduced, and the main objectives had not transpired. Much debate over this has ensued and many have felt that this policy created a small and wealthy Malay elite, as it reduced the Chinese and Indian minorities to second-class citizens. Hence, April 2009, the government removed some of the controversial ethnic Malay affirmative action requirements.

Overall, the government is improving from its already favorable investment climate by allowing 100 percent ownership in the manufacturing industry, liberalizing the financial sector and removing capital controls on overseas investments. Numerous infrastructure projects using state funding also have been initiated. Malaysia's purchasing power remains among the highest in ASEAN.

Myanmar

Unlike most other ASEAN countries, Myanmar is not yet a fully free market economy. After it gained independence, as a reaction to years of colonization, the country adopted central planning, which resulted in a severe decline of the economy. From being one of the wealthiest export nations (rice, teak, mineral, and oil), it experienced severe inflation.

The subsequent military coup of 1962 saw further deterioration of the economy as Myanmar adopted the "Burmese Way of Socialism." Industries were nationalized and the state owned all sectors of the economy, leaving only agriculture to the masses. By 1987, Myanmar made the UN's list of least developed countries.

The country has suffered mismanagement of resources, low productivity, high inflation, large budget deficits and an overvalued currency, government control of financial institutions, poor infrastructure, and rampant corruption. In 1988, the government changed course and opened the economy to expansion of the private sector, encouraging foreign investment and participation in some sectors. Progress has been slow but increased trade with regional neighbors, fellow ASEAN nations, India and China has resulted. There exists a large informal economy, which includes trade in currency and commodities.

Myanmar has immense natural resources but the economy remains essentially agro-based. Over 50 percent of its GDP is derived from rice and other crops such as sesame, groundnuts and sugarcane, livestock and fisheries and forestry. Myanmar has one of the largest teak reserves in the world. It is also a net exporter of oil and natural gas and has substantial confirmed deposits. It has the 10th largest natural gas reserves in the world and the seventh largest in Asia. Precious stones are also abundant; 90 percent of the world's rubies come from Myanmar. It also produces large amounts of sapphires, pearls, and jade, which are exported mainly across the border to Thailand. A large illicit cross-border trade exists, as Western sanctions do not allow major jewelry companies to import gems from Myanmar. Manufacturing remains a small component of the economy, just over 10 percent in 2008. Food processing, mining (copper, tin, tungsten, and gems), cement, fertilizer, oil and natural gas production and garments are its principal industries. The currency, the kyat, remains officially overvalued. A dual exchange rate exists and such inflation is a serious problem, which averaged seven percent in 2009, down from 22 percent in 2008 and 33 percent in 2007.

Myanmar has not received any loans from the World Bank since 1987 or any assistance from the IMF despite its membership to both organizations. It has been a member of the ADB since 1973 but has received no assistance in over 20 years. Its economic indicators, however, are positive, as depicted in Figure 3.8.

Liberalization of the economy is a work in progress. Production controls in agriculture have been removed. Privatization of state-owned enterprises is currently occurring. Over 100 state-owned companies were up for sale in 2010. The government reports that in 2009 it sold

Economic indicator	2008	2009	2010	2011	2012
Per capita GNI, Atlas method ($)	. . .	. . .	. . .	. . .	. . .
GDP growth (% change per year)	3.6	5.1	5.3	5.5	6.3
CPI (% change per year)	22.5	2.3	8.2	2.8	3.5
Unemployment rate (%)	4.0	4.0	4.0	4.0	. . .
Fiscal balance (% of GDP)	(2.5)	(5.2)	(5.4)	(3.9)	(5.4)
Export growth (% change per year)	12.3	(1.4)	25.8	13.3	11.2
Import growth (% change per year)	25.6	1.9	15.8	24.4	22.0
Current account balance (% of GDP)	(3.1)	(2.6)	(1.2)	(2.5)	(4.0)
External debt (% of GNI)	. . .	. . .	. . .	. . .	. . .

() = negative, . . . = data not available, CPI = consumer price index, GDP = gross domestic product, GNI = gross national income.

Figure 3.8 Myanmar's economic indicators, 2008–2012

Source: ADB, 2013 Asian Development Outlook

260 state-owned buildings, factories and land plots. With the opening of the economy, foreign investments from China, South Korea, India, and ASEAN countries, including Singapore, Malaysia, and Thailand have increased.

Tourism has grown and infrastructure is being developed with participation from foreign investors. New industrial zones are being developed. Myanmar is an active participant and member of the Greater Mekong Sub-region Economic Cooperation Program (the GMS Program) together with Cambodia, China, Laos, Thailand, and Vietnam as well as the Bay of Bengal Initiative for Multi-sectorial Technical and Economic Cooperation (BIMSTEC) with Bangladesh, Bhutan, India, Nepal, Sri Lanka, and Thailand. The Shwe Gas Project in the Bay of Bengal is a consortium of Kores Gas Corporation (KOGAS), which has a 51 percent stake; Oil and Natural Gas Corporation (ONGC), GAIL (India); and the Myanmar-state oil company. The government has signed a contract to sell production to China, which is building a pipeline connecting a gas field to China.

Myanmar has the highest potential for hydropower in Southeast Asia and the government has set the goal of generating all electricity from hydropower by 2030. There are over 36 hydropower plants under construction. China has invested $200 million of the total $600 million cost and helped in the construction of the largest hydropower project in Ye Village. Another large project under construction is the Ta Sang project, which involves the building of a dam on the Salween River in the northeast of the country. This is a joint venture with a Thai company MDX Group. The project should be completed by 2022, with the electricity produced being to Thailand. In return, Myanmar will receive a certain percentage of free power.

Myanmar's chief trading partners are Thailand, China, India, Singapore, Japan, Malaysia and Indonesia. It has border trade agreements with China, India, Bangladesh, Thailand and Laos. Several Memoranda of Understandings have been signed with these countries to expand bilateral trade. Myanmar remains isolated from much of the Western world and sanctions are still imposed by the United States, EU, Australia, and Canada. Trade with the United States and the EU were less than seven percent of total trade in 2007. Foreign currency reserves totaled $8.2 billion in 2013 mainly due to gas exports. GDP growth is estimated by the IMF to remain at around five percent for the next few years into 2015.

The Philippines

The Philippines was hit in the fall of 2013 by a natural disaster of tremendous consequences and the level of damage caused by it will most likely slow down its economy for a while, as the effort of its people and government takes priority in creating a robust economy and better conditions for development.

The history of the Philippines economy goes back to the end of World War II. Then, there was strong economic expansion and the Philippines became one of the Asia's strongest economies. Sadly, the economy declined to become one of the poorest in the region due to years of economic mismanagement, political turmoil and misallocation of scarce resources. Oligopolies ruled a legacy of the U.S. colonial period, where farmland was concentrated in large estates.

As a policy, protectionism was used to prevent imports and restrictions were placed, preventing foreign ownership and other assets. This was exacerbated by rampant corruption and tax revenue remained low at only 15 percent of the GDP. There was underinvestment in infrastructure and disproportionate economic development, with the region around Manila producing 36 percent of the output with only 12 percent of the population. The result was economic stagflation during the Marcos era, severe recession in the mid-1980s, and political instability during the Aquino years (1986–1992).

Crumbling infrastructure, trade and investment barriers and a lack of competitiveness hampered long-term economic growth. More than half of GDP came from the service sector (53.5 percent); industry contributed 31.7 percent and agriculture, forestry and fishing accounted for the remaining 14.8 percent. Over 11 percent of the labor force was forced to go abroad to work and send remittances to their families. These remittances totaled $25.1 billion in 2013 and accounted for 8.4 percent of the GDP. A number of economic reforms were implemented during the Ramos presidency to help regain stability and the Philippine economy began to stabilize.

Macroeconomic stability has returned but long-term growth is doubtful due to poor infrastructure and education. GDP grew by 7.1 percent in 2007, the highest in 30 years. In 2008, GDP growth slowed to 3.7 percent. This was mainly the result of high inflation coupled with the worldwide downturn in export demand. Furthermore, the Philippines have suffered from a strong decrease in capital investment. Services grew by 3.1 percent in 2008 and 2.8 percent in 2009. Manufacturing had slightly better growth, despite drops in orders in the fourth quarter. Construction showed strong growth, while mining, metals, and agriculture displayed a sluggish performance.

The budget has shown a deficit every year since 1998, though trends in the last decade have been encouraging. The deficit is a direct result of overspending and poor collection of revenue. Attempts are being made to bring down debt ratios and raising new taxes has helped. Value added tax (VAT) was implemented in 2005 and raised from 10 percent to 12 percent and expanded its coverage. A law passed to increase revenue using a performance-based collection system. Though a deficit remains despite efforts to balance the budget for five consecutive years, deficit spending is considered necessary to cope with the economic crisis. A deficit of 0.9 percent of GDP was seen in 2008 and 3.2 percent in 2009.

Another source of revenue that needs improvement is the extractive industry. It is estimated that the Philippines possesses untapped mineral wealth of $840 billion. Mining has declined from 30 percent to only one percent of GDP but the country was a top mining producer in the 1970s and 1980s. In 2004, the Philippine Supreme Court ruled that foreign companies would be permitted to obtain mining and energy contracts with the Philippine government. Foreign companies now are permitted to own up to 100 percent equity and invest in large-scale exploration, development and utilization of minerals, oils and gas. GDP grew at around 1.1 percent in 2009 and 3.5 percent in 2010.

The government has taken steps to jumpstart the economy by introducing a $7 billion stimulus package. This money will be used to expand welfare, improve infrastructure and provide tax breaks for both private citizens and corporations. The country continues to have strong potential especially in the areas of mining, natural gas production, manufacturing, business process outsourcing (BPO) and tourism.

Inflation and unemployment remain major challenges. Infrastructure must be improved and greater reforms put in place to increase productivity and competitiveness. Tax revenues need to be increased further and reduction of poverty remains a top priority. We believe that trade liberalization to spur investment and increase competitiveness can help achieve greater growth. These reforms would lower cost of doing business and removing obstacles to growth.

Philippine GDP growth, as shown in Figure 3.9, which cooled from 7.6 percent in 2010 to 3.9 percent in 2011, expanded to 6.6 percent in 2012—meeting the government's targeted six to seven percent growth range. The 2012 expansion partly reflected a rebound from depressed 2011 exports and public sector spending levels. The economy has weathered global economic and financial downturns better than its regional peers due to minimal exposure to troubled international securities, lower dependence on exports, relatively resilient domestic consumption, large remittances from four- to five-million overseas Filipino workers, and a rapidly expanding business process outsourcing industry. The current account balance had recorded consecutive surpluses since 2003; international reserves are at record highs; the banking system is stable; and the stock market was Asia's second best performer in 2012.

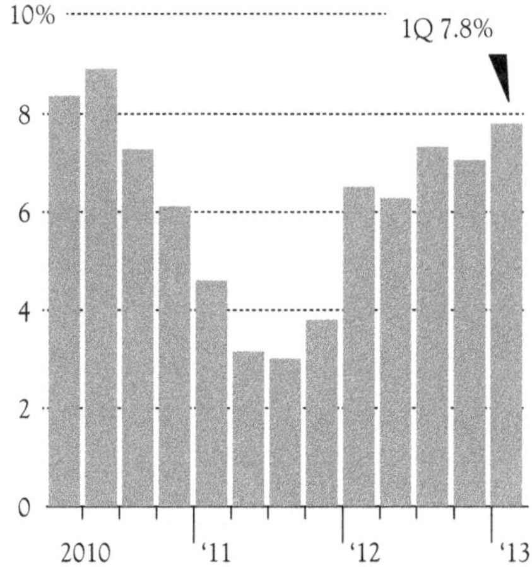

Figure 3.9 Philippines economic growth 2010–2013

Source: National Statistical Coordination Board, the Wall Street Journal

Efforts to improve tax administration and expenditure management have helped ease the Philippines' tight fiscal situation and reduce high debt levels. The Philippines received several credit rating upgrades on its sovereign debt in 2012, and has had little difficulty tapping domestic and international markets to finance its deficits. Achieving a higher growth path nevertheless remains a pressing challenge.

Economic growth in the Philippines averaged 4.5 percent during the Macapagal-Arroyo administration but poverty worsened during her term. Growth has accelerated under the Aquino government, but with limited progress thus far in improving the quality of jobs and bringing down unemployment, which hovers around seven percent. Underemployment is nearly 20 percent and more than 40 percent of the employed are estimated to be working in the informal economy sector. The Aquino administration has been working to boost the budgets for education, health, cash transfers to the poor, and other social spending programs, and is relying on the private sector to help fund major infrastructure projects under its Public-Private Partnership program. Long-term challenges include reforming governance and the judicial system, building infrastructure, and improving regulatory predictability.

Singapore

Singapore has a highly developed and successful free-market economy. It enjoys a remarkably open and corruption-free environment, stable prices, and a per capita GDP higher than that of most developed countries. The economy depends heavily on exports, particularly in consumer electronics, information technology products, pharmaceuticals, and on a growing financial services sector. Real GDP growth averaged 8.6 percent between 2004 and 2007.

The economy contracted one percent in 2009, as shown in Figure 3.10, as a result of the global financial crisis, but rebounded 14.8 percent in 2010, on the strength of renewed exports, before slowing to 4.9 percent in 2011 and 2.1 percent in 2012. This was largely a result of soft demand for exports during the second European recession. Over the longer term, the government hopes to establish a new growth path that focuses on raising productivity, which has sunk to a compounded annual growth

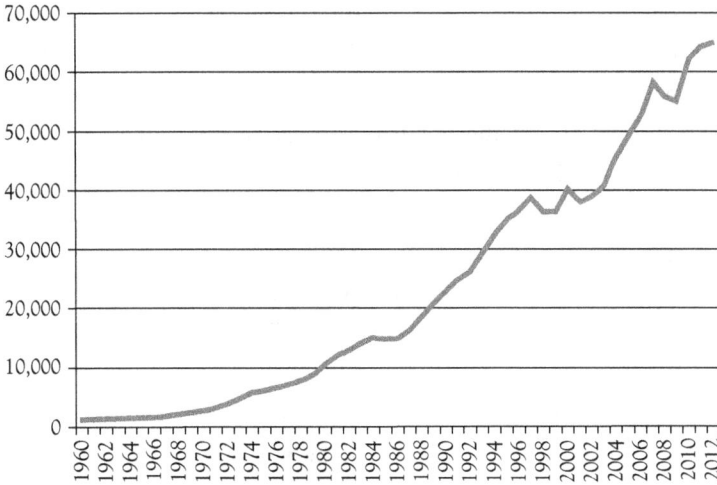

Figure 3.10 *Singapore's annual per capita GDP*

Source: Singapore Department of Statistics

rate of just 1.8 percent in the last decade. Singapore has attracted major investments in pharmaceuticals and medical technology production and will continue efforts to establish itself as Southeast Asia's financial and high-tech hub.

Singapore is poised to undertake a plethora of reforms in order to be one of the hubs of the global economy. Political pressure is forcing Singapore to rethink the liberal immigration policy that was once part of its strategy to become a global city. Although creative foreign workers have contributed greatly to economic development, at the same time its liberal immigration policy creates many non-negligible issues, and ones in which society will need to cope. The government is tightening entry conditions for foreign workers, while at the same time encouraging foreign entrepreneurs. It is investing heavily in development of human capital of indigenous workers, and encouraging businesses to upgrade their technology and production methods.

As part of that investment effort, the government has lent strong backing to small and medium-sized enterprises (SMEs). They account for over half of total enterprise value and employ nearly 70 percent of the workforce. Their rise, though, has been largely driven by government policy, which has funded them and boosted domestic market growth.

This begs the question as to how sustainable this state's SME policy is in the long term. Research and Development (R&D) is considered an important component of Singapore's policy of productivity-driven economic growth. In the last two years since 2013, the government has brought local SMEs into R&D with cash incentives to help them develop.

Combined public and private R&D expenditure have put Singapore among the most R&D-intensive countries. Nevertheless, it lags behind in private R&D spending. As a small city-state with no natural resources, Singapore has been careful in managing its human capital, regarding such management as an important source of competitiveness and strength for the economy. Over the years, public expenditure on education has consistently been the second highest, after defense, in the government's annual fiscal budget. In the 2012 budget, for example, expenditure on education claimed a 17.9 percent share, compared with 20.8 percent for defense. Such emphasis on education has helped contribute to Singapore's stronger record in human capital development than other countries in the region. Over the past decade, a major force shaping the human capital landscape in Singapore has been the increased presence of foreign workers.

As part of the overall strategy to transform Singapore into a global city, the government aggressively liberalized the foreign worker and immigration policy.* From 2000 to 2011, the number of non-residents rose from 754,500 to 1,394,400, representing a jump from 18.7 percent to 26.9 percent of the total population. In contrast, the share of Singapore citizens (excluding permanent residents and non-residents) in the population steadily declined from 74.1 percent in 2000 to 62.8 percent in 2011.† The aggressive pursuit of the global city vision has transformed not only the physical look of the city-state, but also its business environment and production coupled with these changes.

The composition of the labor force has also been significantly altered both in terms of the local-foreign mix and the mix between workers in *old* and *new* industries. While the open-door labor policy brought in a

---

* OECD; ASEAN Secretariat: CIA Faxback (2014).

† Department of Statistics Singapore (2011).

large number of highly skilled, high wage foreign workers, it has also led to a huge influx of low-skilled, low-wage foreign workers. Whereas the former could potentially expand the economy's range of skill sets and raise its productivity level, the latter could substantially offset such positive effects. Indeed, with the readily available of low-wage foreign workers, firms in Singapore might not find many incentives to upgrade their technologies and production structures, or to invest in training or upgrading workers' skills sets.

Thailand

Recent political unrest in Bangkok and other cities, due to deep divisions in Thai society, has created uncertainty for the future of this vibrant economy. With a well-developed infrastructure, a free-enterprise economy, generally pro-investment policies, and strong export industries, Thailand has achieved steady growth largely due to industrial and agriculture exports—mostly electronics, agricultural commodities and processed foods.

Bangkok is trying to maintain growth by encouraging domestic consumption and public investment. Unemployment, at less than one percent of the labor force, stands at one of the lowest levels in the world, which puts upward pressure on wages in some industries. Thailand also attracts nearly 2.5 million migrant workers from neighboring countries. Bangkok is implementing a nation-wide 300 baht per day minimum wage policy and deploying new tax reforms designed to lower rates on middle-income earners.

The Thai economy has both internal and external economic shocks in recent years. The global economic crisis severely cut Thailand's exports, with most sectors experiencing double-digit drops. In 2009, the economy contracted 2.3 percent. However, in 2010, Thailand's economy expanded 7.8 percent, its fastest pace since 1995, as exports rebounded. In late 2011, historic flooding in the industrial areas north of Bangkok, crippled the manufacturing sector and interrupted growth. Industry has recovered since the second quarter of 2012 and GDP expanded 5.8 percent in 2012. The government has invested in flood mitigation projects to prevent similar economic damage.

Vietnam

Vietnam is one of the success stories of Asia's revival, a country marked by tragedy and despair because of the conflict that desecrated the former Indochina and ended three decades ago. The Vietnamese quickly have learned the lessons from the changing international environment. Even before the dissolution of the former Soviet Union, this densely populated developing country has transitioned from the rigidities of a centrally planned economy since 1986. Vietnamese authorities have reaffirmed their commitment to economic modernization in recent years.

Vietnam's economic growth quickened in the second quarter of 2014 as the outlook for exports improved after the dong was devalued for the first time in a year. Despite the global recession, Vietnam's economy continuers to charge ahead, with GDP rising at 5.25 percent in the second quarter from a year earlier, according to data released by the General Statistics Office in Hanoi.* That compares with a revised 5.09 percent pace in the three months through March. The economy expanded 5.18 percent in the first half from a year earlier, compared with a median estimate of 5.2 percent in a Bloomberg News survey of 8 economists.

Agriculture's share of economic output has continued to shrink from about 25 percent in 2000 to less than 22 percent in 2012, while industry's share increased from 36 percent to nearly 41 percent in the same period. State-owned enterprises account for 40 percent of the GDP. Notwithstanding, in terms of nominal GDP, Vietnam's economy has grown consistently since 2000, as shown in Figure 3.11. Likewise, poverty has declined significantly, and Vietnam is working to create jobs to meet the challenge of a labor force that is growing by more than one million people every year.

Unfortunately, what is also depicted in Figure 3.11, the global recession hurt Vietnam's export-oriented economy, with real GDP in 2009–2012 growing less than the seven percent per annum average achieved during the previous decade. In 2012, however, exports increased by more than 12 percent, year-on-year; several administrative actions brought the trade deficit back into balance. Between 2008 and 2011, Vietnam's

---

* http://www.gso.gov.vn/default_en.aspx?tabid=491, (last accessed on 06/21/2014).

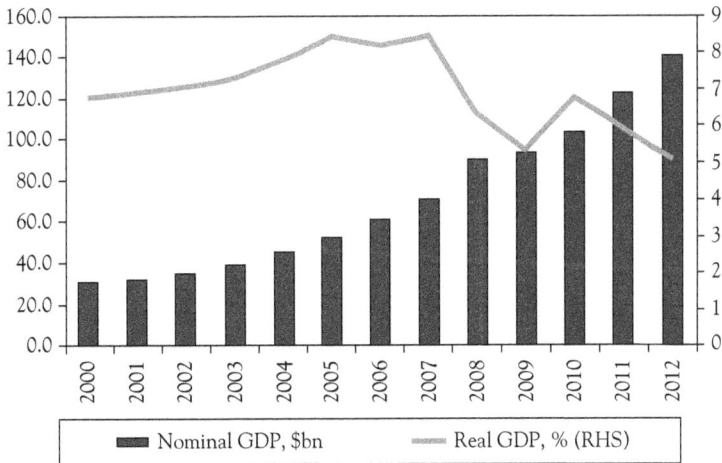

Figure 3.11 *In terms of nominal GDP, Vietnam's economy has grown consistently since 2000*

managed currency, the dong, was devalued in excess of 20 percent, but its value remained stable in 2012.

Foreign direct investment inflows fell 4.5 percent to $10.5 billion in 2012. Foreign donors have pledged $6.5 billion in new development assistance for 2013. Hanoi has vacillated between promoting growth and emphasizing macroeconomic stability in recent years. In February 2011, the government shifted away from policies aimed at achieving a high rate of economic growth, which had fueled inflation, to those aimed at stabilizing the economy, through tighter monetary and fiscal control.

In early 2012 Vietnam unveiled a broad, *three-pillar* economic reform program, proposing the restructuring of public investment, state-owned enterprises, and the banking sector. Vietnam's economy continues to face challenges from an undercapitalized banking sector. Non-performing loans weigh heavily on banks and businesses. In September 2012, the official bad debt ratio climbed to 8.8 percent, though some financial analysts believe it could be as high as 15 percent.

CHAPTER 4

Can MENA's Rise be Powered by BRICS?

Overview of the MENA Region

This chapter provides an overview of the Middle East and North Africa (MENA) region followed by a review of recent trade and investment relations between MENA and BRICS countries. It also reviews and discusses challenges and opportunities for economic development arising from the complementarities and interactions between countries form both blocs.

The people of the MENA region have long played an integral, if somewhat volatile, role in the history of human civilization. MENA is one of the cradles of civilization and of urban culture. Three of the world's major religions originated in this region, including Judaism, Christianity, and Islam. Universities existed in this region long before they did in Europe. In today's world, MENA's politics, religion, and economics have been inextricably tied in ways that affect the world economy. The region's vast petroleum supply, which accounts for two-thirds of the world's known oil reserves, is a major reason for the world's interest, especially from advanced economies. MENA's influence, however, extends beyond its rich oil fields. It occupies a strategically important geographic position between Asia, Africa, and Europe. It has often been caught in a tug-of-war of land and influence that affects the entire world.

According to the World Bank[1] the diversity of countries in the MENA region, as depicted in Figure 4.1, is great, particularly in terms of population and resources, and can be segmented in three groups:

- Oil exporters–these countries are rich in resources and have large shares of foreign residents. It is comprised of the six Gulf Cooperation Council (GCC) members (Bahrain, Kuwait, Oman, Qatar, Saudi Arabia, and the United Arab Emirates) and Libya.

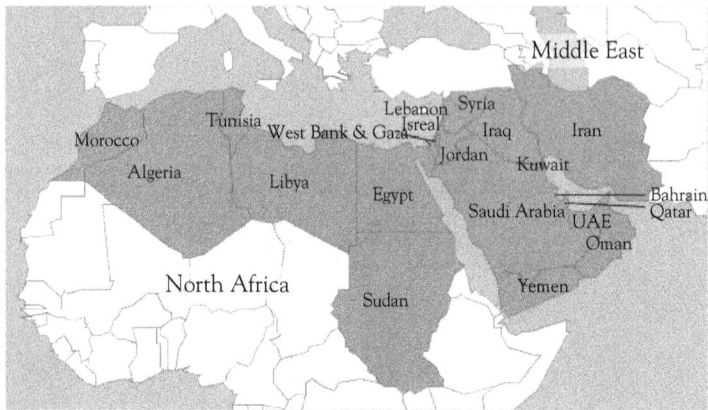

Figure 4.1 *Map of the Middle East and North Africa (MENA) Region*

- Developing countries–these are countries rich in resources with large native populations and include Algeria, Iran, Iraq, Syria, and Yemen.
- Oil importing countries–these are countries poor in resources that are small producers or importers of oil and gas, and include Egypt, Morocco, Tunisia, Jordan, and Lebanon.

In terms of population, the MENA region has quadrupled from 1950 to 2007, and is expected to increase by 60 percent until 2050. MENA's rapid population growth exacerbates the challenges that this region of the world faces as it enters the third millennium. For hundreds of years, the population of MENA hovered around 30 million, but reached 60 million early in the 20th century. Only in the second half of the 20th century the population growth in the region gained momentum. The total population increased from 100 million in 1950 to 380 million in 2000, an extra 280 million people in only 50 years.

As depicted in Figure 4.2, during this period the population of the MENA region increased 3.7 times, more than any other major world region over the past century. MENA's annual population growth reached a peak of 3 percent around 1980, while the growth rate for world as a whole reached its peak of two percent annually more than a decade earlier.* Improvements in human survival, particularly during the second

---

* At a 3 percent rate of growth, a population doubles in size in 23 years.

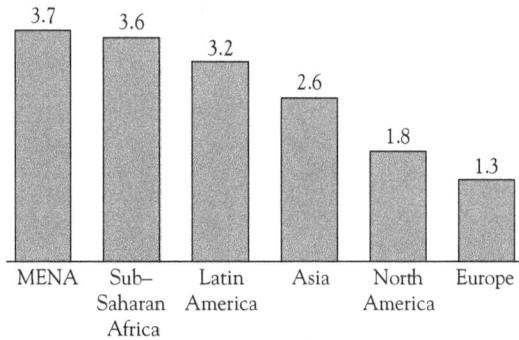

Figure 4.2 *Ratio of population size in 2000 to population size in 1950, by major world regions*

Source: United Nations, World Population Prospects: The 2000 Revision (New York: United Nations, 2001)

half of the 20th century, led to rapid population growth in MENA. The introduction of modern medical services and public health interventions, such as antibiotics, immunization, and sanitation, caused death rates to drop rapidly in the developing world after 1950, while the decline in birth rates lagged behind, resulting in high rates of natural increase (the surplus of births over deaths).[2]

On average, fertility in MENA declined from seven children per woman (1960) to 3.6 children (2001). The total fertility rate, the average number of births per woman, is less than three in Bahrain, Iran, Lebanon, Tunisia, and Turkey, and is more than five in Iraq, Oman, Palestinian Territory, Saudi Arabia, and Yemen. Even though the decline in fertility rates is expected to continue in the MENA region, the population will continue to grow rapidly for several decades. In a number of countries, each generation of young people enters childbearing years in greater numbers than the previous generation, so as a whole they will produce a larger number of births. The population of the region is increasing at two percent per year, the second highest rate in the world after sub-Saharan Africa. Nearly seven million people are added each year. As indicated in Figure 4.3, the population growth is most significant in the Western Asian countries encompassing Iran, Iraq, Israel, Jordan, Lebanon, Palestinian Territory, Syria, and Turkey.

MENA's demographics of a young population pose both strengths and weaknesses as shown in Figure 4.4.

	Pop. mid-2001 (millions)	Births per 1,000 pop.	Deaths per 1,000 pop.	Rate of natural increase (%)	Projected pop. (millions)		Projected pop. change 2001–2050 (%)	Percent urban	Percent of pop. age	
					2025	2050			<>	65+
Middle East and North Africa	385.6	26	7	2	568.7	719.4	87	59	36	4
Algeria	31	25	6	1.9	43.2	51.5	66	49	39	4
Bahrain	0.7	21	3	1.9	1.7	2.9	300	88	31	2
Egypt	69.8	28	7	2.1	96.2	114.7	64	43	36	4
Iran	66.1	18	6	1.2	88.4	100.2	52	64	36	5
Iraq	23.6	37	10	2.7	40.3	53.6	127	68	42	3
Israel	6.4	22	6	1.6	8.9	10.6	64	91	29	10
Jordan	5.2	27	5	2.2	3.7	11.8	128	79	40	5
Kuwait	2.3	20	2	1.8	4.2	6.4	181	100	26	1
Lebanon	4.3	23	7	1.7	5.4	5.8	35	88	29	7
Libya	5.2	23	4	2.4	8.3	10.3	106	36	37	4
Morocco	29.2	26	6	2	40.5	48.4	66	55	33	5
Oman	2.4	39	4	3.5	4.9	7.6	218	72	41	2
Palestine[4]	3.3	42	5	3.7	7.4	11.2	239	–	47	4
Qatar	0.6	31	4	2.7	0.8	0.9	45	91	27	2
Saudi Arabia	21.1	35	6	2.9	40.9	60.3	185	83	43	2
Syria	17.1	31	6	2.6	27.1	35.2	106	50	41	3
Tunisia	9.7	19	6	1.3	12.5	14.2	46	62	31	6
Turkey	66.3	22	7	1.5	85.2	97.2	47	66	30	6
United Arab Emirates	3.3	18	4	1.4	4.5	5.1	54	84	26	1
Yemen	18	44	11	3.3	39.6	71.1	295	26	48	3

Figure 4.3 Population size and growth of MENA region

Source: Carl Haub and Diana Cornelius, 2001 World Population Data Sheet; UNICEF; The State of the World's Children 2001, Table 7.

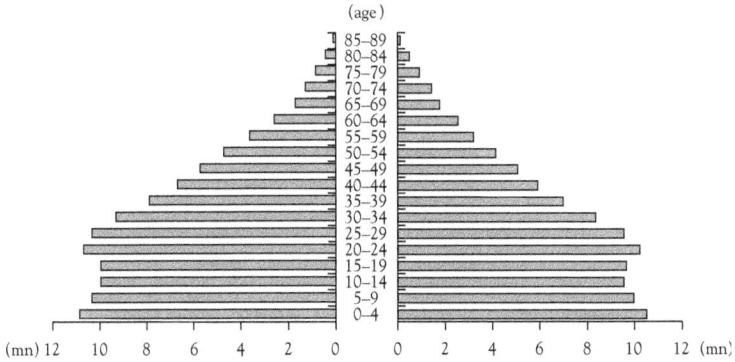

Figure 4.4 MENA's population pyramid, 287 million, 2010

When it comes to economic performance of MENA in terms of GDP, the region has essentially two distinct groups of countries: the Gulf countries that until 2011 have had a GDP per capita above $10,000 dollars, and the North Africa and other Middle East countries which have not exceeded $5,000 dollars per capita, as depicted in Figure 4.5. This variation in development levels indicates the superior performance of the resource-rich labor importing countries. However, as discussed later, the reasons for these outcomes are not solely related to resources but also with the historical and institutional development of the MENA's countries before, during, and post colonial times.[3]

According to IMF Survey Magazine,[4] the healthy growth rates of the region's oil exporters—Algeria, Bahrain, Iran, Iraq, Kuwait, Libya, Oman, Qatar, Saudi Arabia, the United Arab Emirates, and Yemen— are projected to moderate from an average of 5.7 percent in 2012 to 3.2 percent in 2013. This is mainly due to a scaling back of increases in oil production amid modest global demand. The average real GDP per capita from 1980 to 2010, however, lagged significantly behind other regions of the world, as depicted in Figure 4.6. Nevertheless, despite the recent turmoil in the MENA region, GDP is expected to be over five percent by 2016.

By contrast, the region's oil importers—Afghanistan, Djibouti, Egypt, Jordan, Lebanon, Mauritania, Morocco, Pakistan, Sudan, and Tunisia— face a difficult external environment. On average, this group of countries is projected to post moderate growth of three percent in 2013. For the

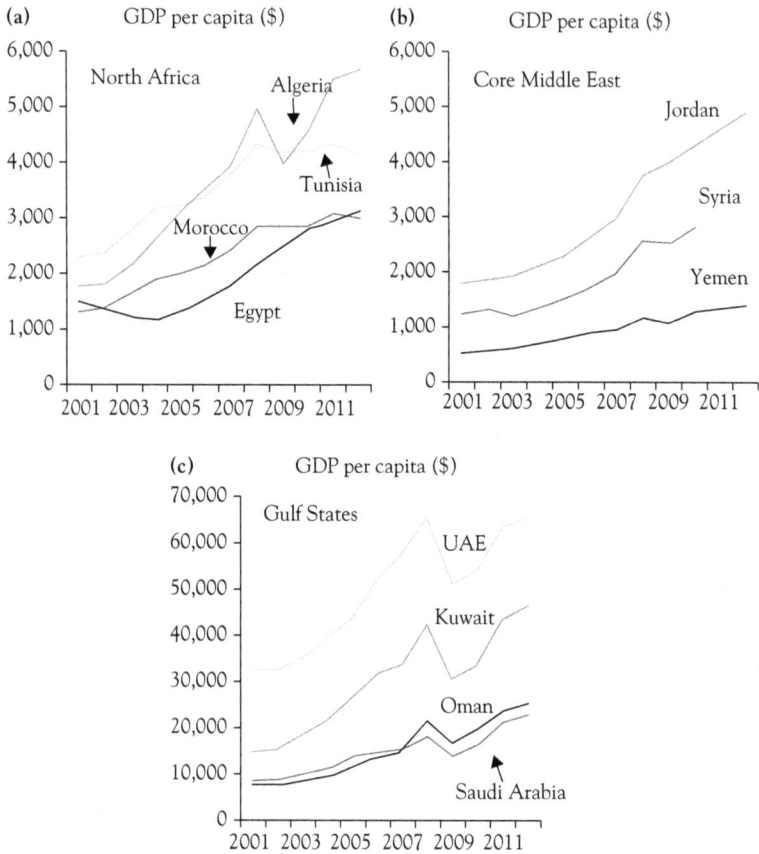

(a) GDP per capita ($)

North Africa
Algeria
Tunisia
Morocco
Egypt

(b) GDP per capita ($)

Core Middle East
Jordan
Syria
Yemen

(c) GDP per capita ($)

Gulf States
UAE
Kuwait
Oman
Saudi Arabia

Figure 4.5 GDP per capita in North Africa, Core Middle East, and Gulf Countries[5]

Arab countries in transition, continued political uncertainty is also pre-venting growth. Hence, to assess to what extent the MENA region has benefited from globalization it is worthwhile to examine exports and FDI flows. In regards to exports we find that the percentage of non-oil exports in MENA region is significantly lower than in emerging countries in Asia and other low and middle income countries, as depicted in Figure 4.7, suggesting that the region is not as globally integrated as others.

Second, in terms of FDI inflows to the region, we find that in the period from 1995 to 2011 the FDI inflow to the MENA region was stag-nant and lower than the world average. This was true again after the 2008 world crisis has declined, as depicted in Figure 4.8.

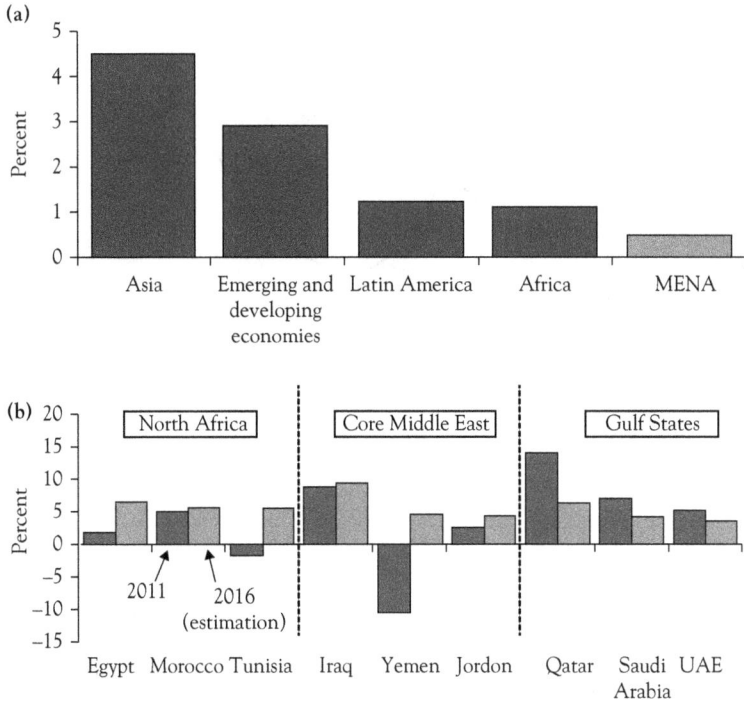

Figure 4.6 Real GDP per capita and expected GDP growth in selected MENA countries

Source: IMF

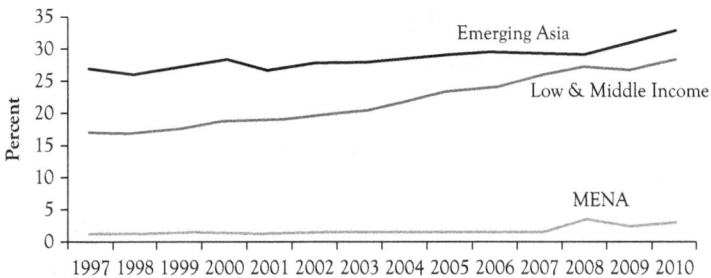

Figure 4.7 Non-fuel exports (percentage of world non-oil exports)

With high fiscal deficits and reduced international reserve buffers, many oil importers have no time to waste embarking on difficult policy choices—considerable fiscal consolidation—implemented in a growth-friendly and socially balanced way—and greater exchange rate flexibility. This should help maintain macroeconomic stability, instill confidence,

(a)

(b)

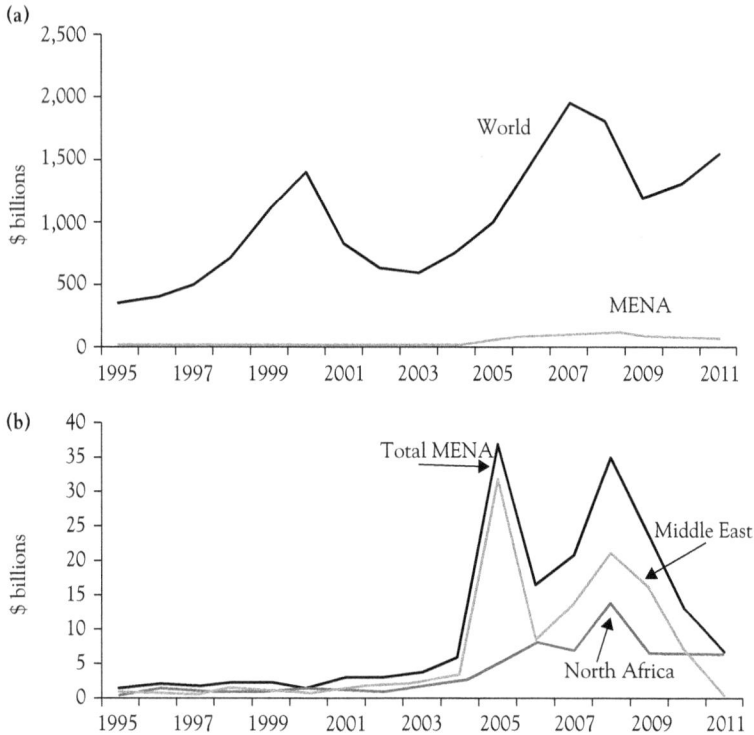

Figure 4.8 *FDI flows to the MENA region relative to the world and after 2008 world crisis*

preserve competitiveness, and mobilize external financing, thus putting in place important preconditions for a healthy economic recovery.*

Finally, it is important to understand the role of tourism as source of revenue in the MENA region. With its world-class combination of cultural and natural attractions, the MENA region, according to the World Bank,[6] has long held a powerful allure for tourists. It has made tourism an important source of revenue and growth. In 2011, the industry contributed an estimated $107.3 billion, representing 4.5 percent of the region's GDP, and accounted for 4.5 million jobs, almost seven percent of total employment. Figure 4.9 illustrates the percentage of tourism revenues for 2010 between the non-Gulf Cooperation Council (GCC) MENA countries, the MENA and other regions of the world.

---

* Ibidem.

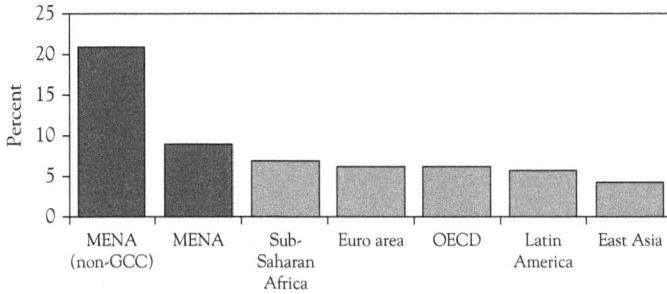

Figure 4.9 International tourism receipts (percent total exports), 2010

Long-term Issues of the MENA Countries

According to O'Sullivan and Galvez[7] at the World Economic Forum (WEF), the Arab Spring has accentuated problems in the MENA region that already existed for some time. These issues include a high level of unemployment, which is more acute among youth, pervasive corruption combined with lack of transparency and accountability, a bloated public sector that hinders the development of private enterprises, limited levels of entrepreneurship, and inflation in resource-poor countries.* Therefore, the MENA bloc could substantially benefit from other blocs, particularly the BRICS.

To understand how MENA could be further connected with the BRICS countries it is important that we take a closer examination of each of these internal issues.

- **Unemployment**—Data from WEF[†] suggests that in the MENA region the Palestinian Authority has the highest unemployment rate (above 20 percent) followed by Yemen, Tunisia, Jordan and Algeria (above 10 percent), whereas the GCC countries have the lowest rates, as depicted in Figure 4.10A. However, unemployment is particularly serious among young people (15–24 years old), as depicted in Figure 4.10B.

---

* Ibidem.
† Ibidem.

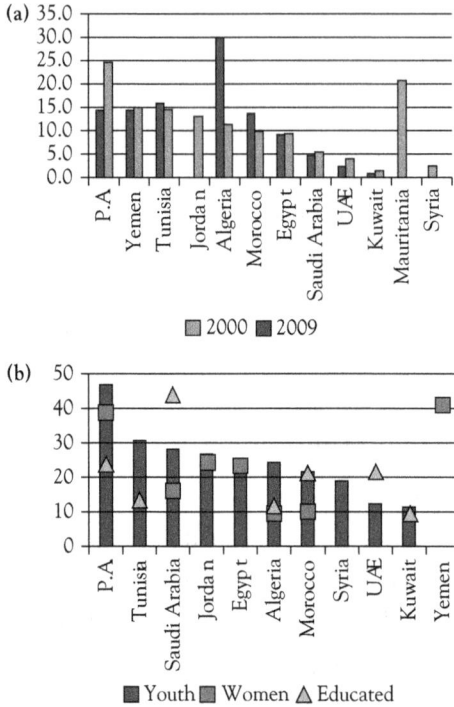

Figure 4.10 Unemployment rates in MENA

Source: O'Sullivan, Rey, and Galvez, 2011, based on World Bank data

As O'Sullivan point out, every year there are about 2.8 million young workers who enter the labor market but they find it increasingly more difficult to procure viable employment. Moreover, few countries, such as Saudi Arabia, Palestine, Morocco, and UAE have a large percentage of unemployed who are educated due to a persistent mismatch between job market requirements and skills acquired at a university. Lastly, the gender gap in unemployment, meaning the very low participation of women in the labor force, indicates another missed opportunity for the optimization of resources for economic development.

- **Corruption, lack of transparency, and poor accountability—** The Arab Spring was motivated in large part for these three issues, the solution to which will invariably mean a change to the political structures in most of the MENA countries.

According to Transparency International* only two MENA countries perform well in the corruption index, Qatar at 7.7, and UAE at 6.3[†], with the average score for the MENA region at 3.1. The reform processes in some MENA countries, such as Egypt and Tunisia, however, promise to change the institutional frameworks, with transparency likely to increase.

- **Bloated public sector distorts labor markets**—Employment in the public sector ranges from 22 percent in Tunisia to about 33–35 percent in Syria, Jordan, and Egypt, but if we exclude the agricultural sector then the public sector employment reaches 42 percent in Jordan and 70 percent in Egypt. The public sector provides higher salaries, job security, and social status that the private sector cannot match, thus reducing the pool of qualified candidates for the private sector. Moreover, during periods of crisis many of the MENA's governments have responded by increasing salaries and creating more jobs to appease discontent and increase consumption. This has short and long term consequences. In the short term it offers relief and an economy with a stimulus; in the long term it has a negative impact on the public budget's sustainability, particularly in resource-poor countries, and inhibits the innovation and entrepreneurship in the private sector.

- **Low entrepreneurship levels**—The World Bank Group Entrepreneurship Survey[‡] suggests that in high-income countries there are about four companies created per 1000 working people, whereas in the MENA the average is only 0.63 new firms. In the BRICS region the rates are 2.17 new firms in Brazil, 4.3 in Russia, 0.12 in India and no available data for China or South Africa. Based on the OECD research O'Sullivan[8] mentioned, low business creation in

---

* http://archive.transparency.org/regional_pages/africa_middle_east/middle_east_and_north_africa_mena, (last accessed on 01/03/2014).

† Scale from low = 1 to high = 10.

‡ http://siteresources.worldbank.org/INTMNAREGTOPPOVRED/Resources/MNA_Gender_EN_Final.pdf, (last accessed on 01/03/2014).

MENA region is due to the high barriers for small firms doing business (e.g. corruption, licenses, rigid laws, taxes, unfair competition), lower social status attached to entrepreneurial activity as compared with public sector, and low participation of women in the workforce.

- **High inflation in resource-poor MENA countries**—The average inflation in the MENA countries from 1999 to 2005 was about three percent but it increased to 6.5 percent in the following five years (2006–2010). While the resource-rich countries found compensatory measures to cope with negative effects of inflation, the resource-poor countries did not. The reason for high inflation in resource-poor countries is mainly due to a spike in import prices of food and fuel. O'Sullivan et al.* note that given the rising incomes of middle class in most emerging economies and the instability in MENA countries, the inflation is likely to continue here.

In addition to the factors described, the economic growth of the MENA region is also due to other economic and structural factors, namely low levels of competitiveness in manufacturing sectors, lack of export-market diversification, and low intra-regional integration.† These issues present opportunities for the BRIC countries, which can provide assistance and complementarities for furthering economic development in the MENA region. Thus, it is important that we review the recent economic developments in the MENA region.

The Economic Impact of the Arab Spring

When comparing the economic performance of the MENA region to other regions, we find that MENA countries have been performing relatively well, on par with Sub-Saharan Africa and Latin America, but below emerging Asian countries, yet above OECD and EU countries as depicted in Figure 4.11.

---

* Ibidem.
† Ibidem.

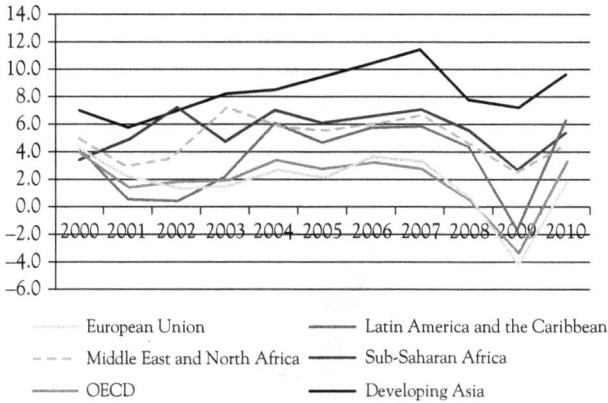

Figure 4.11 GDP growth by region, percent change, constant prices

Source: O'Sullivan et al., 2011, based on IMF and OECD data

The impact of the Arab Spring has had varying effects in the MENA region depending on the extent of the turmoil and economic fundamentals. First, the political and social instability caused an immediate negative effect in the countries affected by the turmoil. However, as O'Sullivan et al.* noted, the countries with stronger economic fundamentals, such as Egypt and Tunisia, are expected to recover faster if a successful political transition and economic reform continue to be implemented. In contrast countries such as Morocco and Jordan did not experience significant tensions but their respective economies are more exposed to negative spill-overs and likely to recover at a slower pace. Second, the turmoil caused a significant rise in oil prices, which indirectly benefited the resource-rich countries. Moreover, the weak economic performance of OECD countries is likely to have a negative impact in MENA countries as trade and investment originated at OECD is likely to remain slow.

Trade Diversification and Intra-Regional Trade are Low

In 2009, the trade of the MENA region was $932 billion in exports and $742 billion in imports, however it was not diversified. The major export category in MENA countries is oil, representing about 62 percent of total

---

* Ibidem.

Exports
Total: $932billion

Imports
Total: $742billion

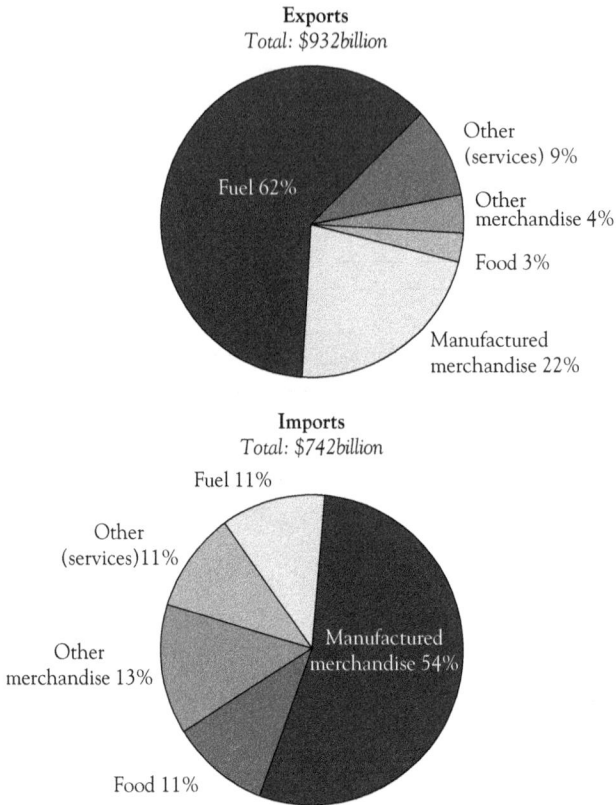

Figure 4.12 **MENA's exports and imports of goods and services with the world, by commodity or type of service, 2009**

Source: Akhtar, Bolle, and Nelson, 2013

exports, while the imports are manufactured goods, 54 percent of the total imports, as depicted in Figure 4.12.

Regarding MENA's partners, as of 2011 the most significant was the EU followed by China and the United States, as depicted in Figure 4.13. Note however that as a single country China is the most influential trading partner of MENA.

MENA has failed, however, to increase its global market share in part because the region's exports flow mainly to Europe and are concentrated in traditional products. Europe has been the main destination for MENA exports, reflecting proximity and long-standing linkages. Since the 1970s, the region's exports to Europe have accounted for close to 60 percent of

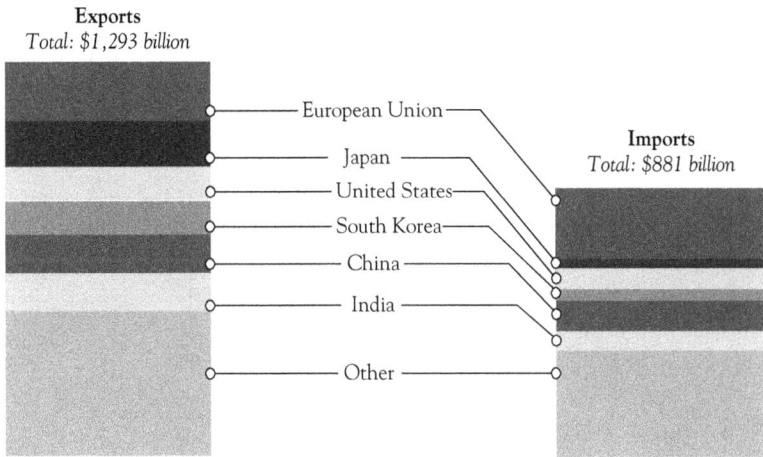

Figure 4.13 MENA's major trading partners, 2011

Source: Akhtar, Bolle, and Nelson, 2013.

total exports, while exports to Asia Pacific and Latin America, respectively, have accounted for 15 percent and one percent of total exports. Until the mid-1970s, the focus on European markets linked the region to an engine of global growth. But, more recently, this focus has implied that MENA has not been benefiting from the high growth rates achieved in emerging Asian and Latin American powerhouses, including Brazil, India, and China.

Notwithstanding, exports from the MENA region have increased significantly in the past years. When considering exports as a percentage of GDP, MENA's exports have increased from 35 percent in 1990, to 39.2 percent in 2000, up to 53 percent in 2009.* However, as O'Sullivan and his colleagues noted, a closer analysis reveals two noteworthy trends. First, the increase of exports is mainly due to increased value of oil exports from resource-rich countries, as depicted in Figure 4.14.

And second that the current account balance of resource-poor countries is worsening, as depicted in Figure 4.15. Looking ahead, there are unknowns as to the timing of Europe's recovery. Moreover, there is a broad consensus that, over the medium term, growth in Europe will lag behind that of emerging Asia and Latin America. As such, it is even more

---

* Ibidem.

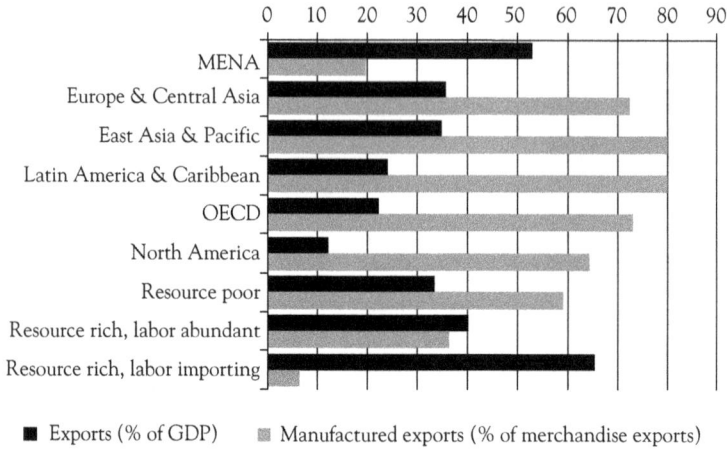

■ Exports (% of GDP)   ▓ Manufactured exports (% of merchandise exports)

Figure 4.14 Exports as a share of GDP are high in MENA, but manufactured exports are comparatively low

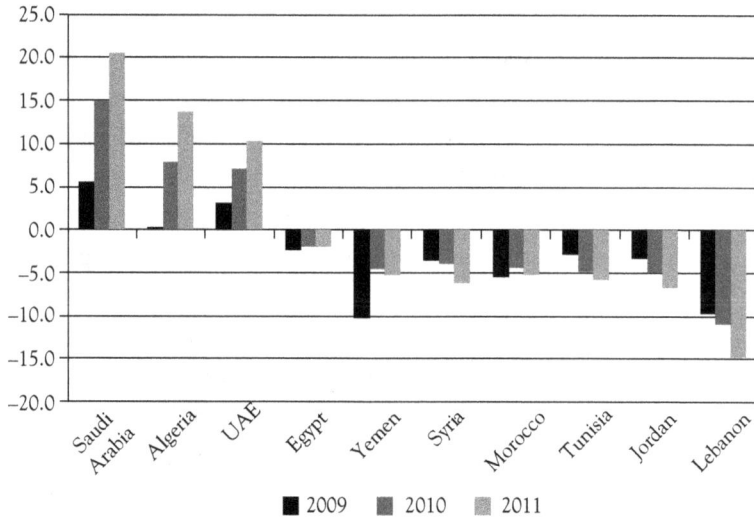

■ 2009   ■ 2010   ▓ 2011

Figure 4.15 Current account balance as percent of GDP

important to redirect MENA's exports to these dynamic regions of the global economy, such as the BRICS and ASEAN, and to allow MENA to link more closely to the new growth engines and thus provide a foundation for high and sustained growth.

MENA exports, according to IMF's Masood Ahmed[9] have primarily concentrated on consumer goods, and less so in high value-added, high technology, intermediate and capital goods, which have seen the most growth in recent years. Consumer and primary goods currently account for 64 percent of total exports in this region, compared to 41 percent for Asian countries, 57 percent for Latin American countries and 66 percent for African countries. Capital goods, on the other hand, account for only six percent of MENA exports, similar to the seven percent in low-income countries, while they account for 37 percent of Asian exports and 11 percent of Latin American exports. These export patterns hold back MENA's potential for trade and, indeed, MENA countries trade less with the rest of the world than could be expected. MENA's total exports in 2009 amounted to only 28 percent of GDP, compared to 30 percent for Asia Pacific, 56 percent when excluding the three largest economies, Japan, India, and China, given that large economies typically have lower export shares.

When examining the export markets for MENA countries we find that the resource-poor countries mostly export to the EU, and that intra-regional trade among MENA countries has increased but compared with EU and other markets it is still modest, as shown in Figure 4.16. Moreover, in terms of trade with the BRICS countries, the exports have increased but are not yet significant, which suggests that there may be opportunities for further exports into the BRICS markets.

A country's export volumes are driven partly by characteristics such as proximity to markets, tariff rates, the establishment of free trade

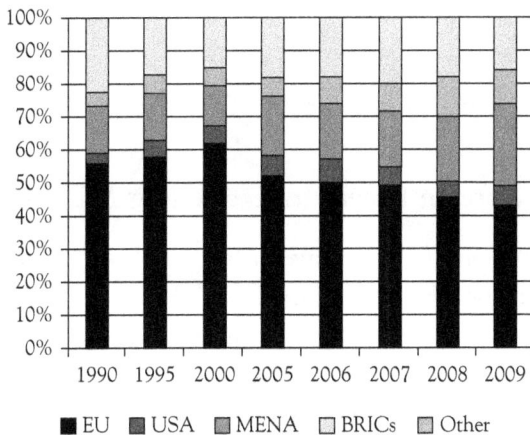

Figure 4.16 *Resource-poor countries' main export market is the EU, and BRIC markets is still modest*

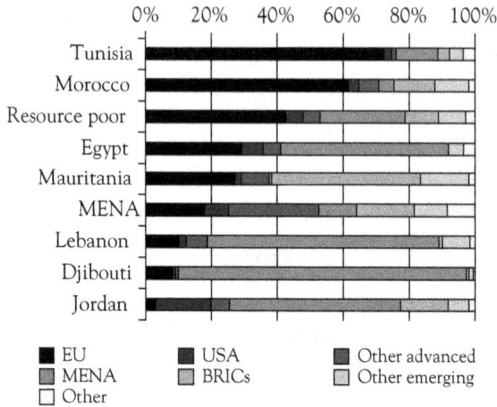

Figure 4.17 Resource-poor countries' main export market is the EU, but to varying degrees

agreements or cultural linkages with trading partners. However, these characteristics do not explain MENA's low export-to-GDP ratio–quite the opposite. Looking at the exports of the each MENA country, as depicted in Figure 4.17, we find other interesting patterns. First, Tunisia and Morocco have a large percentage of exports to EU. Second, Mauritania's exports are concentrated in the BRIC, particularly China, where it exports 40 percent of iron ore. Third, Lebanon, Djibouti, and Jordan send most of their exports to MENA countries. Lastly, Egypt is the country with the most balanced export markets.

Trade variations, as noted by O'Sullivan et al.,[10] are due in part to varying supply and demand chains. In terms of demand, China imports oil, gas and natural resources, and EU manufactured goods.

Foreign Direct Investment at MENA

As of 2010, foreign direct investment (FDI) in MENA countries amounted to $64.5 billion, and nearly two thirds of which derives from resource-rich countries, namely in Saudi Arabia, which attracted over 44 percent of MENA's total FDI.* The resource-poor countries attracted about 25 percent of the FDI, as shown in Figure 4.18, with Egypt and

---

* Ibidem.

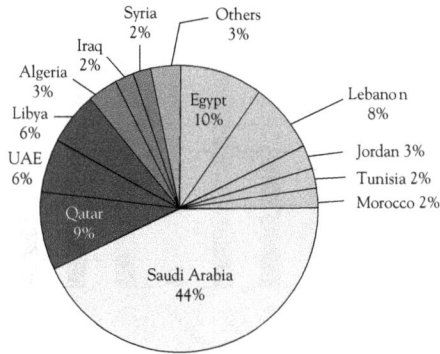

Figure 4.18 FDI inflows to the MENA region, 2010

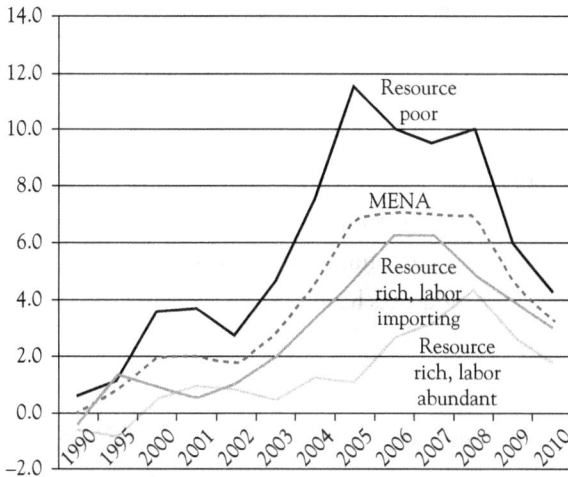

Figure 4.19 FDI as a share of GDP in the MENA region, 2010

Lebanon as the main recipients. The remaining FDI was channeled to resource-rich countries characterized by political instability. Overall the data suggests that investments are attracted by opportunities in resource-rich countries provided they offer a relatively stable context.

Interestingly, when considering FDI as a share of GDP (Figure 4.19), we find that resource-poor countries are performing better than other countries in the region, which points to increasing opportunities for investment. The FDI inflow to resource-poor countries jumped from 0.6 percent of GDP in 1990 to 12 percent in the mid-2000s. Due to the financial crisis of 2008–2009, there was a decline, but the relative performance of the resource-rich countries remained.

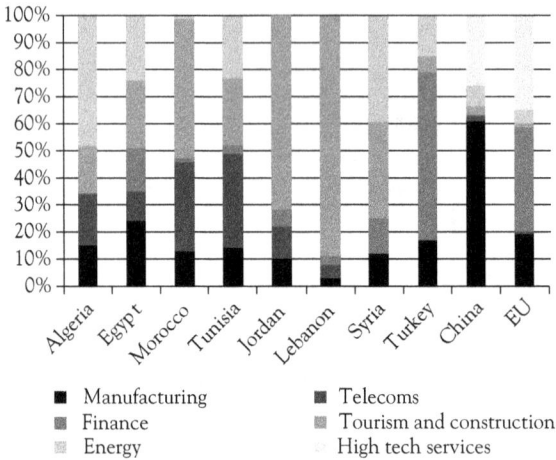

Figure 4.20 FDI by economic sector, cumulative 2000–2007, percent of GDP

When looking at non-energy sectors that have attracted FDI to resource-poor countries we find that it is attributed mostly to service industries, namely telecommunications, tourism and construction, while the manufacturing industries have received a low level of FDI, as depicted in Figure 4.20.

Integration of BRICS with MENA

The economic integration of MENA's region with Brazil, Russia, India, China, and South Africa has increased recently with varying levels of integration. In general this trend brings visible benefits, but it is not without challenges. Benefits include increasing revenues through exports, higher quality consumer welfare by lowering prices on consumption and lowering manufacturing input costs. Challenges consist mainly of increased competition for domestic companies in MENA, particularly, as World Bank's Pigato[11] noted, for unskilled and resource-intensive manufacturing and food items in labor abundant countries.

The prospect of furthering integration seems to combine a mix of economic optimist with political caution. A report by Ernst & Young and Oxford Economics[12] predicts that MENA's trade flows will grow fastest with Russia, India, and China over the period 2011–2020. Researchers of this study expect global trade to grow at about 9.4 percent (p.a.), but MENA's trade flows will grow even faster, specifically trade with Russia will grow at 14.4 percent p.a., with India at 13.5 percent p.a. and with China at 12.5 percent p.a. On the other hand, annual trade with the United States, EU, and Japan will grow at slower pace, respectively: 8.4 percent, 7.7 percent, and 7.3 percent.

Brazil and MENA's integration is based on a growing economic partnership catalyzed in 2003 when President Lula da Silva proposed the creation of the Summit South America and Arab Countries.[13] Since then the volume of trade between Brazil and MENA countries increased at a rate of 13 percent per annum, from $4.9 billion in 2002 to $26 billion in 2012.

Yet all this economic optimism may need to be tempered by political risks to MENA countries. A cursory glance of this issue, namely, the United States changing direction toward the Middle East will be reviewed later on in this chapter. The next section examines the prospect of further economic integration of each BRIC country with MENA region.

Brazil and MENA

In 2010, Brazil's balance of trade with Arab countries was positive. The export volume was $12.5 billion and imports were merely $6.9 billion only. Exports were concentrated mostly on meat, sugar, minerals, and cereals; respectively about 25 percent, 23 percent, 17 percent, and 13 percent of the total exports. The imports were essentially focused in oil resources (84 percent). Inward and outward FDI of Brazil and MENA countries are of little consequence. UAE investors in the hotel sector in Brazil did the most significant investment.*

According to Marcelo Nabih Sallum,[14] President of the Chamber of Commerce Brazil-Arab Countries, the exponential growth in trade between Brazil and the Arab countries is due mainly to the large potential market of MENA countries. Mr Sallum mentioned that there are opportunities to improve bilateral relations not only in trade but also in tourism, financial services and investments, construction, and health.

---

* Ibidem.

Russia and MENA

The cooperation between Russia and the MENA countries benefits from the Soviet legacy. During the 1950 to 1980s the Soviet Union assisted Arab nations in building several infrastructure projects, but that cooperation ceased and only started to pick up again in the 1990s and 2000s particularly after official visits of the Russian presidents to Algeria in 2006 and 2010.[15] According to Senkovich, Russia aims to reestablish cooperation with the traditional partner countries of Algeria, Lybia, Syria, and Iraq, as well as enter in the markets of the GCC monarchies' markets.

Trade between Russia and MENA was about $14 billion in 2011 and was largely dominated by the Russian exports (90 percent of trade) of precious metals and stones, metal products and machines, transport equipment, coal, and arms, as well as oil and petroleum products which are exported to non-oil producing countries in MENA.

In terms of investment, Arab nations are interested in Russian's technology expertise in higher value industries such as oil and gas production, petrochemicals, remote sensing, water demineralization, nuclear power, space, and Information Technology (IT).* On the flip side, Russia is interested in attracting investments from Arab resource-rich countries, however, Senkovich argues, Arabs perceive Russia as a high-risk market.[†] Yet, he adds, both inward and outward investments between Russia and MENA seem to be moving too slowly allegedly due to competition from Western countries and China.

India and MENA

The influence of India and China in the MENA region is growing rapidly and is expected to become critical for the development of the three regions. Two recent studies have examined the recent economic integration of MENA region with India and with China (Al Masah Capital Management Limited, 2010; Pigato 2009).

The MENA countries have been major trading partners in meeting India's energy needs, particularly Saudi Arabia (the largest oil supplier to

---

* Ibidem.

[†] Ibidem.

(a)

Lebanon	0.4%
Tunisia	0.6%
Libya	0.6%
Jordon	0.7%
Bahrain	0.7%
Morocco	0.7%
Syria	0.9%
Sudan	1.2%
Iraq	1.3%
Qatar	1.4%
Algeria	1.5%
Yemen	1.9%
Kuwait	2.1%
Oman	2.8%
Egypt	3.8%
Iran	5.0%
Saudi	10.5%
UAE	64.1%

0%   20%   40%   60%   80%

(b)

Lebanon	0.0%
Syria	0.2%
Tunisia	0.3%
Sudan	0.6%
Bahrain	0.6%
Libya	0.8%
Jordon	1.0%
Morocco	1.1%
Algeria	1.3%
Yemen	2.0%
Egypt	2.1%
Oman	4.4%
Qatar	5.8%
Iraq	8.8%
Kuwait	10.4%
Iran	14.5%
Saudi	21.5%
UAE	24.5%

0%   10%   20%   30%

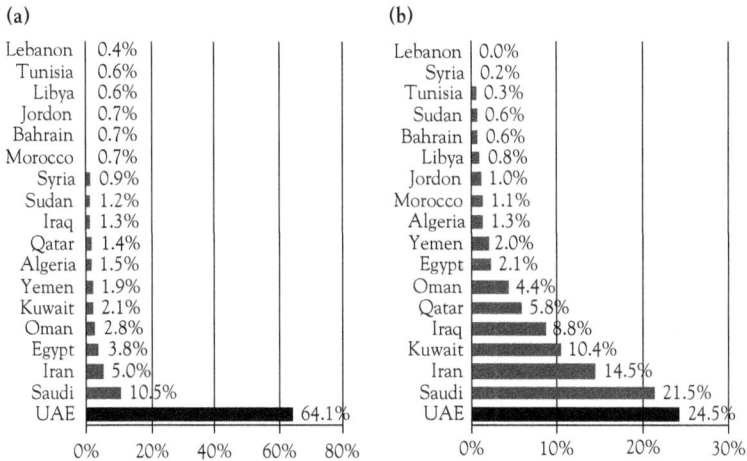

Figure 4.21 India's exports and imports to and from MENA countries, percent share, 2009–2010

Source: Department of Commerce, India

India), as well India's export markets, namely UAE (the largest external MENA market for India). In 2009–2010, total trade between India and MENA countries was $116.9 billion but two thirds of this ($83.9 billion) was trade only with the GCC, as depicted in Figure 4.21.

According to Al Masah Capital,[16] the MENA region can benefit further from India's expertise in services, namely IT related industries, science and technology, and education. To boost economic ties in the MENA region India has been in talks with GCC countries to establish a free trade agreement and is now pushing for a quick conclusion of the negotiation process.

The investments between India and MENA are essentially anchored in Saudi Arabia. Since mid-2000 more than 100 Indian companies have established joint ventures in Saudi Arabia and half of these have reciprocated and established joint ventures in India.* Incorporating Al Masah Capital's report in 2006–2007, more than 82 new licenses were granted to Indian companies in order to establish business in Saudi Arabia. These are expected to be valued at roughly $467 billion in Saudi Arabia, mostly in service industries.

Regarding MENA's FDI in India, the GCC countries are the major investors in India. For example, Saudi investment in India from 1991 to

---

* Ibidem.

2004, was $228 billion, mostly from the industrial sector, (e.g. chemicals, machinery, cement, metallurgy, paper manufacture), as well as in the computer software sector. In just the second and third quarters of 2010, UAE invested $1,792 billion in India and an additional $326.6 billion in Oman.*

In terms of future cooperation, Al Masah Capital points out that 4.5 million Indians already live and work in the Gulf region in a range of jobs from unskilled to professional and highly skilled labors; meaning the human capital from India can be a suitable complement to MENA's countries that lack qualified workers. It is suggested that MENA's oil resources combined with India's technology and human capital may provide the opportunity to create new ventures and cooperation, particularly in four sectors: real estate development, energy, petrochemicals, and transport infrastructure.

To conclude, it is worth noting that despite political risks in the MENA region, India is expected to become its main trading partner by 2013–2015 (HSBC Bank, 2013). The rich MENA countries, particularly Turkey, Saudi Arabia, and Egypt are likely to be the main drivers of India's exports.

China and MENA

China and India's spectacular economic rise over the last two decades has accelerated their trade with Africa, Latin America, and MENA. Their demands for oil, gas, and other natural resources have been forging new relationships with MENA countries based not only on energy but also on trade, investment, and political ties. Indeed, Dubai has become the new Silk Road—the intersection where people, capital, and ideas meet—and Beijing, Shanghai, Hong Kong, Mumbai, Riyadh, and Cairo are the new centers.

The future may well bring new opportunities and faster growth to MENA countries, but the challenges are formidable. For MENA oil-producing countries, faster growth in China and India will increase revenues from oil and the difficult choices associated with their management. For the labor abundant, non-oil producing countries, competition with China and India will spotlight the need for policy measures

---

* Ibidem.

to increase productivity. This may require broader institutional changes seen in China and India—and thus may take time. But the horizon for creating much needed employment is shorter, suggesting the importance of a pragmatic reform agenda that can accelerate productivity, trade, and investment in the region.

Trade between China and MENA has increased significantly in recent years. In 2009, China became the largest exporter to Middle East countries with a two-way trade value of $107 billion.* Saudi Arabia and UAE are the two major trading partners of China in the MENA region, with the former being the major exporter to China and the latter the main importer from China, as depicted in Figure 4.22.

Bilateral trade between Saudi Arabia and China rose to $41.8 billion in 2008 and is estimated to reach $60 billion by 2015 based mostly on oil exports to China.† Trade between China and UAE has been centered mostly on exports of low-cost Chinese goods into UAE and base materials and related materials from UAE to China.

A report focusing on the link between MENA and China (Arabia Monitor, 2012) indicates that there are growing trading synergies between

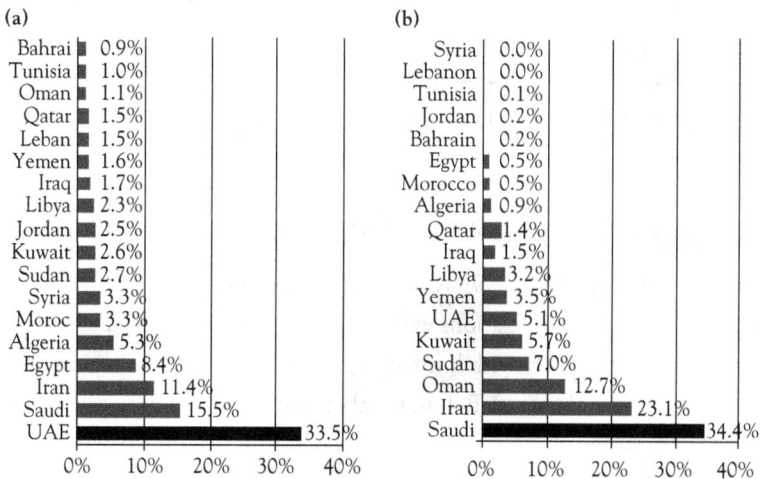

Figure 4.22 *China's exports to MENA (left) and China's import from MENA (right), percent share, Jan–Oct 2008*

Source: Ministry of Foriegn Trade, People's Republic of China

---

* Ibidem.

† Ibidem.

the two regions not only in the traditional oil and resources sectors but also in agriculture and industry. With the decline of exports to Europe MENA's food exporters are expected to capitalize on China's increasing food demand. The same research indicates that Chinese industrial conglomerates (particularly in the automobile industry) also are expected to invest directly in MENA countries in order to gain faster access to the markets in the region. While China's FDI in the region represents just 1.5 percent of its total investment outflow, in terms of MENA's FDI it represents 3.5 percent of the total inflow. Thus the effects of Chinese integration are likely to create significant impact.

South Africa and MENA

For centuries, trade has been integral to most countries that constitute the MENA region. As momentum in global business shifts toward greater intra-emerging markets, or "south-south" trade and investment, the MENA economies are well positioned to benefit. But how far and fast the MENA region integrate into these new economic relationships will depend on how executives from other emerging markets view it, and how such perspectives may differ from those of their peers in the developed world. Hence, it is important to understand a few historical facts regarding the MENA region to better understand its impact on global trade.

Historical Perspectives

At the beginning of the 1990s, just before the end of Apartheid, South Africa had diplomatic relations with no country in the Middle East except Israel, another country with limited ties to nations in its own region until the end of the Cold War.* Before Israel's recognition as a nation in 1948,

---

* It should be noted, however, that Israel had great success in developing relations with independent African states beginning with the decolonization of Ghana in 1957, but due to expanding Arab influence in Africa, especially around the time of the Yom Kippur/Ramadan War of 1973, Israel was drawn closer to white-ruled South Africa, another so-called Pariah state; these ties also included controversial military cooperation.

the same year that Apartheid became official government policy, South Africa had established diplomatic relations with Egypt. Formal relations with Lebanon and Iran came later. Egypt had become a prominent support of African liberation organizations following the establishment of the Arab nationalist regime of Gamal Abdel Nasser in 1956 that lasted until the early 1960s.

According to Michael Bishku, on an essay published at the Middle East Policy Council Journal,[17] in Lebanon's situation, trading relations continued until the mid-1970s, at which time they were formally severed due to pressure from the Arab League states. As for Iran, the Islamic Revolution brought a definitive end to relations with the Apartheid government. Naturally, Jewish and Lebanese ethnic populations in South Africa are factored in, with regard to Israel and Lebanon. As for Egypt, it was the most important African country aside from South Africa and one of only a few independent African states until the late 1950s, the others being Ethiopia and Liberia.

In addition, South Africans were militarily involved in Egypt during WWII as part of British Commonwealth forces fighting the Germans. During that war, Reza Shah Pahlavi, ruler of Iran from the 1920s, was sent into exile on Mauritius—but later moved to South Africa, where he died in 1944—by the British, who accused him of German sympathies; his son and successor, Muhammad Reza Pahlavi, who faced a Soviet threat to his rule following WWII, viewed South Africa as a bulwark against the spread of communism and, like Israel, an important market for Iranian oil. The shah was a rival of Nasser, who looked toward the Soviet Union for military support during the mid-1950s, when Soviet leader Nikita Khrushchev began supporting Third World liberation movements. Diplomatic relations between South Africa and the Soviet Union were severed during his time.

Perspectives on Investments Inflow and Trade

According to a survey conducted by Lewis, Sen, and Tabary for the Economist Intelligence Unit[18] in July 2011, there are striking differences in the way respondents from different regions of the world perceive the MENA region as a place of doing business. Of course, there are similarities too. According to the survey, most multinational companies plan to expand significantly in the region, especially in the Gulf States. And most cite concerns over political risk, bureaucratic red tape and, in particular, a perceived lack of transparency in the region. However, there are major differences in the way that executives from different regions view the prospects for democracy in the Middle East and the likely implications for their own businesses. The culture and norms of respondents' home markets also seem to influence their attitudes toward such factors such as volatility in the business environment, corruption and diversity.

Lewis, Sen, and Tabary* argue that the Middle East region will benefit strongly from accelerating "south-south" business, particularly with increasing trade between emerging markets. While executives from all regions expect the Middle East to feature more prominently in their global business plans over the next five years, it is among Latin American firms, followed by those from Asia-Pacific and North America, where this trend is most pronounced.

Businesses' views on the potential impact of the *Arab Spring* on trade and investment are divided. While investors broadly welcome the outbreak of pro-democracy movements across the Middle East, the upheavals of the Arab Spring create short-term political risk that can dent business confidence. Almost one-half of all respondents of the Economist Intelligence Unit survey report[†] agree that the current unrest in the region is likely to have an adverse effect on their business in the near future.

The UAE is the most favored destination in the Middle East for business expansions and trade, with expansion plans centered on the wealthy Gulf States, probably reflecting the beneficial impact of high oil prices on the economic outlook for these countries. The Gulf States also are favored due to the perception that political risk is lower than in other countries in the region. The UAE is by far the most popular investment and trading location, cited by 63 percent of respondents overall. Latin American executives also showed strong interest in Egypt and Morocco. Emerging-market firms are more likely to focus activities on less saturated markets and sectors.

Latin American firms are less worried about the impact of political turmoil on business in the Middle East than any other region in

---

* Ibidem, pp. 3–4.
† Ibidem.

the world. According to Lewis, Sen, and Tabary survey* 55 percent of total respondents from Latin America say that the political upheaval seen recently in the region (2013) is unlikely to affect business adversely in the medium to long term, compared with 43 percent of respondents from both North America and Asia-Pacific. This could reflect the fact that many Latin American countries have come through their own transitions from authoritarian or military rule to democracy in the past 25 years. Nevertheless, a majority of investors, unsure how to handle rapid change, say that if forced to choose, they would prefer stability over democracy.

Corruption is less of a concern for emerging-market firms than it is for businesses from developed markets. Corruption is a relatively minor concern for emerging-market investors in the Middle East, especially among Asian and Latin American companies. However, for European and North American firms, corruption is cited as having a major impact on operations, possibly reflecting tighter anti-corruption legislation, such as the Foreign Corrupt Practice Act (FCPA), in their home markets.

Cultural factors also present major concerns for emerging-market businesses. A significant minority of the Economist's[†] survey respondents from all regions adheres to the view that businesses and workers may face discrimination on the basis of gender, race or nationality in the Middle East. Attitudes toward women and ethnic minorities significantly deter economic development of the region. Almost half of Latin American businesses believe that the business culture of the Middle East is more suitable for corporations from other emerging markets than for corporations from advanced economies. Some emerging-market investors also expressed concern that their goods, services or employees are not treated on par with those from Western countries.[‡]

The burgeoning youth population that is demanding political change in the Middle East is also valued as an economic resource. Demographics are seen at least as important as oil and gas resources when it comes to driving opportunities for business in the Middle East. Nearly 50 percent

---

* Ibidem, pp. 5–6.
† Ibidem.
‡ Ibidem.

of all Economist's survey* respondents expect business opportunities to emerge from the growth of a new middle class, while 41 percent cite the growing youth population as a source of opportunity. Respondents from Europe are particularly likely to value the region's demographics, probably reflecting concerns about slowing population growth, aging populations and market saturation in their home markets. Fifty-two percent of European respondents cite the growth of young population as a source of opportunity, compared with just 33 percent who cite commodities.

The gradual shift toward emerging markets reflects policy decisions by Middle Eastern governments, including the region's major oil exporters, who are well aware that their future top customers are located in Asia, and not in the G-7 group. Indeed, when the current Saudi ruler, King Abdullah bin Abdel-Aziz Al Saud, came to the throne, his first overseas trip was to Beijing, not to the United States or UK. For a brief period in 2009, China imported more oil from Saudi Arabia than the United States—something that may become a permanent reality in the near future assuming Chinese oil consumption grows and the United States continues its policy of reducing its reliance on Middle East oil. Moreover, some of the region's authoritarian rulers have been particularly attracted to the so-called *China model*: focusing on economic development but not on political reform. In contrast to the United States or Europe, China does not seek commitments on human rights in order to sign trade deals. While China's approach to trade may appeal to authoritarian regimes in the Middle East, this year's Arab Spring of popular uprisings in favor of greater democracy is likely to force governments in the region to reconsider their foreign and trade policies.

South Africa has expressed keen interest in expanding its trade relations with the MENA bloc. In late November 2013, the South African Department of Trade and Industry (DTI) lead a business delegation to the Middle East, one of South Africa's important trade zones, with the objective of enhancing trade and investment relations in that region. According to the news outlet allAfrica,[19] DTI's outward trading mission to Saudi Arabia and Kuwait was aimed at building the commitments made by the DTI to expose South African companies to the Middle East

---

* Ibidem.

market and to deepen bilateral trade and investment relations between these countries.

DTI's Minister, Rob Davies, argues that the Middle East is an important trade zone for South Africa, holding great potential for South Africa as an export market, and serving as a potential source of FDI, as he sees the Middle East as one of the world's fastest growing markets for manufactured products and services.* Indeed, Saudi Arabia is South Africa's largest trading partner and second largest export destination in the Gulf region. In 2012 alone, total bilateral trade between the two countries amounted to R61.7 billion rand. Kuwait is one of South Africa's major trading partners, and is the sixth largest export destination in the Middle East, with a total bilateral trade between the two countries amounted to R246 million rand in 2012.

Turkey also has a role to play in South African DTI's trade mission, as its Deputy Minister, Elizabeth Thabethe, has been focusing on an outward selling and investment mission to that country. According to Thabethe both South Africa and Turkey are featured in one another's top 40 lists of imports and export trade partners. The two countries are regional powerhouses in their respective regions. South Africa's exports to Turkey have been steadily increasing to an extent that the trade deficit in favor of Turkey has been significantly reduced.

Currently, South Africa conducts trade with MENA in various industrial sectors including agro-processing, manufacturing machinery and equipment, and capital equipment. Turkey has targeted the following sectors for the mission: energy, mining, infrastructure, information and communication technology, capital equipment and engineering, and textiles.

In concluding this section, it is worth mentioning that, according to Cashin, Mohaddes and Raissi,[20] the MENA countries are more sensitive to macroeconomic developments in China than to shocks in the EU or the U.S. According to McKinsey Consulting,[21] trade flows between China and the GCC are expected to rise to between $350 and $500 billion dollars by the year 2020. This supports the idea that the interconnectedness between China and MENA region will be a significant force shaping the world economic environment.

---

* Ibidem.

Rising Together?

In March 2013, the fifth BRICS summit was held in Durban, South Africa. The heads of these governments acknowledged the need to operationalize the recommendations received by the think tanks of their countries. There is a need to accelerate from talk into action. One idea shared during the meetings was the possibility of the BRICS countries to create a new development bank, one mandated to assist developing nations (south-south development). Deen[22] mentioned that one area of intervention of this bank could be to assist some MENA countries, specifically Egypt, who is seen as having significant influence in the Arab world.*

Certainly, companies around the globe recognize the long-term economic potential of the Arab world. Trade between Middle East countries and others, particularly those from emerging markets, has been increasing for years, and is likely to grow further as part of a broader trend of greater economic exchange between non-OECD countries. Political authoritarianism and instability have forced many investors to think twice about their plans in the short term, although many emerging-market firms appear less worried about volatile operating conditions. A significant minority of executives in all regions (except the Middle East itself) believes that local attitudes toward women and ethnic minorities would hold back the region's economic development. Nevertheless, the current upheavals of the Arab Spring are giving hope to investors from all regions that, despite obvious short-term difficulties inherent in political transition, a more transparent business environment will emerge eventually.

MENA Countries Attract Less FDI
Than Other Emerging Markets

While concerns about corruption, infrastructure and political uncertainty will remain worrisome in the medium term, the opportunities deriving

---

* Ibidem.

from a young and growing population are all too evident, and our survey shows that investors from all regions are planning major expansion into the MENA region. Firms from other emerging markets are increasingly seeking opportunities outside the oil and gas industry, in the less-developed sectors and countries across the region. Latin American firms are leveraging their expertise in fostering innovation in agriculture. Others are finding a niche in providing goods and services by competing on price or quality.

For companies from industrialized countries and emerging markets alike, significant challenges remain in doing business and attracting FDI in the Middle East. But the region is changing in visible ways, as made clear from the Arab Spring, and in ways that are more imperceptible, as in the recalibration of policies and attitudes toward business. The region today represents opportunities that businesses around the world are keen to grasp. Given the trends in global trade and investment, it is more than likely that the attractiveness of the opportunities will outweigh the risks over time.

According to Daniele and Marani,[23] however, the underperformance of MENA countries to attract FDI is due to several major factors, namely: the small size of local markets and lack of real economic integration; changes in international competition for FDI; slow institutional and trade reforms; and political and macroeconomic instability. However, to overcome these obstacles MENA countries need to improve their governance systems that, according to various indicators, display poor performance, as depicted in Figure 4.23.

The MENA region encompasses countries with diverse wealth concentrations and resource levels, widely divergent economic structures and trajectories ranging from wealthy Gulf monarchies to poor countries such as Yemen.[24] As Cammett* pointed out the development of MENA countries is shaped not only by economic and institutional factors but also by the culture and history of these countries. While most of the explanations regarding development in MENA countries are valid there is still no clear

---

* Ibidem.

	Voice accountability	Political stability	Government effectiveness	Regulatory quality	Rule of law	Control corruption
Algeria	160	192	133	173	152	124
Egypt	166	157	107	154	97	105
Israel	85	177	41	62	55	49
Jordan	149	116	79	95	84	70
Lebanon	155	161	121	142	117	127
Libya	203	112	157	197	145	175
Morocco	142	126	92	120	101	93
Syria	201	151	153	187	122	153
Tunisia	171	101	64	118	89	78
Turkey	123	144	89	110	96	106

Figure 4.23 MENA governance indicators

Source: Daniele and Marani, 2006

understanding of what are the most important factors, and more importantly of how political and economic institutions in MENA region will reproduce and change in the future. The future presents opportunities for both the MENA and BRIC countries to cooperate further but not without uncertainties and risks.

Opportunities in the MENA Region

Growth and trade in the MENA region is constrained by several factors. On the one hand, growth is hindered by difficulties in access to finance, labor skill disparities and shortages, and electricity constraints.[25] On the other hand, underperformance in MENA's trade is constrained by logistics and transport limitations and inefficiencies in custom clearance processes.[26] Despite such huge challenges, O'Sullivan and colleagues[27] noted that there are some clear opportunities in the MENA region to consider, and which the BRIC countries should be aware of when developing relations with MENA. The opportunities are as follows:

- The young population as a market and labor force. As the average age in the MENA countries is just 25 years, well below other emerging regions, there will soon be a larger labor force and consequently a rise in consumption levels. However, for this opportunity to materialize governments need to develop institutional frameworks that promote essential social needs, namely education, employment, health, and housing. Renewable energies, including solar sources in all MENA countries, hydropower (Egypt, Iran, Iraq, and Syria) and wind (along the Red Sea and Morocco's Atlantic coast). The International Energy Agency forecasts that by 2035 the use of renewables for electricity generation could reach 33 percent and FDI reach $400 billion provided that adequate policies and institutions are implemented.

- The tourism sector already represents a large industry in some MENA countries and provides significant sources of employment and exports. MENA countries have traditionally targeted tourists from European and Gulf markets, however, with increased purchasing power of people in emerging countries MENA can expand into new tourism markets.

- Agro-industries in MENA countries with sufficient water resources also offer significant growth potential. Such countries include Iraq, Lebanon, Morocco, Egypt, and Syria. The opportunities will exist in both domestic and emerging markets essentially due to demographic trends and economic growth. Internally, the demographic trend in the MENA region and its subsequent expected consumption (as described earlier), there will be higher demand for food products. The same phenomenon can already be seen in other emerging countries, such as China. One particular benefit of the agro-industries is that it will open up business opportunities and create employment in related industries upstream (farming) and downstream (handling, packaging, processing, transporting, and marketing).

- And of course there will be a plethora of opportunities in the energy sector. The resource-rich countries of the MENA region account for nearly 60 percent of the world's oil reserves and 45 percent of the natural gas reserves. This sector will continue to attract investments, technology, and know-how.

The United States Changes Direction
in the Middle East

By M.K.Bhadrakumar*

The politics of the Middle East are undergoing a period of great turbulence emanating from changes in direction of the regional policies pursued by the United States. When the ship makes a turnaround, it has to be over an arc, and it is now possible to discern the reset of the compass.

This is primarily being felt in the Obama administration's rethink on the Syrian conflict and its decision to constructively engage with Iran. Neither is an afterthought, but rather they took time to mature. . .

To take Syria first, Leslie Gelb, President Emeritus at the Council on Foreign Relations in New York needs no introduction as an influential voice in the U.S. foreign policy establishment. His views on the Syrian conflict will always merit attention—especially when aired through the Voice of America (VOA).

Gelb made four key points on Syria in an exclusive interview with the VOA. First, the specter that haunts all the parties inside Syria as well as the U.S.' friends and allies who neighbor Syria—Iraq, Turkey, Jordan, Israel—is the rise of the *jihadi*. Second, the elimination of the *jihadis* will take time because they are seasoned fighters and it is best achieved through cooperation between the Syrian regime and the moderate rebels. The basis of such cooperation could be through a "power-sharing arrangement, mainly along federal lines," as stated by Gelb. Third, there is urgency to lay the basis of cooperation between the regime and the moderate rebels—that is, as argued by Gelb, "how they could compromise and live together." Or else, Geneva 2 may not prove productive. And fourth, the United States is according to Gelb, "beginning to change direction" as it has "finally figured out... that the only way to stop this

---

* Mr. Bhadrakumar is a former career diplomat in the Indian Foreign Service whom devoted much of his three-decade long career to the Pakistan, Afghanistan and Iran desks in the Ministry of External Affairs and in assignments on the territory of the former Soviet Union. After leaving the diplomatic service, he took to writing and contributing to The Asia Times, The Hindu, and Deccan Herald. I, Dr. Goncalves, appreciate his valuable contribution to this chapter. Mr. Bhadrakumar lives in New Delhi, India.

fighting is to work something out between the moderate rebels and the Alawites."*

For example, the United States has stopped saying that Syria's president, Assad, must go. That used to be the hallmark of U.S. policy. The United States no longer says that anymore. The U.S. administration says only he has lost legitimacy, and that it wants him and his government to come and participate in negotiations. So that's changed. Also changed is the notion that the United States can simply help the rebels, as it finally realized that it does not exactly know who these rebels are and what they can do. After all, they have never gotten fully organized. And there's a big gap, it seems, between the rebels the U.S. deals with and that council [Syrian National Coalition] in Turkey and the good rebels fighting in the field.

Indeed, it is palpable that the United States is currently supportive of the series of diplomatic initiatives Moscow has been taking during early fall 2013 in a renewed push for a Syrian peace conference. The Russian Deputy Foreign Minister Mikhail Bogdanov met the Syrian National Coalition (SNC) representatives in Istanbul during that time. The SNC also had come under American pressure to accept Russia's invitation to go to Moscow to discuss the peace conference.

Equally, there has been a sea change in the U.S. Iran standoff. The probability that the ongoing negotiation of the P5+1† is high and

---

* Today, Alawites represent 12 percent of the Syrian population and are a significant minority in Turkey and northern Lebanon. The Alawites, also known as Alawis, are a prominent mystical religious group centered in Syria who follow a branch of the Twelver school of Shia Islam (the largest branch of Shi'a Islam), but with syncretistic elements. Alawites revere Ali (Ali ibn Abi Talib), and the name "Alawi" means followers of Ali. The sect is believed to have been founded by Ibn Nusayr during the 8th century. For this reason, Alawites are sometimes called "Nusayris," though this term has come to have derogatory connotations in the modern era.

† The P5+1 is a group of six world powers, which in 2006 joined the diplomatic efforts with Iran with regard to its nuclear program. The term refers to the P5 or five permanent members of the UN Security Council, namely U.S., Russia, China, United Kingdom, and France, plus Germany. P5+1 is often referred to as the E3+3 (or E3/EU+3) by European countries.

Iran may produce an interim nuclear deal. Contrary to the widely held view that the Obama administration's push to reach an interim agreement with Iran would be torpedoed on Capitol Hill, the Democratic leadership in the U.S. Senate, in particular the heads of the Armed Services Committee, Carl Levin, and Intelligence Committee, Dianne Feinstein, have concurred that this would be a bad time to impose new sanctions against Iran when negotiations are under way.

The former U.S. national security advisors Zbigniew Brzezinski and Brent Scowcroft have written a letter to the Senate Majority Leader Harry Reid strongly pleading, "If more sanctions are enacted now, as these unprecedented negotiations are just getting started, this would reconfirm Iranians' belief that the United States is not prepared to make any agreement with the current government of Iran. We call on all Americans and the U.S. Congress to stand firmly with the President in the difficult but historic negotiations with Iran."[28]

Indeed, Gelb himself is on record that a short-term deal "would lead to the Mideast equivalent of ending the Cold War with the Soviet Union . . . [and] could reduce, even sharply, the biggest threat to regional peace, an Iranian nuclear bomb, and open pathways to taming dangerous conflicts in Syria, Iraq, and Afghanistan."[*]

Therefore, there is cautious optimism that an agreement can be finalized. The leaders of Russia, China, and UK have had telephone conversations with Iranian President Hassan Rouhani. After a fall 2013 meeting President Obama, Secretary of State John Kerry, and National Security Advisor Susan Rice called with key U.S. senators, the White House issued the following statement, "We have the opportunity to halt the progress of the Iranian (nuclear) program and roll it back in key respects, while testing whether a comprehensive resolution can be achieved."[29] It warned that if there is not an initial agreement, Iran will continue making progress on increasing enrichment capacity, growing its stockpiles of enriched uranium, installing new centrifuges, and developing a plutonium reactor in the city of Arak.

Meanwhile, Iran's surprise announcement that relinquishing its insistence that the world powers should acknowledge explicitly its right to

---

[*] Ibidem.

enrich uranium deftly sidesteps a potentially tendentious aspect of the dispute and shifts the emphasis to practical steps that can be agreed on the interim.

Of course, it is not going to be a cakewalk for the Obama administration and a showdown is still very much possible between the White House and Congress regarding Iran. The conflict in Syria is not so much a contentious (and emotive) issue for the U.S. political establishment as the situation around Iran is, but everything converges ultimately on how the Obama administration will handle U.S. foreign policy in the Middle East for remainder of his presidency.

What makes this a high stakes contestation is that this is both a real time fight as well as a struggle over long-term issues. Let's not forget, relations between the Obama administration and the Israeli government led by Prime Minister Benjamin Netanyahu have entered uncharted waters and the latter has launched a full-scale attack on the entire trajectory of Obama's Middle East policies. Compounding matters further, Israel's concerns are not exclusively its own, but are shared by other U.S. key allies in the region, especially Saudi Arabia.

Due to a combination of circumstances including the searing experience in Iraq, crisis of the U.S. economy, and the U.S. public's lack of support for war, all against the backdrop of a rebalance in Asia, Washington wants to reduce its military "footprint" in the Middle East, whereas, U.S.' alliances in the region tried to pressure the Obama Administration into launching new wars against Syria and Iran. In his United Nations General Assembly speech in September 2013, President Obama virtually admitted the United States' helplessness in modulating the Arab Spring and spelled out that Washington's core concern in the Middle East would narrow down to four areas: protect allies from external aggression, ensure the free flow of oil, prevent proliferation of weapons of mass destruction, and counter the al-Qaeda threat.

Conceivably, the United States appears to be distancing itself from its entangled alliances so as to avoid being cajoled into conflicts from its closest regional allies. In a manner of speaking, the Obama Administration is seeking an optimal regional policy to suit U.S. interests rather than Israeli or Saudi interests. This is not tantamount to a "strategic retreat" from the region and it does not necessarily mean that U.S. interventionism is gone forever. It means simply that Washington's actions will be guided by a range of U.S. interests rather than succumbing to Israeli demands or Saudi Arabia's regional ambitions. If this reset is carried to its logical conclusion, the balance of forces in the Middle East will be transformed beyond recognition.

CHAPTER 5

Frontier Markets

The Next Emerging Markets

Overview

Two thousand years ago, everything outside of Rome was a frontier market. Three hundred years ago, everything outside of Europe was a frontier market. The emerging countries of today were the frontier as recently as 30 years ago. Now, we'd say that any country outside of the MSCI All Country World Index is a frontier market, at least from the perspective of investors in the advanced economies and especially in the United States.

Lawrence Speidell* argued that the United States, as the leading economy in the world as measured by both capitalization and trading volume, was a frontier market in 1792. At the time, the Buttonwood Agreement was executed at an outdoor location, under a buttonwood tree in New York City. It required brokers to trade only with each other and to fix commission rates. China too was a frontier market by the late 70's and early 80's, and today, it is the second largest economy in the world, although it is classified as an emerging market.

The same was true for Argentina, once a frontier market, but by 1896, it was about three-quarters as prosperous as the United States and had one of the world's leading stock markets. The country's long decline, at least in relative standing, resulted in purchasing power parity GDP per capita in 2002 that was only double the 1896 level, whereas the United States grew sevenfold over the same period. Even though Argentina has enjoyed a strong recovery and is a solidly middle-income economy, as of

---

* Speidell, Lawrence (2011-05-13). Frontier Market Equity Investing: Finding the Winners of the Future (Kindle Locations 67–68). CFA Institute. Kindle Edition.

this writing, its equity market is still classified as a frontier market because of capital controls that were imposed in 2005. In 2011, the country was in the process of removing these controls, but in 2013 and 2014 much of its progress was derailed, and inflation is accelerating and projected to hit 40 percent in 2014. Nonetheless, most frontier markets are more developed than we think, and set for fast economic growth.

Frontier markets are sometimes referred to as "pre-emerging markets." These are countries with equity markets that are less established, such as Argentina, Kuwait, and Bangladesh. They tend to be characterized by lower market capitalization, less liquidity and, in some cases, earlier stages of economic development. But such markets are not just growth markets in distant places; they represent more than 1.2 billion people. These emerging and frontier countries are also placing increasing demands on the world's resources, as they become intensive consumers of basic commodities to support their infrastructure development and manufacturing. In the 1950s, the U.S. Interstate Highway System was built, and China is building its equivalent now. This trend is echoed in railway construction, power plant construction, and new building and bridge construction. And it is not just China either. Developing countries around the world are undertaking such projects.

In the words of Speidell,

> It is easy to read articles with negative headlines and decide to avoid these markets. It is easy to think of only "big men" dictators and desperate poverty. But a traveler who reads only the headlines might also avoid Los Angeles and New York City. The truth is that most people in frontier countries are hard workers. They are trying to get an education, get a job, raise a family, and live in peace. They know all about Hollywood movie stars, basketball, and the World Cup. And they know a lot about getting by with less. It has been said, "they've been doing so much with so little for so long, they could do anything with nothing."*

---

* Speidell, Lawrence (2011-05-13). Frontier Market Equity Investing: Finding the Winners of the Future (Kindle Locations 132–136). CFA Institute. Kindle Edition.

For several decades, frontier markets have been caught in a vicious circle of poverty, with little ability to develop savings for investment in future growth. What investment occurred in frontier countries was done by colonial powers that took out more than they put in. Foreign direct investment (FDI) is highly correlated with GDP growth and can be used as a measure of how the developing economies are faring in globalization. As FDI inflows increase in these markets, we believe that the frontier market growth opportunity is similar in many ways to the opportunity that existed 20 years ago for emerging markets, especially taking into consideration many of the mineral resources these countries have, as depicted in Figure 5.1.

Nonetheless, due to its small, unpopular, and illiquid economies these countries have not yet *fully* joined the global investment community. Nonetheless, many have already joined the global economic community, as several of these countries have matured, improved their economic and trading policies, strengthen their institutions, achieved greater global credibility, and, in various cases, hoarded substantial foreign exchange reserves.

Country	Rank	Resource
Algeria	6	Barite
Algeria	1	Lead
Algeria	1	Zinc
Armenia	6	Molybdenum
Armenia	2	Rhenium
Botswana	8	Copper
Botswana	2	Diamonds
Botswana	15	Nickel
Botswana	2	Soda
Bulgaria	14	Barite
Guinea	1	Bauxite
Guyana	8	Bauxite
Kazakhstan	11	Bauxite
Kazakhstan	8	Bismuth
Kazakhstan	9	Boron

Figure 5.1 Mineral resource ranks for some of the frontier countries

Source: Speidell, Lawrence*

---

* Speidell, Lawrence (2011-05-13). Frontier Market Equity Investing: Finding the Winners of the Future (Kindle Locations 612–615). CFA Institute. Kindle Edition.

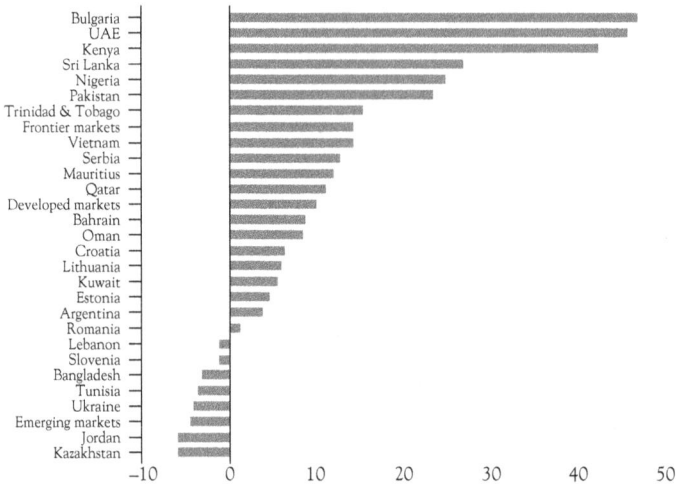

Figure 5.2 Percentage change in MSCI frontier market index for 2013

Source: MSCI, Reuters

Figure 5.2 shows how frontier markets such as Kenya, Bulgaria, and the United Arab Emirates (UAE) have improved more than 40 percent during 2013. Note that most of them experienced much more growth than developed markets (advanced economies), which averaged about 12 percent, and emerging markets at negative five percent.

When assessing frontier markets one should consider purchasing power parity (PPP) figures because they take into account the living standards of local people who may earn little but can live well because their money can go far when they buy inexpensive local products and services. When evaluating a country's GDP at PPP exchange rates it takes into consideration the sum value of all goods and services produced in the country valued at prices prevailing in the United States. This is the measure most economists prefer when looking at per-capita welfare and when comparing living conditions or use of resources across countries.

For instance, as shown in Figure 5.3, in Cambodia, Malawi, and Bangladesh, local prices are extremely cheap, whereas in Kuwait, Slovenia, and Cyprus, they are close to world levels. In contrast to these countries, Denmark's GDP per capita in nominal 2008 dollars is $46,314, but prices are so high that on a PPP basis, it is only $32,333.*

---

* According to Trading Economics as of 06/13/2014: http://www.tradingeconomics.com/denmark/gdp-per-capita

Country	CUP per capita (nominal $)	CUP per capita (PPP-adjusted $)	Difference
Cambodia	$ 651	$ 1,905	192%
Malawi	299	837	180
Bangladesh	494	1,334	170
Vietnam	1,052	2,785	165
Tanzania	482	1,263	162
Pakistan	1,013	2,644	161
Uzbekistan	1,022	2,656	160
Uganda	459	1,165	154
Sri Lanka	2,020	4,560	126
Zambia	1,134	1,356	20
Latvia	14,909	17,100	15
Venezuela	11,230	12,804	14
Kuwait	42,102	46,575	11
Slovenia	26,779	27,605	3
Cyprus	24,895	24,789	0

Figure 5.3 GDP per capita comparison: nominal dollars and PPP-adjusted dollars, 2008

Source: Speidell, Lawrence*

An analysis of PPP GDP per capita over the past 30 years shows that China started behind India ($250 versus $415 in 1980) but has now surpassed it ($5,962 versus $2,972 as of 2008). China is in a quest for continuous and significant geopolitical gains through its investments in frontier countries, whereas many advanced economies (particularly in the West) have cut back because of political preferences and budget pressure from the current economic slowdown. India is another emerging country that is active in Africa, which is no coincidence because for generations, a large number of Africa's entrepreneurs have been of Indian heritage. Even Russia has joined the skirmish, with then President Medvedev touring Egypt, Nigeria, Angola, and Namibia back in June 2009 in search of trade and investment deals.

---

* Speidell, Lawrence (2011-05-13). Frontier Market Equity Investing: Finding the Winners of the Future (Kindle Location 243). CFA Institute. Kindle Edition.

The breakup of the Soviet Union dramatically affected the economies of the constituent members. By far the largest is Russia, where GDP per capita fell from $9,052 in 1989 to $6,303 in 1996 (a 31 percent decrease, which is more severe than the Great Depression in the United States) before more than doubling to $13,392 in 2008. In contrast, Botswana, a frontier country that fortunately discovered diamonds shortly after gaining independence in 1962, has shown dramatic improvement in its GDP per capita.

Progress, however, has not been across the board, as monetary and fiscal policies, FDI inflow imbalances, and stock vulnerabilities vary widely across these economies. This situation is aggravated by the fact the mainstream media tend to emphasize negative news of conflicts, violence, drought, flood, and human suffering in frontier markets, causing public opinion to categorize them with negative connotations. Behaviors such as of Robert Mugabe, president of Zimbabwe, who allowed inflation to reach an absurd 231,000,000 percent in 2008 is an example of such news that foster the development of a general prejudice, such as not trusting any government in Africa.

We believe each country should be judged on its own merits. For instance, in the frontier countries of Africa and Asia, the financial sector for consumers is almost totally undeveloped. According to Speidell, "Ghana, for example, has 22 million people but only 1.5 million bank accounts, fewer than 500,000 debit cards, and almost no credit cards. Nigeria has 148 million people and only 20 million bank accounts. Mortgages and auto loans are practically unheard of in these countries. Many banks in frontier countries take customers' deposits and pay low interest rates of 2–4 percent."* Then, they simply make government and commercial loans at 10 percent or more. Net interest margins are often greater than five percent, and one bank in Malawi recently told me that its net interest margin is 15 percent.

Below is a brief highlight of some of the most important frontier markets. This list is not extensive and not necessarily in any order of

---

* Speidell, Lawrence (2011-05-13). Frontier Market Equity Investing: Finding the Winners of the Future (Kindle Locations 493–498). CFA Institute. Kindle Edition.

magnitude. It just provides an overall picture of the typical opportunities and challenges faces by these countries. For more in depth information, please refer to our other book titled "*Frontier Markets, the Next Emerging Bloc*," by the same publisher.

Bangladesh

Bangladesh is a country the size of the state of Iowa in the United States. It is a moderate, secular, and democratic society, ranked the seventh most populated nation in the world, with 160 million (larger than Russia). Bangladesh has a big potential market for foreign investors, with a growing garment sector providing steady export-led economic growth and a rapidly developing market-based economy, on the cusp of attaining lower-middle income status of over $1,036 GDP per capita, thanks to consistent annual GDP growth averaging six percent since the 90s.

Since 1976, the Investment Corporation of Bangladesh (ICB) has been a catalyst in fostering rapid economic growth. Now the local economy is growing at full tilt, and depicted in Figure 5.4, with GDP growth projected to climb from about 5.8 percent in 2012 to around 7.2 percent in 2017. Bangladesh's economy grew by above six percent on average over the last four years and is set to continue growing by six percent in 2014.

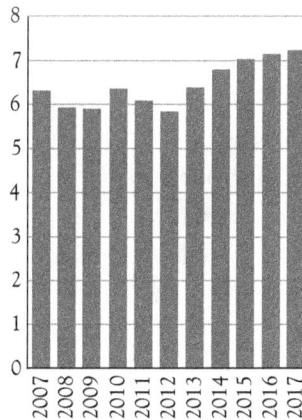

Figure 5.4 Bangladesh GDP growth projection through 2017

Source: IMF

Bangladesh has a lot of potential for rapid economic growth, as show in Figure 5.4. Over the past 20 years the country's GDP has expanded on average five percent a year and is now considered one of the most attractive destinations for investment in the region. It has already surpassed other South East Asian countries in a number of fundamental economic and development indicators.

The country has gone through an extensive restructuring of its economy. Since the 1970s it has been fighting to modernize its systems, produce top entrepreneurs and broaden the base of investments in the country—and the hard work is paying off. Fostering development is still a main challenge in Bangladesh, and for some time the government strategy has been to privatize the numerous companies that were nationalized after independence. The country had a socialist economy after its independence in 1971, and around that time it nationalized all industries. However, the country has since revisited its economic policy as it undergoes reforms to stimulate at the creation of experienced entrepreneurs, managers, administrators, engineers, and technicians due to lack of private initiative.

The Bangladesh Chamber of Commerce and Industry (BCCI) has recently announced that it expects that by 2030 Bangladesh should be among the 30 largest economies in the world; it currently is the 58th largest.

Egypt

Egypt is another overlooked economy, which has lately been politically unstable as a result of the Arab Spring that spread through the Middle East, causing massive damage to its economy. After the ouster of President Mohamed Morsi in July 2013, one year after he took office, Egypt entered another phase of political uncertainty.

According to the African Development Bank Group (AEBG),* Egypt's economic growth has moderated, standing at just above two percent in both the 2011–2012 and 2012–2013 fiscal years. In 2012–2013, the resilience of private consumption (81.2 percent of GDP) and the munificence

---

* http://www.afdb.org/en/countries/north-africa/egypt/egypt-economic-outlook/

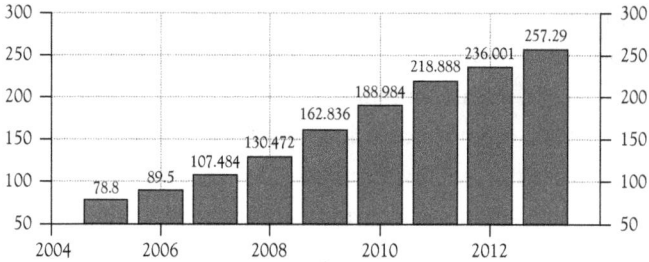

Figure 5.5 Egypt's GDP growth forecast

Source: TradingEconomics.com, World Bank, AEBG

of government consumption (11.7 percent of GDP) kept the economy from sliding into recession, as investment (14.2 percent of GDP) and exports (17.6 percent of GDP) remained weak. Unceasing violent protests and political instability have adversely affected manufacturing (15.6 percent of GDP), trade (12.9%) and tourism (3.2 percent). Only traditional sectors such as agriculture (14.5 percent of GDP) and mining (17.3 percent) have remained relatively unscathed.

Egypt is, however, the third largest economy in Africa, and remains an important emerging market in that region, as it controls and draws significant revenues from the Suez Canal. Also according to the AEBG* projections, as depicted in Figure 5.5, the countries economy is expected to continue to grow at consistent pace.

The country's GDP was worth $257.29 billion in 2012, and about 0.41 percent of the world economy. The country's ability to withstand the financial burden of the revolution, for now at least was helped by the remarkable growth it posted up until December 2011. A financial reform program that began in 2003 had also helped create a well-capitalized and well-managed banking system. But for Egypt's economy to pick up, much will depend on how the political process evolves over the coming months.

Indonesia

Indonesia, the fourth-largest country in the world by population, not only is a G-20 economy, but it also boasts an already significant and

---

* http://www.africaneconomicoutlook.org/en/

growing middle class transitioning to democracy. The country has relatively low inflation and government debt, is rich in natural resources
including oil, gas, metals, and minerals. Recently, with the fall of its currency, the rupiah, exports received a major boost. The country is less reli-
ant on international trade, which enabled it to grow despite the global
financial crisis, as domestic demand constituted the bulk of output in
Indonesia, about 90 percent of real GDP.

The Indonesian economy has recorded strong growth over the past few
decades, notwithstanding the sharp economic contraction that occurred
during the 1997–1998 Asian financial crises, as depicted in Figure 5.6. In
recent years, the firm pace of economic expansion has been accompanied
by reduced output volatility and relatively stable inflation. Indonesia's
economic performance has been shaped by government policy, the country's endowment of natural resources and its young and growing labor
force. Alongside the industrialization of its economy, Indonesia's trade
openness has increased over the past half century.

This strong pace of growth has seen Indonesia become an increasingly important part of the global economy. It is now the fourth largest
economy in East Asia*—after China, Japan, and South Korea—and the

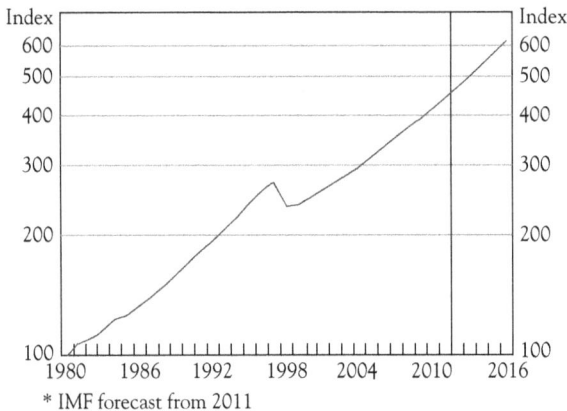

Figure 5.6 Indonesia real GDP from 1980 through 2016 (log scale)

Source: IMF

---

* Unless otherwise specified, East Asia refers to the economies of China, South
Korea, Taiwan, Hong Kong, Singapore, Indonesia, Thailand, Malaysia, and the
Philippines.

15th largest economy in the world on a PPP basis. Furthermore, its share of global output, currently just under 1½ per cent, is expected to continue to rise over the years ahead.

Nigeria

As the largest African nation by population, Nigeria is projected to have the highest GDP growth in the next few years and perhaps for the next several decades as depicted in Figure 5.7. In 2014, the National Bureau of Statistics (NBS) recalculated the value of GDP based on production patterns in 2010, increasing the number of industries it measures to 46 from 33 and giving greater weighting to sectors such as telecommunications and financial services. The revised figure surpassed South Africa's as the largest on the continent after the West African nation overhauled its gross domestic product data for the first time in two decades.

Oil and agriculture account for more than 50 percent of its GDP, while petroleum products account for 95 percent of exports, while the industrial and the service sectors are also on the rise. This economic growth potential invites a number of FDI initiatives, mostly from China, the United States, and India. The challenge, however, is with its legal framework and financial markets regulations, which leave much to be desired.

Nonetheless, while the revised figure makes Nigeria the 26th-biggest economy in the world, the country lags in income per capita, ranking 121 with $2,688 for each citizen.

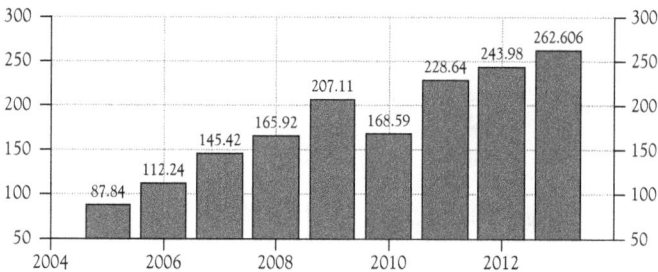

Figure 5.7 Nigeria's GDP growth

Source: TradingEconomics.com, World Bank

Pakistan

Pakistan is another frontier market, which we believe has a lot of potential for growth based on its rising population and middle class, rapid urbanization and industrialization, and ongoing, even though slowly, economic reforms. The country has important strategic endowments and development potential, as it is located at the crossroads of South Asia, Central Asia, China, and the Middle East and is thus at the fulcrum of a regional market with a vast population, large and diverse resources, and untapped potential for trade. The increasing proportion of Pakistan's working-age population provides the country with a potential demographic dividend but also with the critical challenge to provide adequate services and increase employment.

The country has experienced significant progress for several decades now, at an average rate of 4.9 percent GDP growth, as depicted in Figure 5.8. But, despite such positive economic indicators, Pakistan is still one of the poorest and least developed countries in Asia, with political instability, widespread corruption and lack of law enforcement hampering private investment and foreign aid.

Nonetheless, the country faces significant economic, governance and security challenges to achieve durable development outcomes. The persistence of conflict in the border areas and security challenges throughout the country is a reality that affects all aspects of life in Pakistan and impedes development. A range of governance and business environment indicators suggest that deep improvements in governance are needed to unleash Pakistan's growth potential.

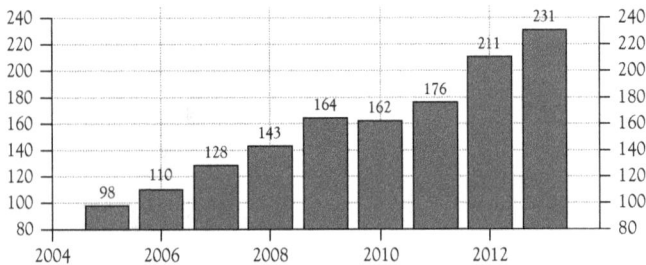

Figure 5.8 Pakistan GDP growth

Source: TradingEconomics.com, World Bank

Pakistan also faces significant economic challenges. The sharp rise in international oil and food prices, combined with recurring natural disasters like the 2010 and 2011 floods had a devastating impact on the economy. As Pakistan recovered from the 2008 global crisis, its GDP grew 3.8 percent in 2009–2010. The 2010 floods, with an estimated damage of over $10 billion, caused growth to slow down to 2.4 percent. In 2011–2012, however, the Pakistan economy grew by an estimated 3.7 percent, against the pre-flood targeted growth rate of 4.2 percent.

The Philippines

The Philippines has shown a strong economic progress in the past few years, as shown in Figure 5.9, posting the highest GDP growth rates in Asia for most of 2013. The country weathered the global economic crises very well owing to significant progress made in recent years on fiscal consolidation and financial sector reforms, which contributed to a marked turnaround in investor sentiment, fostering significant FDI inflows. The challenges, as a newly industrialized country, are that the Philippines are still an economy with a large agricultural sector, although services are beginning to dominate the economy.

Robust private consumption and investment drove economic growth in the Philippines higher in 2013. Strong growth is expected to continue in the forecast period, though moderating from last year. Rehabilitation and reconstruction in areas hit by natural disasters may have a significant impact on the economy in late 2014 or 2015. Inflation is forecasted

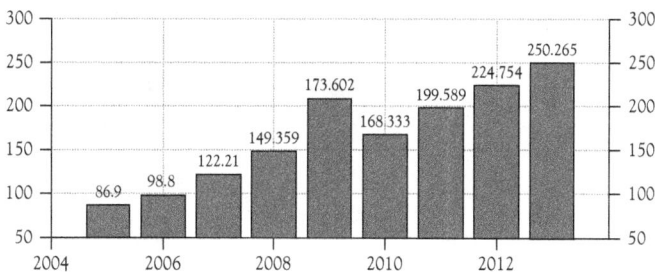

Figure 5.9 Philippines GDP growth

Source: TradingEconomics.com, World Bank

to pick up this year but remain within the central bank's target range. The challenge is to translate solid economic growth into poverty reduction by generating more and better jobs.

Turkey

Turkey's economy, as depicted in Figure 5.10, much like the Philippines, has been growing at a fast pace, and for much of the same reasons. Rapid industrialization coupled with steady economic reforms has made Turkey an attractive emerging market. In the summer of 2013, however, Turkish economy suffered with civil unrest and the United States taper talk. The country's political stability, unique geographical location on the border of Europe and Asia, market maturity and economic growth potential, positions Turkey's economy to remain prone for FDI inflows.

The ruling Development and Justice Party (AKP) secured a clear victory in the local elections on March 30, 2014, confirming the prime minister, Recep Tayyip Erdogan's dominance of the AKP and Turkish politics. Mr. Erdogan and his party are well placed ahead of the presidential and legislative elections due in August 2014 and June 2015, respectively. But deep social and political polarization risks exacerbate economic difficulties arising from shifting global financial flows and a weaker lira.

Economic growth lost momentum in the course of 2013, as capital market tensions pushed interest rates up. Credit and private demand decelerated. Export growth fell, notably due to rapidly declining gold sales. Political tensions have dented confidence, provoking capital

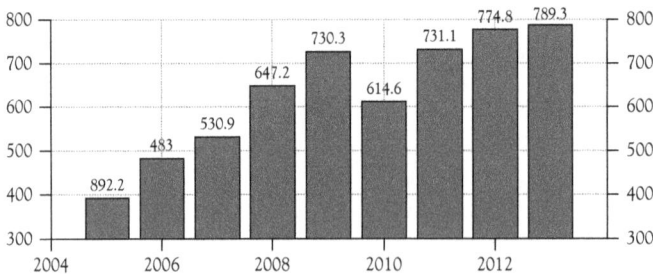

Figure 5.10 Turkey's GDP growth

Source: TradingEconomics.com, World Bank

outflows, and forcing the central bank to raise interest rates sharply in early 2014. Growth is projected to remain subdued through mid-2015, while the current account deficit will remain very high.

Vietnam

Vietnam, with agriculture still accounting for 20 percent of its GDP, has an industry and services sector that continues to grow. The major challenge with Vietnam is still its authoritarian regime, which causes its economy to be split between state planned and free market sections. In addition, its economy is still volatile, despite the much progress, due to relatively high inflation, lack of transparency into government policy, and the fact that the country virtually lacks large enterprises.

Vietnam is a development success story. Political and economic reforms launched in 1986 have transformed Vietnam from one of the poorest countries in the world, with per capita income below $100, to a lower middle-income country within a quarter of a century with per capita income of $1,130 by the end of 2010. The ratio of population in poverty has fallen from 58 percent in 1993 to 14.5 percent in 2008, and most indicators of welfare have improved. Vietnam already has attained five of its ten original Millennium Development Goal targets and is well on the way to attaining two more by 2015.

Vietnam has been applauded for the equity of its development, which has been better than most other countries in similar situations. The country has been growing at a sturdy pace, as depicted in Figure 5.11.

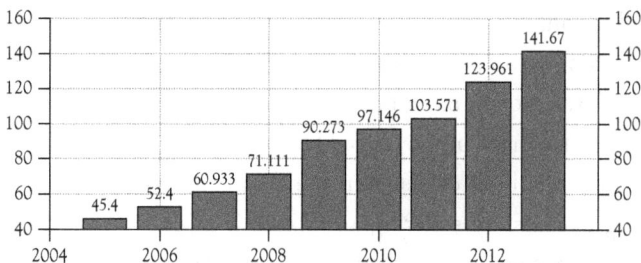

Figure 5.11 Vietnam's GDP growth

Source: TradingEconomics.com, World Bank

The country is playing a more visible role on the regional and global stage, having successfully chaired the 2009 Annual Meetings of the Boards of Governors of the World Bank Group and the IMF, and carried out the Chairmanship of the ASEAN in 2010.

Vietnam now has a love affair with the motorbike, which started 10 years ago with cheap imports from China. The cheapest ones cost as little as $300, but the more coveted Hondas and Suzuki's are about $1,000, and luxury models cost twice that amount. The government has wisely discouraged car sales by implementing a 250 percent tax, so the streets of Saigon are not nearly as hopelessly clogged as those of Dhaka or Mumbai.

Recommendations

Overall, we see significant opportunities in frontier markets, especially considering its solid capital base, young labor pool, and improving productivity, particularly in Africa, where we believe the sub-Saharan region eventually will overtake China and India. It is plausible to assume that Africa's economy will grow from $2 trillion to $29 trillion by 2050, greater than the current economic output of both the United States and the eurozone.

We must consider, however, the frontier market's deepening economic ties to China, which make it vulnerable to a slowing Chinese economy. Also, frontier markets are not without risks, as local politics are complex, and there are still several pockets of corruption and instability. Further, liquidity is scarce, transaction costs can be steep, and currency risk is real. As if that's not enough to worry about, there's also the risk of nationalization.

That said, we do not subscribe to the idea that emerging markets are in "crisis." The growth economic index for these countries has soared up 20.2 points, far ahead of the United States, Europe and Japan's 12 points. In our view, the hard evidence in the data contradicts the notion that emerging markets are suffering an economic crisis, especially considering that most emerging markets also have a fast-growing middle class of consumers. The so-called Fragile-Five (Brazil, India, Indonesia, South Africa, and Turkey) and other emerging economies that run chronic current-account deficits may be at risk, but due to a liquidity crunch. There are many other emerging markets performing very well economically, reflected in their stock markets, which continue to outperform the S&P 500 Index year-to-date.

As the emerging markets of today move on to become part of the advanced economies of the world, the stage is set to bring along a new set of emerging candidates from the frontier markets.

About the Authors

Marcus Goncalves, EdD, is an international management consultant with more than 25 years of experience in the U.S., Latin America, Europe, Middle East, and Asia. Mr. Goncalves is the former CTO of Virtual Access Networks, which under his leadership was awarded the *Best Enterprise Product* at Comdex Fall 2001, leading to the acquisition of the company by Symantec. He holds a master's degree in Computer Information Systems and a doctorate in Educational Leadership from Boston University. He has more than 45 books published in the U.S., many translated into Portuguese, German, Chinese, Korean, Japanese, and Spanish. He's often invited to speak on international business, global trade, international management and organizational development subjects worldwide. Marcus has been lecturing at Boston University and Brandeis University for the past 11 years. He has also been a visiting professor and graduate research adviser/examiner at Saint Joseph University, in Macao, China for the past three years. He is an Associate Professor of Management, and the International Business Program Chair at Nichols College, in Dudley, MA, USA. Dr. Goncalves can be contacted via e-mail at marcus.goncalves@nichols.edu or at marcusg@mgcgusa.com.

José Alves, PhD, is an Associate Professor of Management at the Faculty of Business, Government, and Social Work of the University of Saint Joseph, Macau. He holds a Ph.D. in Business Administration from the University of Massachusetts Amherst. He is currently based in Macau, China, but has lived in Europe and U.S. His major research interests include leadership and management in international contexts, namely in Asia and China. His research has been published in journals and conference proceedings, such as the Journal of Managerial Psychology, Human Resources Management Review, and International Journal of Leadership Studies. He has also presented at various conferences, including the Academy of Management, Iberoamerican Academy of Management, International Association for Chinese Management Research, and Academy of Human Resource Development. He is an entrepreneur and advisor to European companies intending to enter into Asia and China. Dr. Alves can be contacted via email at jose.alves@usj.edu.mo.

Advance Quotes for *Emerging and Frontier Markets*

The book written by Marcus Goncalves and Jose Alves is an excellent compilation of knowledge about the process of changing of the emerging and frontier markets. In a clear and structured way they show groups of countries (i.e. BRICS CIVETS, ASEAN, MENA also included frontier markets) and each country individually. I highly recommend this publication to any person who would like a better understanding of how those markets operating in the global trade and how they affect each other. In the perspective of their history, politics, cultural habits, economy challenges, threats, successes, but also problems, such as corruption. This book will give you a simple and practical answer supported by scientific facts. It's good to have a book like that in your own library because you never know where you will have a chance to do business in future.

— *Ewelina Kroll, Public Relations Manager at East Europe Consulting,*
Gdynia, Pomeranian District, Poland

Goncalves and Alves' work is a very interesting and promising book for the development themes of emerging markets. The style and quality of the material is worthy of respect, providing a clear analysis of the international markets and global development of various economic and commercial relations and trading routes.

— *Yurii Pozniak, International Management Consultant*
at Ukroboronservis, Kiev, Ukraine

Emerging and Frontier Markets: The New Frontline for Global Trade brings together a collection of insights and a new outlook of the dynamics happening between the emerging and the advanced markets. The book provides also an excellent, easy to read and straight-to-the point economic and political description of the MENA, BRICS, ASEAN, and CIVETS markets. A description that should interest every person willing to invest, work or just acquire a deep understanding of the emerging markets economic and political conditions.

—*Réda Massoudi, BU Director Management and Transformation*
Consulting, LMS Organization & Human Resources.
Casablanca, Morocco.

Notes

Chapter 1

1. O'Neill, Jim (2001). Building Better Global Economic BRICs.
2. Garcia-Herrero, Alicia (2012).
3. IMF (2013). World Economic Outlook, April 2013, http://www.imf.org/external/pubs/ft/weo/2013/01/weodata/index.aspx, last accessed on 04/12/2013.
4. Marquand, Robert (2011).
5. IMF (2013). Transitions and Tensions.
6. Hawksworth, John and Dan Chan (2013).
7. IMF, (2013). World Economic Outlook, April 2013, http://www.imf.org/external/pubs/ft/weo/2013/01/weodata/index.aspx, (last accessed on 04/12/2013).
8. Schwab, Klaus (2013).
9. https://www.cia.gov/library/publications/the-world-factbook/geos/rs.html.
10. World Bank (2012). World Development Indicators Database.
11. Schwab, Klaus (2013).
12. Nilekani, Nandan (2008).
13. Mookerji, Nivedita (2013).
14. Schwab, Klaus (2013).
15. Amin, M. (2009).
16. Schwab, Klaus (2013).
17. Rai, V. and W. Simon (2008), pg. xi.
18. Blanke, Jennifer (2013).
19. Rai, V. and W. Simon (2008), pg. 245.
20. O'Neill, Jim. (2005). How solid are the BRICS.
21. https://www.cia.gov/library/publications/the-world-factbook/geos/ch.html.
22. Schwab, Klaus (2013).
23. https://www.cia.gov/library/publications/the-world-factbook/geos/rs.html.
24. Schwab, Klaus (2013).
25. Evans-Pritchard, Ambrose (2013).
26. Cartas, Jose (2010).
27. Business Standard of India Staff Writers (2011).
28. Clinton, Hillary (2011).
29. Zoffer, Joshua (2012).

30. The RT Staff Writers (2013).
31. Kelly, L. and P. Simao (2014).
32. International News of Pakistan Staff Writers, (2012).

Chapter 2

1. Stern, Melanie (2012).
2. Hutchinson, Martin (2010).
3. Embassy of Colombia in Washington D.C. (2013).
4. Central Intelligence Agency (2013). The World Factbook.
5. Grewal, Kevin (2010).
6. The World Bank Staff Writers (2013). "Doing Business: Ease of Doing Business in Colombia."
7. Markey, Patrick (2010).
8. The Economists Staff Writers. (2012). Gushers and guns.
9. Colombo, Jesse (2013).
10. American Chamber of Commerce, International Affairs, (2013).
11. Hayton, Bill (2006).
12. Khaithu (2012).
13. The World Bank Staff Writers (2013). "An Update on Vietnam's Recent Economic Development July 2013: Key Findings."
14. The Economist's Writers (2013). "It's the politics, stupid."
15. Ghanem, Hafez and Salman Shaikh (2013).
16. Werr, Patrick (2013).
17. Geromel, Ricardo (2013).
18. The World Bank (2012). "World Development Indicators Database."
19. OECD (2013). "Economic Outlook: Analysis and Forecast."
20. IMF (2013). "Transitions and Tensions."
21. IMF (2013) Survey. "Economic Health Check."
22. OECD (2013). "Economic Surveys and Country Surveillance."
23. The Fox News Staff Writers (2013).
24. Blanke, Jennifer (2013).
25. Kowalczyk-Hoyer, Barbara and Susan Côté-Freeman (2013).
26. http://www.pwc.com/us/en/view/issue-15/succeed-emerging-markets.jhtml.

Chapter 3

1. Qiang, Hou (2013).
2. Shahminan, Fitri (2013).
3. The Oxford Business Group's Staff Writers (2013).

4. Chheang, Vannarith (2008).
5. Wallace, Julia (2013).
6. Heng, Dyna (2011).
7. Gronholt-Pedersen, Jacob (2012).
8. Ministry of Economy and Finance of Cambodia (2013) Council for the development of Cambodia (CDC), Economic Trends, http://www.cambodiainvestment.gov.kh/investment-enviroment/economic-trend.html, (last accessed on 11/04/2013).
9. Weggel, Oskar (2006).
10. Jeong Chun Hai @Ibrahim, and Nor Fadzlina Nawi. (2007).

Chapter 4

1. World Bank (2008).
2. Roudi, Farzaneh (2001).
3. Cammett, M. (2013).
4. IMF Staff Writers (2013). "Economic Growth Moderates Across Middle East."
5. "Two, Three, Many Middle Easts: A Region's Economic Prospects," April 29, 2013, http://www.milkeninstitute.org/events/gcprogram.taf?function=detail&eventid=gc13&EvID=3959, (last accessed on 12/20/2013).
6. World Bank Staff Writers (2013). "Tourism in the Arab World can mean more than Sun, Sand and Beaches."
7. O'Sullivan, A., M.E. Rey, and M.J. Galvez (2011).
8. O'Sullivan, A., M.E. Rey, and M.J. Galvez (2011).
9. Ahmed, Masood (2010).
10. O'Sullivan, A., M.E. Rey, and M.J. Galvez (2011).
11. Pigato, M. (2009).
12. Ernst & Young, and Oxford Economics (2011).
13. Montibeler, E.E. and Gallego, E.S. (2012).
14. Sallum, M.N. (2013).
15. Senkovich, V. (2013).
16. Al Masah Capital Management Limited (2010).
17. Bishku, Michael B. (2010). Fall 2010, Vol. XVII, No. 3.
18. Lewis, P., Sen, A., and Tabary, Z. (2011).
19. Africa Staff Writers (2013). http://allafrica.com/stories/201311220292.html, (last accessed on 01/03/2013).
20. Cashin, P., Mohaddes, M.K., and Raissi, M.M. (2012).
21. Al Masah Capital Management Limited (2010).
22. Deen, E.S. (2013).
23. Daniele, V. and Marani, U. (2006).

24. Cammett, M. (2013).
25. Bhattacharya, R. and Wolde, H. (2010a).
26. Bhattacharya, R. and Wolde, H. (2010b).
27. O'Sullivan, A., Rey, M.E., and Galvez, M.J. (2011).
28. Lobe, Jim (2013).
29. Condon, Stephanie (2013).

References

Abulof, Uriel. 2011. "What Is the Arab Third Estate?" *Huffington Post*, http://www.huffingtonpost.com/uriel-abulof/what-is-the-arab-third-es_b_832628.html, (last accessed on 11/12/2013).

Afrol News of Morocco Staff Writers. 2011. "Morocco King on holiday as people consider revolt," *Afrol News*, http://www.afrol.com/articles/37175, (last accessed on 11/01/2013).

Afrol News Staff Writers. 2011. "New clashes in occupied Western Sahara," *Afrol News*, http://www.afrol.com/articles/37450, (last accessed on 10/25/2013).

Ahmed, Masood. 2010. "Trade Competitiveness and Growth MENA," *World Economic Forum's Arab World Competitiveness Review*, http://www.imf.org/external/np/vc/2010/103010.htm, (last accessed on 01/03/2014).

Akhtar, S.I., M.J. Bolle, and R.M. Nelson. 2013. "U.S. Trade and Investment in the Middle East and North Africa: Overview and Issues for Congress," *Congress Research Service*, http://fpc.state.gov/documents/organization/206138.pdf, (last accessed on 02/12/2014).

Al Jazeera Staff Writers. 2011. "Tunisia's Ben Ali flees amid unrest," *Al Jazeera*, http://www.aljazeera.com/news/africa/2011/01/20111153616298850.html, (last accessed on 11/15/2013).

Al Jazeera Staff Writers. 2011. "Sudan police clash with protesters," *Al Jazeera*, http://www.aljazeera.com/news/africa/2011/01/2011130131451294670.html, (last accessed on 09/12/2013).

Al Masah Capital Management Limited. 2010. "China and India's Growing Influence in the MENA Region: Their Legacy and Future Footprint." http://s3.amazonaws.com/zanran_storage/ae.zawya.com/ContentPages/142996358.pdf, (last accessed on 01/03/2014).

Al-Ansary, Khalid. 2011. "Iraq's Sadr followers march against Bahrain crackdown," *Reuters*, http://www.reuters.com/article/2011/03/16/us-bahrain-iraq-idUSTRE72F4U220110316, (last accessed on 11/12/2013).

Aljazeera Staff Writers. 2011. "Thousands protest in Jordan," *Al Jazeera*, http://www.aljazeera.com/news/middleeast/2011/01/2011128125157509196.html, (last accessed on 10/25/2013).

allAfrica Staff Writers. 2013. *South Africa: SA to Enhance Trade, Investment Relations in Middle East, 11/21/2013*, http://allafrica.com/stories/201311220292.html, (last accessed on 01/03/2013).

Alternative Economic System. Al Jazeera Center for Studies. Retrieved from http://studies.aljazeera.net/en/reports/2013/06/20136474134190632.htm, (last accessed on 12/19/2013).

Amadeo, K. 2013. "What Is a Currency War?" http://useconomy.about.com/od/tradepolicy/g/Currency-Wars.htm, (last accessed on 02/12/2014).

Amartya Sen. 1999. *Development as Freedom*, Oxford, United Kingdom: Oxford University Press, 1999.

Ambrose, S. and D. Brinkley. 2011. *Rise to Globalism*, Penguin Group: New York City, NY.

American Chamber of Commerce, International Affairs. 2013. "ASEAN Business Outlook Survey," *Singapore Business Federation*, http://www.amcham.org.sg/wp-content/uploads/2013/08/2014ABOS.pdf, (last accessed on 10/24/2013).

Amin, M. 2009. "Labor Regulation and Employment in India's Retail Stores," *Journal of Comparative Economics* 37 (1): 47–61.

Arabia Monitor. 2012. "Shifting Sands, Shifting Trade: Building a New Silk Route," *Middle East and North Africa Outlook Q4 2012*. www.arabiamonitor.com, (last accessed on 12/19/2013).

Arkalgud, A.P. 2011. "Filling "institutional voids" in emerging markets," *Forbes*. http://www.forbes.com/sites/infosys/2011/09/20/filling-institutional-voids-in-emerging-markets/

Asian Development Bank. 2013. "Asian Development Outlook 2013 Update," *ADB*. Manila, http://www.adb.org/countries/pakistan/economy, (last accessed on 12/20/2013).

Associate Press Staff Writers. 2011. "Algeria protest draws thousands," *CBC News World/Associate Press*. http://www.cbc.ca/news/world/algeria-protest-draws-thousands-1.1065078, (last accessed on 11/02/2013).

Axworthy, T. 2010. *Who Gets to Rule the World?* Canada: Macleans. 1 July 2010.

Bain & Company's Staff Analysts. 2012. "A world awash in money," *Bain & Company*. http://www.bain.com/publications/articles/a-world-awash-in-money.aspx, (last accessed on 12/07/2013).

Bakri, N. and D. Goodman. 2011. "Thousands in Yemen Protest against the Government," *The New York Times*. http://www.nytimes.com/2011/01/28/world/middleeast/28yemen.html?_r=0, (last accessed on 11/11/2013).

Barrera, C. and T. Dobbyn. 2012. "U.S. says BizJet settles foreign bribery charges," *Reuters*. http://www.reuters.com/article/2012/03/14/us-mexico-lufthansa-idUSBRE82D1H220120314, (last accessed on 10/28/2013).

Barstow, David. 2012. "Vast Mexican Bribery Case Hushed Up by Wal-Mart After High-Level Struggle," *The New York Times*. http://www.nytimes.com/2012/04/22/business/at-wal-mart-in-mexico-a-bribe-inquiry-silenced.html?_r=0, (last accessed on 05/13/2012).

BBC News Middle East Staff Writers. 2011. "Man Dies After Setting Himself on Fire in Saudi Arabia," *BBC News*. http://www.bbc.co.uk/news/world-middle-east-12260465, (last accessed on 11/04/2013).

BBC News Staff Writers. 2011. "News Corp shares hit two-year low on hacking arrest," *BBC World News*, http://www.bbc.co.uk/news/business-14181119, (last accessed on 02/04/2012).

Bhattacharya, R. and H. Wolde. 2010a. "Constraints on Growth in the MENA Region," *IMF Working Papers*, 1–21.

Bhattacharya, R. and H. Wolde. 2010b. "Constraints on Trade in the MENA Region," *IMF Working Papers*, 1–18.

Bishku, Michael B. 2010. "South Africa and the Middle East," *Journal Essay Middle East Policy Council*. Fall 2010, Vol. XVII, No. 3.

Blanchart, Olivier. 2013. "Advanced Economies Strengthening, Emerging Market Economies Weakening," *IMF Direct*. http://blog-imfdirect.imf.org/2013/10/08/advanced-economies-strengthening-emerging-market-economies-weakening/, (last accessed on 10/15/2013).

Blanke, Jennifer. 2013. "The Global Competitiveness Report 2013–2014," *World Economic Forum*. http://www.weforum.org/issues/global-competitiveness, (last accessed on 11/24/2013).

Bonham, C., B. Gangnes, and A.V. Assche. 2004. "Fragmentation and East Asia's Information Technology Trade," *Department of Economics at the University of Hawaii at Manoa, and University of California at Davis*. Working Paper No. 04.09. http://www.economics.hawaii.edu/research/workingpapers/WP_04–9.pdf, (last accessed on 12/01/2013).

Boone, Elisabeth. 2007. "Political Risk in Emerging Markets," *The Rough Notes Company, Inc.* http://www.roughnotes.com/rnmagazine/2007/october07/10p060.htm, (last accessed on 11/11/2013).

Brahmbhatt, M., O. Canuto, and S. Ghosh. 2010. "Currency Wars Yesterday and Today." *Economic Premise*, 43.

Bremmer, Ian. 2009. *State Capitalism and the Crisis*. Eurasia Group.

Bremmer, Ian. 2013. *Every Nation for Itself: Winners and Losers in a G-Zero World*. Portfolio/Penguin: New York City, NY.

Bukharin, N. 1972. *Imperialism and World Economy*. London: Merlin.

Business Standard of India Staff Writers. 2011. "BRICS is passé, time now for 3G: Citi," *Business Standard*. New Delhi, India. http://www.business-standard.com/india/news/brics-is-passe-time-now-for-percent5C3gpercent5C-citi/126725/on, (last accessed on 11/01/2013).

Caballero, Ricardo. 2009. "Sudden Financial Arrest." *10th Jacques Polak Annual Research Conference*. http://www.imf.org/external/np/res/seminars/2009/arc/pdf/caballero.pdf, (last accessed on 11/30/2013).

Cammett, M. 2013. "Development and Underdevelopment in the Middle East and North Africa." In *Handbook of the Politics of Development*, eds. Carol Lancaster and Nicolas van de Walle. New York, NY: Oxford University Press, 2013 (Forthcoming). Available at SSRN: http://ssrn.com/abstract=2349387, (last accessed on 12/20/2013).

Canuto, O. 2010. "Toward a Switchover of Locomotives in the Global Economy." *Economic Premise*, 33.

Canuto, O. and M. Giugale (Eds). 2010. *The Day After Tomorrow—A Handbook on the Future of Economic Policy in the Developing World*. Washington, DC: World Bank.

Cartas, Jose. 2010. "Dollarization Declines in Latin America," *Finance and Development* 47, no. 1. http://www.imf.org/external/pubs/ft/fandd/2010/03/pdf/spot.pdf, (last accessed on 11/05/2013).

Carton, Bruce. 2011. "Company Allegedly Bumped Out of Contract by Rival's Corruption Recovers $45 Million in Civil Settlement," *Compliance Week*, Oct. 5, 2011. http://www.complianceweek.com/company-allegedly-bumped-out-of-contract-by-rivalscorruption-recovers-45-million-in-civil-settlement/article/213666/, (last accessed on 12/10/2013).

Cashin, P., M.K. Mohaddes, and M.M. Raissi. 2012. "The Global Impact of the Systemic Economies and MENA," *Business Cycles* (Working Paper No. 12–255). International Monetary Fund.

Cavusgil, S. Tamer, Tunga Kiyak, and Sengun Yeniyurt. 2004. "Complementary Approaches to Preliminary Foreign Market Opportunity Assessment: Country Clustering and Country Ranking," *Industrial Marketing Management*, 33, no. 7, pp. 607–617.

Cavusgil, S. Tamer. 1997. "Measuring The Potential of Emerging Markets: An Indexing Approach," *Business Horizons* 40, no. 1, pp. 87–91.

Central Intelligence Agency. 2013. "The World Factbook," https://www.cia.gov/library/publications/the-world-factbook/, (last accessed on 09/23/13).

Cheema, Faisal. 2004. "Macroeconomic Stability of Pakistan: The Role of the IMF and World Bank (1997–2003)," *Programme in Arms Control, Disarmament, and International Security (ACDIS)*. University of Illinois at Urbana-Champaign. http://acdis.illinois.edu/assets/docs/250/MacroeconomicStabilityofPakistanTheRoleoftheIMFandWorldBank19972003.pdf, (last accessed on 12/14/2013).

Cheewatrakoolpong, K., C. Sabhasri, and N. Bunditwattanawong. 2013. "Impact of the ASEAN Economic Community on ASEAN Production Networks," *IDBI*, No. 409. http://www.adbi.org/files/2013.02.21.wp409.impact.asean.production.networks.pdf, (last accessed on 03/12/2013).

Chheang, Vannarith. 2008. "The Political Economy of Tourism in Cambodia," *Asia Pacific Journal of Tourism Research* 13 (3): 281–297. Retrieved 9 February 2013.

China The People's Daily. 2011. "Asia to play bigger role on world stage, G-20: ADB report." *The People's Daily*. April 26, 2011. http://english.people.com.cn/90001/90778/98506/7361425.html, (last accessed on 10/01/2013).

Clinton, Hillary. 2011. "America's Pacific Century," *Foreign Policy*. http://www.foreignpolicy.com/articles/2011/10/11/americas_pacific_century, (last accessed on 11/12/2012).

CNN. 2009. "Officials: G-20 to supplant G-8 as international economic council." *CNN*, http://edition.cnn.com/2009/US/09/24/us.g.twenty.summit/, (last accessed on 10/03/2013).

Colombo, Jesse. 2013. "Why The Worst Is Yet To Come For Indonesia's Epic Bubble Economy," *Forbes.* http://www.forbes.com/sites/jessecolombo/2013/10/03/why-the-worst-is-yet-to-come-for-indonesias-epic-bubble-economy/2/, (last accessed on 10/05/2013).

Condon, Stephanie. 2013. "Obama appeals to senators to hold off on more Iran sanctions," *CBSNews.* http://www.cbsnews.com/news/obama-appeals-to-senators-to-hold-off-on-more-iran-sanctions/, (last accessed on 12/19/2013).

Corrigan, Terence. 2007. "Mauritania: Country Made Slavery Illegal Last Month," *The East African Standard.* http://www.saiia.org.za/opinion-analysis/mauritania-made-slavery-illegal-last-month, (last accessed on 11/10/2013).

Crawford, David, and Dionne Searcey. 2010. "U.S. Joins H-P Bribery Investigation." *The Wall Street Journal.* http://online.wsj.com/news/articles/SB10001424052702304628704575186151115576646, (last accessed on 12/28/2012).

Daniele, V. and U. Marani. 2006. "Do institutions matter for FDI? A comparative analysis for the MENA countries." *University Library*, Munich, Germany.

Das, Satyajit. 2013. "The new economic nationalism," *ABC Australia.* http://www.abc.net.au/news/2013–09-30/das-the-new-economic-nationalism/4988690, (last accessed on 12/12/2013).

Deen, Ebrahim Shabbir. 2013. "BRICS & Egypt: An Opportunity to Begin Creating an Alternative Economic System." *Al Jazeera Center for Studies.* http://studies.aljazeera.net/en/reports/2013/06/20136474134190632.htm, (last accessed on 12/19/2013).

Department of Justice. 2010. "Innospec Inc. Pleads Guilty to FCPA Charges and Defrauding United Nations; Admits to Violating the U.S. Embargo Against Cuba." http://www.justice.gov/opa/pr/2010/March/10-crm-278.html, (last accessed on 12/10/2013).

Department of Justice. 2011. "Innospec Inc. Pleads Guilty to FCPA Charges and Defrauding United Nations; Admits to Violating the U.S. Embargo Against Cuba." Second Amended Complaint 1, Newmarket Corp. v. Innospec Inc., No. 3:10-cv-00503 (E.D.Va. Jan. 27, 2011) (ECF No. 41).

Dilip S. Mutum, Sanjit Kumar Roy, and Eva Kipnis (eds). 2014. *Marketing Cases from Emerging Markets.* New York, NY: Springer.

Donnison, Jon. 2011. "Palestinians emboldened by Arab Spring," *Ramallah: BBC News.* http://www.bbc.co.uk/news/world-middle-east-13417788, (last accessed on 11/16/2013).

Dooley, Emily C. 2010. "Richmond firm claims in suit that competitor paid kickbacks to Iraqis," *Richmond Times-Dispatch.* B-03.

Dresen, F.J. 2011. "BRICS: Shaping the New Global Architecture," *Woodrow Wilson International Center for Scholars.* http://www.wilsoncenter.org/publication/

brics-shaping-the-new-global-architecture, (last accessed on 4/5/2012).

Durand, M., C. Madaschi, and F. Terribile. 1998. "Trends in OECD countries' international competitiveness: the influence of emerging market economies," *OECD Economics Department Working Paper, No. 195.*

Economists Staff Writers. 2013. "The gated globe," *The Economist.* http://www.economist.com/news/special-report/21587384-forward-march-globalisation-has-paused-financial-crisis-giving-way, (last accessed on 11/12/2013).

Economists Staff Writers. 2010. "BRICS and BICIS." *The Economist.* http://www.economist.com/blogs/theworldin2010/2009/11/acronyms_4, (last accessed on 11/9/2012).

Economists Staff Writers. 2012. "And the winner is…." *The Economist.* http://www.economist.com/node/21542926, (last accessed on 12/13/2013).

Economists Staff Writers. 2012. "Gushers and guns," *The Economist.* http://www.economist.com/node/21550304, (last accessed on 12/11/2013).

Economists Staff Writers. 2012. "Pros and cons: mixed bags," *The Economist.* http://www.economist.com/node/21542929, (last accessed on 12/13/2013).

Economists Staff Writers. 2012. "The rise of state capitalism," *The Economist.* http://www.economist.com/node/21543160, (last accessed on 12/13/2013).

Economists Staff Writers. 2013. "It's the politics, stupid," *The Economist.* http://www.economist.com/news/leaders/21574495-economy-faces-collapse-broader-based-government-needed-take-tough-decisions-its, (last accessed on 11/12/2013).

Economists Staff Writers. 2013. "Taking Europe's pulse," *The Economist.* http://www.economist.com/blogs/graphicdetail/2013/11/european-economy-guide, (last accessed on 12/13/2013).

Economists Staff Writers. 2013. "The perils of falling inflation," *The Economist.* http://www.economist.com/news/leaders/21589424-both-america-and-europe-central-bankers-should-be-pushing-prices-upwards-perils-falling, (last accessed on 11/12/2013).

Economists Staff Writers. 2013. "When giants slow down," *The Economist.* http://www.economist.com/news/briefing/21582257-most-dramatic-and-disruptive-period-emerging-market-growth-world-has-ever-seen, (last accessed on 12/13/2013).

Embassy of Colombia in Washington D.C. 2013. *About Colombia.* http://www.colombiaemb.org/overview, (last accessed on 10/30/2013).

Ernst & Young, and Oxford Economics. 2011. *Trading Places: The Emergence of New Patterns of International Trade. Growing Beyond Series.* Ernst Young & Oxford Economics.

Evans-Pritchard, Ambrose. 2013. "IMF sours on BRICs and doubts eurozone recovery claims," *The Telegraph.* http://www.telegraph.co.uk/finance/

financialcrisis/10365206/IMF-sours-on-BRICs-and-doubts-eurozone-recovery-claims.html, (last accessed on 11/08/2013).

Faulconbridge, G. 2008. "BRICs helped by Western finance crisis: Goldman," *Reuters.* http://www.reuters.com/article/2008/06/08/us-russia-forum-bric-idUSL 071126420080608, (last accessed on 07/12/2012).

Forbes. 2000. "Global 2000." http://www.forbes.com/lists/2007/18/biz_07forbes 2000_The-Global-2000_Rank.html.

Forbes. 2007. "Forbes' billionaire's." http://www.forbes.com/lists/2007/10/07 billionaires_The-Worlds-Billionaires_Rank.html.

Foroohar, R. 2009. "BRICs Overtake G7 By 2027," *Newsweek.* http://www. newsweek.com/brics-overtake-g7–2027-76001, (last accessed on 04/12/2009).

Fox News Staff Writers. 2013. "IMF issues warning on South African economy," *Fox News.* http://www.foxnews.com/world/2013/10/01/imf-issues-warning-on-south-african-economy/, (last accessed on 10/24/2013).

Freeland, Chrystia. 2012. *Plutocrats: The Rise of the New Global Super-Rich and the Fall of Everyone Else.* New York City, NY: Penguin Press.

Freeman, R. 2006. "The Great Doubling: The Challenge of the New Global Labor Market," *European Central Bank.* http://eml.berkeley.edu/~webfac/ eichengreen/e183_sp07/great_doub.pdf, (last accessed on 11/02/2013).

Garcia-Herrero, Alicia. 2012. "BBVA EAGLES Emerging and Growth-Leading Economies," *BBVA Research.* http://www.bbvaresearch.com/KETD/fbin/mult/ 120215_BBVAEAGLES_Annual_Report_tcm348–288784.pdf?ts=164 2012, (last accessed on 11/01/2013).

Garcia-Palafox, Galia. 2012. "Walmart Bribery Allegations: Watchdog Group Says Mexican Government Should Investigate Claims of Vast Bribery Campaign," *Huffington Post.* http://www.huffingtonpost.com/2012/04/22/ walmart-bribery-allegations-watchdog-urges-probe_n_1444488.html, (last accessed on 04/23/2012).

Geromel, Ricardo. 2013. "Forbes Top 10 Billionaire Cities - Moscow Beats New York Again," *Forbes.* http://www.forbes.com/sites/ricardogeromel/2013/03/14/ forbes-top-10-billionaire-cities-moscow-beats-new-york-again/, (last accessed on 10/30/2013).

Ghanem, Hafez and Salman Shaikh. 2013. "On the Brink: Preventing Economic Collapse and Promoting Inclusive Growth in Egypt and Tunisia," *Brookings.* http://www.brookings.edu/research/papers/2013/11/economic-recovery-tunisia-egypt-shaikh-ghanem, (last accessed on 12/12/2013).

Ghosh A.R., M. Chamon, C. Crowe, J.I. Kim, and J.D. Ostry. 2009. "Coping with the Crisis: Policy Options for Emerging Market Countries," *International Monetary Fund.* http://www.imf.org/external/pubs/ft/spn/2009/spn0908.pdf, (last accessed on 12/12/2013).

GlobalEdge. 2013. "Market potential index (MPI) for emerging markets—2013," *Michigan State University*, International Business Center. Retrieved from http://globaledge.msu.edu/mpi/2013

Golf, E., R. Boccia, and J. Fleming. 2012. "Federal Spending per Household Is Skyrocketing, Federal Budget in Pictures," *The Heritage Foundation*. http://www.heritage.org/federalbudget/federal-spending-per-household, (last accessed on 01/23/2013).

Golf, E., R. Boccia, and J. Fleming. 2013. "2013 Index of Economic Freedom," *The Heritage Foundation*. http://www.heritage.org/index/ranking, (last accessed on 01/23/2013).

Graph from Milken Institute. 2013. *Two, Three, Many Middle Easts: A Region's Economic Prospects*. http://www.milkeninstitute.org/events/gcprogram.taf?function=detail&eventid=gc13&EvID=3959, (last accessed on 12/20/2013).

Grewal, Kevin. 2010. "CIVETS: The next gateway to growth," *Daily Markets*. http://www.dailymarkets.com/stock/2010/08/24/civets-the-next-gateway-to-growth/, (last accessed on 02/13/2011).

Gronholt-Pedersen, Jacob. 2012. "Cambodia aims for offshore production next year." *The Wall Street Journal*. http://online.wsj.com/news/articles/SB10000872396390443507204578020023711640726, (last accessed on 02/11/2013).

Guerrera, Francesco. 2013. "Currency war has started." *The Wall Street Journal*. http://online.wsj.com/news/articles/SB10001424127887324761004578283684195892250, (last accessed on 12/13/2013).

Halpin, Tony. 2009. "Brazil, Russia, India and China form bloc to challenge U.S. dominance," *The Times*. http://www.timesonline.co.uk/tol/news/world/us_and_americas/article6514737.ece, (last accessed on 23/03/2011).

Hamburger, T., B. Dennis, and J.L. Yang. 2012. "Wal-Mart took part in lobbying campaign to amend anti-bribery law," *The Washington Post*. http://www.washingtonpost.com/business/economy/wal-mart-took-part-in-lobbying-campaign-to-amend-anti-bribery-law/2012/04/24/gIQAyZcdfT_story_1.html, (last accessed on 11/19/2012).

Haub, Carl. 2012. "The BRIC Countries," *Population Reference Bureau*. http://www.prb.org/Publications/Articles/2012/brazil-russia-india-china.aspx, (last accessed on 12/05/2012).

Hauser, Christine. 2013. "Iraq: Maliki demands that protesters stand down," *The New York Times*. http://www.nytimes.com/2013/01/03/world/middleeast/iraq-maliki-demands-that-protesters-stand-down.html?_r=1&, (last accessed on 02/16/2013).

Hawksworth, J. 2011. "The world in 2005: How big will the major emerging market economies get and how can the OECD compete," *Price Waterhouse Coopers*. http://www.pwc.com/en_GX/gx/psrc/pdf/world_in_2050_carbon_emissions_psrc.pdf, (last accessed on 01/02/2011).

Hawksworth, John and Dan Chan. 2013. "World in 2050: The BRICS and Beyond: Prospects, Challenges, and Opportunities," *PWC Economics*. http://www.pwc.com/en_GX/gx/world-2050/assets/pwc-world-in-2050-report-january-2013.pdf, (last accessed on 03/12/2013).

Hayton, Bill. 2006. "Vietnam: ¿comunista o consumista?," *BBC Mundo*, Hanoi. http://news.bbc.co.uk/hi/spanish/business/newsid_5308000/5308298.stm, (last accessed on 07/22/2012).

Heng, Dyna. 2011. "Managing Cambodia's economic fragility," *CamproPost*. http://campropost.org/2011/07/15/managing-cambodia-s-economic-fragility.html, (last accessed on 10/10/2013).

Hood, Michael. 2013. "The Stubborn Inflation in Emerging Markets," *Institutional Investors*. http://www.institutionalinvestor.com/gmtl/3279243/The-Stubborn-Inflation-in-Emerging-Markets.html, (last accessed on 11/15/2013).

Hoti, Ikram. 2004. "Pakistan ends ties with IMF tomorrow," *PakistaniDefence.com*. http://forum.pakistanidefence.com/index.php?showtopic=36120, (last accessed on 10/12/2013).

HSBC Bank. 2013. "India Trade Forecast Report–HSBC Global Connections," *HSBC Global Connections Report*. India. https://globalconnections.hsbc.com/global/en/tools-data/trade-forecasts/in, (last accessed on 12/19/2013).

Human Rights Watch Staff Writers. 2012. "Iran: Arrest Sweeps Target Arab Minority," *Human Rights Watch*. http://www.refworld.org/docid/4f34de412.html, (last accessed on 11/03/2013).

Hutchinson, Martin. 2010. "The CIVETS: Windfall Wealth From the NewBRIC Economies," *European Business Review*. http://www.europeanbusinessreview.eu/page.asp?pid=829, (last accessed on 11/02/2013).

IMF Report. 2006. "Globalization and inflation," *World Economic Outlook*. Washington D.C. http://www.imf.org/external/pubs/ft/weo/2006/01/pdf/weo0406.pdf, (last accessed on 11/08/2013).

IMF Report. 2010. Global Financial Stability Report. April.

IMF Staff Writers. 2013. "Economic Growth Moderates Across Middle East," *IMF Survey Magazine*. http://www.imf.org/external/pubs/ft/survey/so/2013/car052113a.htm, (last accessed on 01/03/2014).

IMF Report. 2013. "South Africa Searches for Faster Growth, More Jobs," *IMF Survey Magazine*. http://www.imf.org/external/pubs/ft/survey/so/2013/car080713a.htm, (last accessed on 11/05/2013).

IMF Report. 2013. "Transitions and tensions," *World Economic Outlook*. http://www.imf.org/external/pubs/ft/weo/2013/02/, (last accessed on 11/02/2013).

IMF Report. 2013. *World Economic Outlook*. http://www.imf.org/external/pubs/ft/weo/2013/01/weodata/index.aspx, (last accessed on 04/12/2013).

IMF Reports. 2013. "Middle East and North Africa: Defining the Road Ahead, Regional Economic Outlook Update," *Middle East and Central Asia*

Department. http://www.imf.org/external/pubs/ft/reo/2013/mcd/eng/pdf/mcdreo0513.pdf, (last accessed on 11/02/2013).

IMF. 2013. Survey, Economic Health Check, South Africa Searches for Faster Growth, More Jobs, 10/01/2013. http://www.imf.org/external/pubs/ft/survey/so/2013/car080713a.htm, (last accessed on 11/05/2013).

International News of Pakistan Staff Writers. 2012. "Asia Nations to Double Currency Swap Deal," *Pakistan.* http://www.thenews.com.pk/Todays-News-3–98519-Briefs, (last accessed on 11/05/2013).

Jahan, S. 2012. "Inflation Targeting: Holding the Line," *IMF.* Washington DC.

Jeong Chun Hai @Ibrahim, and Nor Fadzlina Nawi. 2007. *Principles of Public Administration: An Introduction.* Kuala Lumpur: Karisma Publications.

Johnson, A.G. 2000. *The Blackwell Dictionary of Sociology.* Oxford: Blackwell Publishing.

Kelly, L. and P. Simao. 2014. "BRICS aim to finish development bank preparations by July summit," *Reuters.* http://in.reuters.com/article/2014/04/10/g20-economy-brics-idINDEEA390GA20140410, (last accessed on 06/11/2014).

Khaithu. 2012. "Traditional Market in Vietnam: A Social and Economic Angle," 10/15/2012. http://khaithu.wordpress.com/2012/10/15/traditional-market-in-vn-a-social-and-economic-angle/, (last accessed on 11/01/2013).

Khanna, T. and K.G. Palepu. 2010. *Winning in Emerging Markets: A Roadmap for Strategy and Execution.* Boston, MA: Harvard Business School Publishing.

Koelbl, Susanne. 2011. "It Will Not Stop: Syrian Uprising Continues Despite Crackdown," *Der Spiegel.* http://www.spiegel.de/international/world/it-will-not-stop-syrian-uprising-continues-despite-crackdown-a-753517.html, (last accessed on 11/10/2013).

Kose, M.A., P. Loungani, and M.E. Terrones. 2012. "Tracking the Global Recovery," *IMF Finance and Development Magazine.* Vol. 49, no. 2.

Kowalczyk-Hoyer, Barbara and Susan Côté-Freeman. 2013. "Transparency in corporate reporting: Assessing emerging market multinationals," *Transparency International.* http://transparency.org/whatwedo/pub/transparency_in_corporate_reporting_assessing_emerging_market_multinational, (last accessed on 11/02/2013).

Lewis, P., A. Sen, and Z. Tabary. 2011. "New routes to the Middle East: Perspectives on inward investment and trade," *Economist Intelligence Unit.* https://www.business.hsbc.co.uk/1/PA_esf-ca-app-content/content/pdfs/en/new_routes_to_middle_east.pdf, (last accessed on 01/03/2014).

Lobe, Jim. 2013. "Scowcroft, Brzezinski Urge Iran Accord," *Lobe Log: Foreign Policy.* http://www.lobelog.com/scowcroft-brzezinski-urge-iran-accord/, (last accessed on 12/16/2013).

Manson, Katrina. 2011. "Pro-democracy protests reach Djibouti," *Financial Times.* http://www.ft.com/intl/cms/s/0/001f94f6–3d18–11e0-bbff-00144feabdc0.html?siteedition=intl, (last accessed on 10/25/2013).

Manyika, J., et al. 2012. "Manufacturing the future: The next era of global growth and innovation," *McKinsey Global Institute*, http://www.mckinsey. com/insights/manufacturing/the_future_of_manufacturing, (last accessed on 12/01/2013).

Markey, Patrick. 2010. "Colombia's Santos takes office with strong mandate," *Reuters.com*. http://www.reuters.com/article/2010/08/07/us-colombia-santos -idUSTRE6760DD20100807, (last accessed on 10/30/2012).

Marquand, Robert. 2011. "Amid BRICS' rise and 'Arab Spring', a new global order forms," *Christian Science Monitor*. http://www.csmonitor.com/World/ Global-Issues/2011/1018/Amid-BRICS-rise-and-Arab-Spring-a-new-global-order-forms, (last accessed on 01/02/2013).

Matsui, Kathy. 2012. "A View from Japan," *Goldman Sachs*. http://www.youtube. com/watch?v=bfkqe4vLdFY, (last accessed on 11/10/2013).

Maxwell, John. 2012. "Beyond the BRICS: How to succeed in emerging markets (by really trying)," *PWC*. http://www.pwc.com/us/en/view/issue-15/succeed-emerging-markets.jhtml, (last accessed on 11/27/2013).

McCrummen, Stephanie. 2011. "13 killed in Iraq's 'Day of Rage' protests," *The Washington Post*. http://www.washingtonpost.com/wp-dyn/content/ article/2011/02/24/AR2011022403117.html, (last accessed on 06/12/2011).

McKinnon, Ronald I. 1973. *Money and Capital in Economic Development*. Washington, DC: Brookings Institution Press.

Middle East Online Staff Writers. 2011. "Kuwaiti stateless protest for third day," *Middle East Online*. http://www.middle-east-online.com/english/?id=44476, (last accessed on 10/25/2013).

Ministry of Economy and Finance of Cambodia. 2013. "Council for the development of Cambodia (CDC)," *Economic Trends*. http://www. cambodiainvestment.gov.kh/investment-enviroment/economic-trend.html, (last accessed on 11/04/2013).

Mitchell, Jared. 2013. "Why Emerging Markets are tough to enter," *HSBC Global Connections*. https://globalconnections.hsbc.com/canada/en/articles/ why-emerging-markets-are-tough-enter, (last accessed on 12/16/2013).

Moghadam, Reza. 2010. "How Did Emerging Markets Cope in the Crisis? The Strategy, Policy, and Review Department, in consultation with other IMF departments," *IMF.* http://www.imf.org/external/np/pp/eng/2010/061510. pdf, (last accessed on 11/15/2013).

Montibeler, E.E. and E.S. Gallego. 2012. "Relaciones Bilaterales Entre Brasil y Liga Árabe: Un Análisis a Partir de la Teoría de la Internacionalización de la Producción y de la Diversificación Comercial." *Observatorio de la Economía Latinoamericana*, 163.

Mookerji, Nivedita. 2013. "Walmart continues to bide its time over Bharti investment," *Business Standard*. http://www.business-standard.com/article/ companies/walmart-continues-to-bide-its-time-over-bharti-investment-113081600670_1.html, (last accessed on 12/15/2013).

Moore, M. 2005. "Signposts to More Effective States: Responding to Governance Challenges in Developing Countries," *Institute of Developing Studies, The Centre for the Future State, UK,* http://www2.ids.ac.uk/gdr/cfs/pdfs/SignpoststoMoreEffectiveStates.pdf, (last accessed on 12/10/2013).

Mortished, Carl. 2008. "Russia shows its political clout by hosting BRIC summit." *The Times.* http://www.thetimes.co.uk/tto/business/markets/russia/article2143017.ece, (last accessed on 05/12/2012).

Mutum, D.P., S.K. Roy, and E. Kipnis (Eds.). 2014. *Marketing Cases from Emerging Markets.* New York, NY: Springer.

Nath, Ravindra. 2011. "Qaboos fires 10 ministers," *Khaleej Times,* Muscat, UAE. http://www.khaleejtimes.com/displayarticle.asp?xfile=data/middleeast/2011/March/middleeast_March140.xml&section=middleeast&col=, (last accessed on 10/12/2013).

New York City Bar Association. 2011. "The FCPA and Its Impact on International Business Transactions—Should Anything be Done to Minimize the Consequences of the U.S.'s Unique Position on Combating Offshore Corruption?," *New York City Bar Association.* http://www2.nycbar.org/pdf/report/uploads/FCPAImpactonInternationalBusinessTransactions.pdf, (last accessed on 12/18/2013).

Nilekani, Nandan. 2008. *Imagining India: The Idea of a Renewed Nation.* New York, NY: Penguin Group.

O'Neill, J. 2011. *The Growth Map: Economic Opportunity in the BRICs and Beyond.* New York, NY: Penguin Group.

O'Neill, Jim. 2001. "Building Better Global Economic BRICs," *Global Economics Paper No. 66,* Goldman Sachs. http://www.goldmansachs.com/our-thinking/archive/archive-pdfs/build-better-brics.pdf, (last accessed on 12/17/2011).

O'Neill, Jim. 2005. "How Solid Are the BRICS," *Goldman Sachs' Global Economics Paper No. 134.* http://www.goldmansachs.com/our-thinking/archive/archive-pdfs/how-solid.pdf, (last accessed on 11/14/2012).

O'Sullivan, A., M.E. Rey, and M.J. Galvez. 2011. "Opportunities and Challenges in the MENA Region." *The Arab world competitiveness report, 2011–2012, World Economic Forum.* http://www.weforum.org/reports/arab-world-competitiveness-report-2011–2012, (last accessed on 01/02/2014).

OECD. 2007. Overview by the DAC Chair, In Development Co-operation Report. Vol. 8(1), chapter 1 (Paris, France: OECD, 2007).

Organization for Economic Co-operation and Development. 2013. "Economic outlook: analysis and forecast: Turkey Economic forecast summary," May 2014, *OECD,* http://www.oecd.org/eco/outlook/turkey-economic-forecast-summary.htm, (last accessed on 11/04/2013).

Organization for Economic Co-operation and Development. 2013. "Economic surveys and country surveillance: Economic Survey of Japan 2013," *OECD.*

http://www.oecd.org/eco/surveys/economic-survey-japan.htm, (last accessed on 11/05/2013).

Organization for Economic Co-operation and Development. 2013. "Economic surveys and country surveillance: Economic Survey of South Africa 2013," *OECD,* http://www.oecd.org/eco/surveys/economic-survey-south-africa.htm, (last accessed on 11/05/2013).

Organization of American States: Inter-American Convention Against Corruption, Mar. 29, 1996, 35 I.L.M. 724. http://www.unicri.it/topics/organized_crime_corruption/

Orgaz, L., L. Molina, and C. Carrasco. 2011. "In El Creciente Peso de las Economias Emergentes en la Economia y Gobernanza Mundiales, Los Paises BRIC", *Documentos Ocasionales numero 1101*, Banco de Espana, Eurosistema. http://www.bde.es/f/webbde/SES/Secciones/Publicaciones/Publicaciones Seriadas/DocumentosOcasionales/11/Fich/do1101.pdf, (last accessed on 12/12/2012).

Oxford Business Group's Staff Writers. 2013. "Brunei Darussalam looks to its labs for growth," *Brunei Darussalam*, http://www.oxfordbusinessgroup.com/economic_updates/brunei-darussalam-looks-its-labs-growth, (last accessed on 11/02/2013).

Pacek, N. and D. Thorniley. 2007. *Emerging Markets: Lessons for Business and the Outlook for Different Markets (2nd edition)*. London: The Economist and Profile Books.

Pain, N., I. Koske, and M. Sollie. 2006. "Globalization and inflation in the OECD Economies," *Economics Department Working Paper No. 524*, OECD, Paris. http://www.oecd.org/eco/42503918.pdf, (last accessed on 11/12/2013).

Papademos, Lucas. 2006. "Globalization, inflation, imbalances and monetary policy," *Bank for International Settlement*, St. Louis, U.S., http://www.bis.org/review/r060607d.pdf, (last accessed on 11/09/2013).

Peterson, S. 2011. "Egypt's revolution redefines what's possible in the Arab world," *The Christian Science Monitor*, http://www.csmonitor.com/layout/set/r14/World/Middle-East/2011/0211/Egypt-s-revolution-redefines-what-s-possible-in-the-Arab-world, (last accessed on 11/10/2013).

Pettis, Michael. 2013. *The Great Rebalancing: Trade, Conflict, and the Perilous Road Ahead for the World Economy*, Princeton University Press.

Pigato, Miria. 2009. *Strengthening China's and India's Trade and Investment Ties to the Middle East and North Africa*. Washington DC: The World Bank.

Portes, R. 2010. *Currency Wars and the Emerging-Market Countries. Vox*EU, http://www.voxeu.org/article/currency-wars-and-emerging-markets, (last accessed on 01/21/2014).

Posadas, Alejandro. 2000. "Combating Corruption Under International Law," *Duke University Journal of Comparative and International Law*, pp. 345–

414, http://scholarship.law.duke.edu/djcil/vol10/iss2/4, (last accessed on 12/02/2013).

Qatar National Bank (QNB Group). 2013. "Economic and International Affairs." http://www.qnb.com.qa/cs/Satellite/QNBQatar/en_QA/AboutQNB/CorporateSocialResponsibility/enEconomicandInternationalAffairs, (last accessed on 11/02/2013).

Qatar National Bank (QNB Group). 2013. "US, eurozone deflation calls for 'expansionary policy.'" http://www.gulf-times.com/business/191/details/374 694/us,-eurozone-deflation-calls-for-'expansionary-policy'

Qiang, Hou. 2013. "ASEAN businesses see integration as opportunity, not threat: survey," *The English News*, Xinhua, China, http://news.xinhuanet. com/english/business/2013–12/11/c_132960344.htm, (last accessed on 12/11/2013).

Radu, Paul C. 2008. "The Investigative Journalist Handbook," *International Center for Journalist.* https://reportingproject.net/occrp/index.php/en/cc-resource-center/handbook/191-the-investigative-journalist-handbook, (last accessed on 09/08/2012).

Rai, V. and W. Simon. 2008. *Think India.* New York, NY: Penguin Group.

Rashid, Ahmed, 2012. *Pakistan on the Brink: The Future of America, Pakistan, and Afghanistan.* New York, NY: Viking/Penguin Group.

Reinhart, C.M. and M.B. Sbrancia. 2011. "The Liquidation of Government Debt," *NBER Working Paper 16893.* http://www.nber.org/papers/w16893, (last accessed on 03/02/12).

Reinhart, C.M. and J.F. Kirkegaard. 2012. "Financial Repression: Then and Now," *Vox.* http://www.voxeu.org/article/financial-repression-then-and-now, (last accessed on 04/23/12).

Rich, Ben R. and Leo Janos. 1994. *Skunk Works: A Personal Memoir of My Years at Lockheed.* New York, NY: Little Brown & Co., 1994, p. 10.

Richter, Frederick. 2011. "Protester killed in Bahrain 'Day of Rage,'" *Reuters,* http://uk.reuters.com/article/2011/02/14/uk-bahrain-protests-idUKT RE71D1G520110214, (last accessed on 11/02/2013).

Rickards, J. 2011. *Currency Wars: The Making of the Next Global Crisis,* Penguin/Portfolio Group.

Rodrik, D. 2009. *Growth After the Crisis.* Cambridge, MA: Harvard Kennedy School.

Roudi, Farzaneh. 2001. "Population Trends and Challenges in the MENA," *PRB.* http://www.prb.org/Publications/Reports/2001/PopulationTrendsand ChallengesintheMiddleEastandNorthAfrica.aspx, (last accessed on 12/20/2013).

RT Staff Writers. 2013. "BRICS agree to capitalize development bank at $100bn," *RT.* http://rt.com/business/russia-brics-bank-g20–468/, (last accessed on 11/06/2013).

Sallum, M.N. 2013. "Potencial a explorar é enorme." *Agência de Notícias Brasil-Árabe*. http://www.anba.com.br/, (last accessed on 01/03/2014).

Saseendran, Sajila. 2013. "Shaikh Mohammed inaugurates solar power park phase-1," *Khaleej Times*. http://www.khaleejtimes.com/kt-article-display

Schmidt, V. 2003. "French Capitalism Transformed; yet still a Third Variety of Capitalism." *Economy and Society*, 32(4). http://www.vedegylet.hu/fejkrit/szvggyujt/schmidt_frenchCapitalism.pdf

Schwab, Klaus. 2013. "The Global Competitiveness Report 2012–2013," *World Economic Forum*, http://www3.weforum.org/docs/WEF_Global CompetitivenessReport_2012–13.pdf, (last accessed on 08/12/2013).

Schwartz, Nelson. 2013. "Growth Gain Blurs Signs of Weakness in Economy," *New York Times*, http://www.nytimes.com/2013/11/08/business/economy/us-economy-grows-at-2–8-rate-in-third-quarter.html?_r=0, (last accessed on 11/10/2013).

Senkovich, V. 2013. "The Arab World's Potential Importance to Russia's Economy." *Russian International Affairs Council*, http://russiancouncil.ru/en/inner/?id_4=1548#top, (last accessed on 01/03/2014).

Seyid, Seyid Ould. 2011. "Mauritania police crush protest–doctors announce strike," *Radio Netherlands Worldwide*, Africa Desk, Mauritania. http://www.rnw.nl/africa/article/mauritania-police-crush-protest-doctors-announce-strike, (last retrieved on 12/12/2012).

Shahminan, Fitri. 2013. "Brunei economy to grow 2.4pc in next four years," *Dawn.com*, http://www.dawn.com/news/1048280/brunei-economy-to-grow-24pc-in-next-four-years, (last accessed on 10/10/2013).

Smith & Nephew Corporate. 2012. "Smith & Nephew reaches settlement with US Government," *Smith & Nephew*, http://www.smith-nephew.com/news-and-media/news/smith-and-nephew-reaches-settlement-with-us-gover/, (last accessed on 12/12/2013).

Snyder, Michael. 2012. "45 Signs That China Is Colonizing America," *End of The American Dream*, http://endoftheamericandream.com/archives/45-signs-that-china-is-colonizing-america, (last accessed on 09/08/2013).

Soubbotina, Tatyana P. and Katherine A. Sheram. 2004. *Beyond Economic Growth: An Introduction to Sustainable Development*, World Bank, 2nd edition.

Spencer, R., 2011. "Libya: Civil war breaks out as Gaddafi mounts rearguard fight," *The Telegraph*, http://www.telegraph.co.uk/news/worldnews/africaand indianocean/libya/8344034/Libya-civil-war-breaks-out-as-Gaddafi-mounts-rearguard-fight.html, (last accessed on 11/12/2013).

Stern, Melanie. 2012. "International Trade: CIVETS Economies," *Financial Director Newspaper*, London, UK. http://www.financialdirector.co.uk/financial-director/feature/2169190/international-trade-civets-economies, (last accessed on 11/03/2013).

Stout, David. 2009. "Ex-Rep. Jefferson Convicted in Bribery Scheme," *The New York Times*. p. A14. http://www.nytimes.com/2009/08/06/us/06jefferson.html, (last accessed on 06/14/2013).

Svensson, L.E.O. 2008. "Inflation Targeting," I *The New Palgrave Dictionary of Economics, 2nd edition*, eds. S.N. Durlauf & L.E. Blume. New York, NY: Palgrave Macmillan.

Taborda, Joana. 2013. "Death of the Dollar 2014: Euro Area GDP Growth Rate," *Trading Economics*, http://www.tradingeconomics.com/euro-area/gdp-growth, (last accessed on 12/15/2013).

Tarun Khanna and Krishna G. Palepu. 2010. *Winning in Emerging Markets: A Roadmap for Strategy and Execution*. Boston: Harvard Business School Publishing.

Telegraph Staff Writers. 2013. "Next chief Lord Wolfson launches £250,000 prize to solve housing crisis." *The Telegraph*, http://www.telegraph.co.uk/finance/newsbysector/constructionandproperty/10448303/Next-chief-Lord-Wolfson-launches-250000-prize-to-solve-housing-crisis.html, (last accessed on 12/11/2013).

The FCPA Blog. 2012, "Biomet Pays $22.8 Million To Settle Bribe Charges," *The FCPA Blog*, http://www.fcpablog.com/blog/2012/3/26/biomet-pays-228-million-to-settle-bribe-charges.html, (last accessed on 09/09/2012).

Transparency International Secretariat. 2013. "Media advisory: Major exporters still lag in enforcing rules against foreign bribery," *Transparency International*, http://www.transparency.org/news/pressrelease/bribe_paying_still_very_high_worldwide_but_people_ready_to_fight_back, (last accessed on 12/14/2013).

U.S. Department of Justice. 2012. "Marubeni Corporation Resolves Foreign Corrupt Practices Act Investigation and Agrees to Pay a $54.6 Million Criminal Penalty," *U.S. Department of Justice*, http://www.justice.gov/opa/pr/2012/January/12-crm-060.html, (last accessed on 07/02/2013).

Vaidya, Sunil. 2011. "One dead, dozens injured as Oman protest turns ugly," *Gulf News*, Oman, http://gulfnews.com/news/gulf/oman/one-dead-dozen-injured-as-oman-protest-turns-ugly-1.768789, (last accessed on 11/01/2013).

Vale Columbia Center on Sustainable International Investment. 2009. "First ranking survey of Mexican multinationals finds grey diversity of industries," *Columbia Law School*, http://www.vcc.columbia.edu/files/vale/documents/EMGP-Mexico-Report-Final-09Dec09.pdf, (last accessed on 11/30/2013).

Wagstyl, S. 2013. "Eurasia: emerging markets are world's 'top risk' for 2013," *Financial Times*, http://blogs.ft.com/beyond-brics/2013/01/07/eurasia-emerging-markets-are-worlds-top-risk-for-2013/#axzz2nkpeGUB7, (last accessed on 12/17/2013).

Wallace, Julia. 2013. "Development and Its Discontent," *International New York Times*, http://latitude.blogs.nytimes.com/2013/04/12/development-and-its-discontent/?_r=0, (last accessed on 10/10/2013).

Weggel, Oskar. 2006. "Cambodia in 2005: Year of Reassurance." *Asian Survey* 46 (1): 158.

Welch, D., and T. Weidlich. 2012. "Wal-Mart Bribery Probe May Exposes Retailer to U.S. Fines," *Bloomberg,* http://www.bloomberg.com/news/2012–04-23/wal-mart-bribery-probe-may-exposes-retailer-to-u-s-fines.html, (last accessed on 04/23/2012).

Werr, Patrick. 2013. "Egypt's economy to miss government growth forecasts: Reuters poll," *Reuters* Cairo, Egypt, http://www.reuters.com/article/2013/10/01/us-economy-egypt-poll-idUSBRE99012O20131001, (last accessed on 10/30/2013).

Wheatley, Alan. 2013. "Emerging markets thrive as eurozone suffers," *The International News,* http://www.thenews.com.pk/Todays-News-3–167386-Emerging-markets-thrive-as-eurozone-suffers, (last accessed on 11/10/2013).

Wiley Online Library. 2013. "Shlomit, Tourre, and Planton," http://onlinelibrary.wiley.com/doi/10.1029/2003GL017862/abstract, (last accessed on 11/01/2013).

Williams, R. 1983. *Capitalism (Revised Edition).* Oxford: Oxford University Press.

Wilson, D. and R. Purushothaman. 2003. "Dreaming with BRICs: The Path to 2050," *Global Economics Paper No. 99,* Goldman Sachs, http://www.goldmansachs.com/our-thinking/archive/archive-pdfs/brics-dream.pdf, (last accessed on 04/05/2011).

World Bank Staff Writers. 2013. "Tourism in the Arab World can mean more than Sun, Sand and Beaches," *The World Bank,* http://www.worldbank.org/en/news/feature/2013/02/11/tourism-in-the-arab-world-can-mean-more-than-sun-sand-and-beaches, (last accessed on 01/03/2014).

World Bank Staff Writers. 2012. "Doing Business 2014: Ease of Doing Business in Pakistan," *The World Bank.* http://www.doingbusiness.org/data/exploreeconomies/pakistan, (last accessed on 11/10/2012).

World Bank Staff Writers. 2012. "World Development Indicators Database. Gross Domestic Product 2011," *The World Bank,* http://data.worldbank.org/data-catalog/world-development-indicators, (last accessed on 09/22/2012).

World Bank Staff Writers. 2013. "An Update on Vietnam's Recent Economic Development July 2013: Key Findings," *The World Bank,* http://www.worldbank.org/en/news/feature/2013/07/12/taking-stock-july-2013-an-update-on-vietnams-recent-economic-development-key-findings, (last accessed on 11/05/2013).

World Bank Staff Writers. 2013. "Doing Business: Ease of Doing Business in Colombia," *The World Bank,* http://www.doingbusiness.org/data/exploreeconomies/colombia/, (last accessed on 06/12/2013).

World Bank Staff Writers. 2013. "Doing Business: Measuring Business Regulations," *The World Bank,* http://www.doingbusiness.org/rankings, (last accessed on 09/22/2012).

World Bank. 2008. *Middle East and North Africa Region 2007 Economic Developments and Prospects: Job Creation in an Era of High Growth.* Washington, DC: World Bank. http://documents.worldbank.org/curated/en/2008/06/9520526/middle-east-north-africa-region-2007-economic-developments-prospects-job-creation-era-high-growth, (last accessed on 02/12/2014).

Young, V. 2006. "Macquarie launches Australia's first BRIC funds," *InvestorDaily,* http://www.investordaily.com.au/25542-macquarie-launches-australias-first-bric-funds, (last accessed on 05/23/2007).

Zoffer, Joshua. 2012. "Future of Dollar Hegemony," *The Harvard International Review,* http://hir.harvard.edu/crafting-the-city/future-of-dollar-hegemony, (last accessed on 10/12/2012).

Index

Announcing the Business Expert Press Digital Library

Concise E-books Business Students Need
for Classroom and Research

This book can also be purchased in an e-book collection by your library as
- a one-time purchase,
- that is owned forever,
- allows for simultaneous readers,
- has no restrictions on printing, and
- can be downloaded as PDFs from within the library community.

Our digital library collections are a great solution to beat the rising cost of textbooks. E-books can be loaded into their course management systems or onto students' e-book readers.

The **Business Expert Press** digital libraries are very affordable, with no obligation to buy in future years. For more information, please visit **www.businessexpertpress.com/librarians**. To set up a trial in the United States, please email **sales@businessexpertpress.com**.

.

www.ingramcontent.com/pod-product-compliance
Lightning Source LLC
Chambersburg PA
CBHW060529210326
41519CB00014B/3177